Horse
Management

The Official Handbook of the
German National Equestrian Federation

Published in 1987 by Half Halt Press, Box 3512, Gaithersburg, Maryland 20878.

Library of Congress Cataloging in Publication Data

Richtlinien für Reiten und Fahren. Bd. 4. English.
  Horse management.

Translation of: Richtlinien für Reiten und Fahren, Bd. IV.
  Includes index.
  1. Horses. 2. Horses—Diseases. 3. Horses—Germany (West)—Breeding. I. Deutsche Reiterliche Vereinigung. II. Title.
  SF285.3.R5313 1987   636.1   87–23625
  ISBN 0–939481–04–9

Printed in Great Britain

Foreword

The *Richtlinien für Reiten und Fahren* (*The Principles of Riding*) first appeared in 1954 as a set of guidelines on basic training intended for club members. Twelve years later it was expanded with the addition of the chapter 'Assessing and keeping the riding horse'. It became apparent during the comprehensive revision of the *Richtlinien* undertaken in 1978–79 that the only way to deal with the wealth of material, and to present it to the reader in a form that was easy to understand, was to divide it up into sections. This book, Volume IV of the *Richtlinien*, originated in this way.

The horse is a valuable cultural possession, to be cherished and guarded. Anyone lucky enough to own a horse and to look after him must recognise and fulfil the horse's biological requirements. The knowledge required to do this is the subject of this volume of the *Richtlinien*. It is aimed in the first instance at young riders, who will prove their knowledge in the graded tests, and at prospective instructors preparing for their examinations. However, this volume will also serve as an indispensable reference book for the experienced horse person, who will consult it with ever-growing enthusiasm. It is hoped that this little book will achieve its aim, to the benefit of our horses and our sport.

Deutsche Reiterliche Vereinigung e.V. (FN),
Sports Division
Warendorf, Westphalia

Contributors to *Horse Management*

Biological Requirements, Dr K. Zeeb
Systems of Management, Dr H. Haring
Anatomy and Physiology, Dr B. Hertsch
Feeding, members of the 'Horse feeds and feeding
    methods' study circle of the Deutsche Reiterliche
    Vereinigung
Grooming, C. Endres and Dr B. Hertsch
Ailments, Dr B. Hertsch
Identification, Assessment and Description, Dr W.
    Uppenborn
Advice on Buying a Horse, Deutsche Reiterliche
    Vereinigung Horse Purchasing Committee
Horse Breeding, Dr H. Haring

Contents

Contents

Contents

Contents

1. Biological Requirements

1(1) Evolution

It has long been acknowledged that as far as their inherent needs are concerned, animals are only in a position to fulfil their potential if they are in harmony with their environment. The needs of wild animals have evolved from the past, on the principle that over the centuries each species has adapted to a particular habitat. Selective breeding occurred naturally; only those animals which could adapt survived.

With domestic animals the situation is different. Man practises selective breeding according to his requirements, and in so doing he brings about changes in the wild species. However, knowledge of wild creatures is essential to an understanding of domesticated ones, as it is ostensibly the wild form that provides the foundation upon which man builds. If man is to make use of the horse and to form a relationship with him he must understand his behaviour. He must also know how to provide adequately for the horse's biological needs. Behaviour patterns, just as much as the animal's general system and individual organs, are conditioned by heredity, and are thus shaped to fit in with the fundamental plan of the species.

Bearing this in mind, let us look at the history of the horse. Between the Pleistocene period (1 million years BC) and the Holocene period (10,000 years BC), four distinct wild forms of horse developed quite separately in response to four quite different habitats. Later, that is after the Ice Age, from 10,000 BC onwards, hybrid forms again developed. Some 5,000 years ago, man thus found himself heir to very varied forms of wild horse, the behaviour of which contained certain deviations from that of the standard form of *equus caballus*. It is only with

11

the standard form that we shall be dealing in this book, but it should be borne in mind that the often very individual behavioural variations encountered in horses today are reminiscent of the different wild forms.

As a basic format we must take *equus caballus* to be a single-toed herd animal, highly specialised in running and flight, with a highly efficient, highly developed respiratory and circulatory system and a tendency towards seasonal migrations in search of grazing. Depending on its particular evolution, or on selective breeding, it is suited to life in places ranging from tundra, marshes, steppes and savannah, and forest to deserts.

1(2) Management, Training and Use

Environment, which played a decisive role in the evolution of the horse, is equally important in its management. Roughly speaking, patterns of behaviour can be divided into the following categories, which have their counterparts in the areas of operation that make up horse management:

Areas of Operation	*Patterns of Behaviour*
Feeding	Feeding
Provision of an area for lying down	Resting
Provision of exercise facilities	Exercise
Removal of droppings and urine	Excretion
Keeping horses in a group	Social activity
Provision of comfortable surroundings	Comfort

Feeding

Large quantities of roughage are essential for the horse's digestive system. Horses in fields will spend up to sixteen hours per day grazing, with sunrise and sunset as peak eating times. Horses fed on hay alone spend up to twelve hours per day eating.

The so-called 'complete feeds' used on their own do not fulfil feeding requirements: too little time is spent eating, and there is too little chewing involved. They also fail to meet the requirements of the digestive system.

Horses in herds keep their places in the social hierarchy while grazing.

Lying Down Area

Horses also observe the rules of social hierarchy while resting.

Areas of the following dimensions are necessary:

For horses kept in groups: approx 6m^2 per horse;

in looseboxes: (2 x height at withers)^2;

in stalls: length: 1·6 x height at withers*

width: height at withers + 20cm.

Dry, draught-free areas are preferred for lying down. Wet bedding reduces the time spent lying down by 60 per cent upwards. The lying down area must be ventilated. In high temperatures horses like to lie down in the wind.

Exercise Facilities

As a highly specialised creature of flight and action, the horse needs to spend plenty of time exercising and, being a migratory animal, needs the space in which to do so.

Where horses are not worked for several hours per day it is helpful to turn them out in groups. The stimulation provided by the other horses conditions the legs, circulation and respiratory system. Keeping horses tied up is only suitable if they are worked for many hours per day. Even the smallest of exercise areas – minimum 2 x (2 x height at withers)^2 – is better than none at all.

Allowing the horse some exercise at liberty makes for surefootedness when he is ridden across country.

Droppings and Urine

Unlike an animal such as the pig, it is not in the horse's nature to remain in one place. Hence he urinates and

*German: 'stick height'. In Germany horses are also measured with a tape over the withers, which works out at about 10cm more than the 'stick height'.

deposits his droppings everywhere. Areas containing droppings are avoided when grazing and horses do not like urinating where they are likely to get splashed. The best bedding from this point of view is straw on top of peat.

If an exercise compound is to remain usable all the year round, it is usual to construct it on a drained foundation, and a permeable membrane can be used.

Droppings and wet bedding must be removed regularly from the stable and exercise compound to prevent reinfection.

Keeping Horses in Groups

Horses' innate social instincts lead them to form a hierarchy or 'pecking order', which becomes established by conditioning. For meeting social, exercise and ambient requirements, running out in groups is the most satsifactory and natural form of management. Bullying can be avoided by setting up several strategically composed groups. If there are two routes out of the stable, there is less bullying, and subordinates suffer less ill effects.

Comfortable Ambient Conditions

The horse's highly sensitive respiratory apparatus is particularly susceptible to the effects of harmful gases, and unventilated stables cause disease.

Extremes of heat and cold are well tolerated by all breeds of horse once they have become conditioned to them. A constant environment in the stables is wrong.

The surroundings in the stables should be a moderated version of outside conditions. The following are most desirable in the immediate proximity of the animals:

air temperature   5–15°C
relative humidity   60–75 per cent ·
air speed   not below 0·1m/sec
             not above 0·3m/sec

Since draughts are cooler than the surrounding air and

play unevenly on the horses' bodies, ventilation in this form should be avoided.

Many breeds of horse can be kept exclusively at grass all the year round provided dry, draught-proof protection against the weather is available.

Training and Use

Only if the following twelve commandments are obeyed in the training and use of the horse can it be said that his inherent needs have been respected:

1 Physically and in his behaviour the horse is a highly specialised creature of flight who, although he is able to jump, prefers to run. He only feels safe in company with others of his own kind.

2 The horse takes man to be one of his own kind who is either higher, equal or lower in the pecking order, or he considers him to be an enemy. As a teacher, man must take the place of other horses. It is in the horse's nature to be submissive.

3 Man must be superior to the horse in his social hierarchy, but he must achieve this by intelligence, not by force. When the horse makes mistakes whilst under man's influence it means that he has not understood man correctly.

4 In order to understand man, the horse must have confidence in him. Confidence is the basis for understanding.

5 The means of communication between man and horse are: voice aids, touch aids, steering aids, correcting aids, weight aids and rewards of food. Correcting aids should *never* consist of thrashing!

6 In order to learn the aids, the horse must first understand them. Being a highly specialised creature he must be accustomed slowly and deliberately to anything new. If, during training, the horse shows signs of insecurity or even fear, the training must be started again from the beginning.

7 The capacity for learning is governed by the horse's

15

physical and mental development. Overtaxing the body and the learning capacity will only set him back in his training.

8 The exercises must be performed daily and in a different order each time. They should only last as long as it takes for the horse to understand. Stopping the exercise is the reward for doing it correctly.

9 The aim of the horse's training is:

balance: expressive rhythmical movement which is without tension;

'durchlässigkeit': unconstrained readiness to accept the aids;

equilibrium: symmetrical development and functioning of the musculature;

roundness = collection: malleable movements incorporating alertness, 'durchlässigkeit', balance and equilibrium.

This aim can only be achieved if man does not hamper or disturb the horse.

10 Each movement performed by the horse is not artificially produced by man but developed from the horse's natural capabilities.

11 The training of the horse comprises his gymnastic training, i.e. his physical and mental development in keeping with his nature and behavioural characteristics, aimed at perfecting the equilibrium to which he is naturally suited.

12 The horse is only in a position to develop his innate talents to the full if he is so in harmony with his environment (which includes man) that his requirements, as a horse, are met. Association with man should mean security for the horse in all situations.

2. Systems of Management

The words of Paragraph 2 Section 1 of the German Animal Protection Act can be taken as a guide for the keeping of any animal:

'Anyone who keeps a horse, cares for one, or causes one to be cared for, must ensure that the animal receives adequate, suitable food and care, as well as accommodation in keeping with its behavioural characteristics, and should not restrict an animal's natural requirement for exercise for such a period or to such an extent that he is subjected to unnecessary pain, suffering or injury.'

2(1) Keeping a Horse at Grass

Keeping a horse or pony at grass is the most satisfactory method from the point of view of 'accommodation in keeping with its behavioural characteristics' and 'suitable food'. However, it is not possible in the majority of cases. Nevertheless, every horsekeeper should try to procure some time out in a field for his four-legged companion now and then – as little as half an hour per day pays dividends.

It is quite impossible to rear horses successfully without turning them out in a field, because it is in the field, particularly through the continuous exercise, that bones, muscles, heart and lungs are developed. Tendons and ligaments, too, are strengthened.

During the growing season, depending on the quality of the grazing, an adult horse weighing 500kg needs an area of 0·25–0·50 hectares. Young horses require correspondingly less. However, at this point it should be added that the field should not be below a certain size if it is to serve the purposes mentioned above. For young horses a

17

field below 2 hectares in size poses as many problems as raising horses in a vegetable garden or rearing one horse on his own.

The most suitable paddocks are large, flat enclosures with natural boundaries of hedges or trees which give the horse sufficient protection against the wind. Forest pastures are not suitable because of the plagues of insects, neither are fields alongside busy roads or in tourist areas owing to the increased risk to the horses from their environment. A supply of fresh, clean water must always be available.

Wooden post and rail fence
with rounded corner and gateway

2(1)i FENCING

Horse paddocks must be enclosed by a strong fence or natural boundary. To reduce the risk of injury to the horses, the corners should be rounded and the gateways

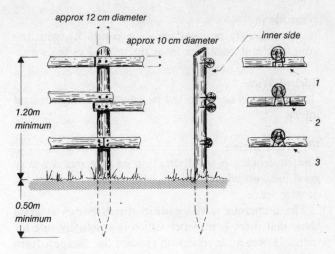

approx 12 cm diameter

approx 10 cm diameter

inner side

1.20m
minimum

0.50m
minimum

1

2

3

Post and rail fence, showing different construction methods:
1, 2 and 3

should, if possible, be situated away from the corners. A natural boundary of trees, hedges and bushes is a useful adjunct to a fence.

Timber Fencing
A well-proven type of timber fence consists of two or three horizontal wooden rails, the top one of which should be a minimum height of about 1·20m. Applying a coat of the foulest possible smelling wood preservative stops the horse chewing it and prolongs the life of the fence.

Fences Made of Tubular Steel and Reinforced Concrete
Such fences are used successfully in some studs, but they are expensive. Fences made of two strands of plain, heavy-gauge wire are often recommended. The bottom strand should be not less than 60cm from the ground.

19

Wire Mesh

Wire mesh may be used for some paddocks, with the same minimum distance from the ground as for wire.

Barbed Wire

Barbed wire is best rejected because of the high risk of injury.

Electric Fencing

Electric fencing is insufficient on its own but is a very good back-up when used in conjunction with a wooden or wire fence.

The numerous mishaps which befall horses at grass show that there is no fence which is absolutely safe for them. However, anyone who chooses the cheapest form of fencing in order to save money will find out when the first accident happens, if not before, just how expensive such economies can be.

2(1)ii FERTILIZING AND MANAGEMENT OF GRASSLAND

The nutritional composition and the palatability of the pasture depend on its botanical composition and on climate, fertilizing and soil. More than 100 different types of plants, grasses, clovers and herbs can grow in meadowland. A ley containing a mixture of plants is the most commonly used, and for horses a grass content of 70 to 80 per cent is the most desirable. The stalky grasses are the most sought after by horses; for example, rye grass, timothy, cocksfoot and meadow fescue are popular, while black bent, red fescue, bromes and couch are not found very attractive. In paddocks used exclusively by horses the tastiest grasses die out because they are eaten down to the roots, while white clover and weeds such as dandelions, buttercups and daisies gain a hold: the paddock becomes 'horse-sick'. This can be prevented, or at least delayed, by appropriate management

and by grazing the field with horses and cattle alternately. Horses and cattle have different grazing habits,
and the level of parasite infestation in both species will
also be reduced.

If the paddock has become 'horse-sick' through being
grazed only by horses, it may be necessary to plough and
reseed. A seed mix consisting of 5kg creeping red fescue,
5kg smooth stalked meadow grass (Kentucky blue grass),
2kg rye grass and 1kg common bent per hectare (two and
a half acres) (Könekamp), and a 'complete' chemical
fertilizer (NPK), will usually fulfil every requirement.

The best mixture for reseeding depends so much on
the soil and the climate that local farmers and professional bodies such as the Ministry of Agriculture should
be consulted if you are in any doubt.

Only through the judicious application of fertilizers
can the plants receive an optimal supply of nutrients, the
main ones being nitrogen, phosphate, potash and lime.
The amount of fertilizer required depends on the soil
balance, the climate and the level or usage. The following
figures can be taken as a general guide but it is best to
have a soil analysis completed. In Britain this can be done
through the Ministry of Agriculture.

Fertilizer Requirements of Permanent Pasture

Type	Quantity/ hectare	Season	Remarks
Nitrogen	60-120kg	The whole of the growing season (in favourable conditions not necessary in the spring)	Higher levels required if meadow grazed simultaneously by cattle
Phosphate	approxi- mately 40kg	Late autumn or spring	

21

Type	Quantity/hectare	Season	Remarks
Potash	approximately 80kg	Early spring	If high levels applied, should be spread over the whole of the growing season, otherwise it can accumulate in the plants and suppress the Na, Ca and Mg
Lime	1,000–1,500kg	Every three to four years, autumn, early winter	On acid soil: the amount depends on the pH-value. pH-values: sandy soils 5–5·5; loams and clay soils 6-6·5; marshy land 4·5

Soils which are low in minerals (sandy soils, marshy land and granite and gneiss based soils) are best treated with a compound fertilizer containing additional trace elements. Organic fertilizers can be used within limits. Liquid manure and slurry contain high levels of nitrogen and potash. Stable manure is in itself a good general-purpose fertilizer, but it tends to increase the levels of certain parasites, namely ascarids, in the fields. Only thoroughly rotted stable manure should be used. After the application of chemical fertilizers the field should not be grazed by stock for at least ten days.

Other forms of management are harrowing and rolling the pasture, which should be done before the grass starts to grow in the spring. During the time the horses are in the field, the droppings should be regularly removed, as far as the work-load will permit, so as to keep worm levels as low as possible. Patches of rank grass and other ungrazed areas must be topped, otherwise the unpopular plant forms and the rank patches will take up larger and larger areas.

2(1)iii USE OF THE PADDOCKS

Transition from stable to field; when to turn out/bring in different age-groups; resting the paddocks:

The transition from the stables to the field should be gradual so as to avoid not only digestive disturbances (diarrhoea, flatulence, colic), but also other diseases such as laminitis. Problems in this transition are caused by the fact that in the stable the food is dry, high in fibre and low in protein, while in the field, especially in the spring, the food has a high water content and is low in fibre and high in protein. Green food should therefore be fed beforehand while the horse is still in the stable, and the horse should be turned out for only a few hours a day to start with. If this is not possible, hay should continue to be fed for a few days after the horse has been turned out. For similar reasons the transition from field to stable should be carried out just as carefully.

The horse should be turned out as early in the year as possible, since however excellent the stable care it is no substitute for being turned out in the field. For climatic reasons, in Germany horses can rarely be turned out before the beginning of May. At this time of the year mares with foals should only be out in the daytime. Only in the summer months, if at all, should they be out day and night. As a rule, a mare with foal at foot should receive a concentrate ration, since otherwise her nutritional requirements may not be fully covered. After weaning, foals should not be left out at night, since the intake of concentrates must be controlled, and a foal turned out alone may not satisfy all its nutritional requirements. Horses should be moved regularly to give the grass a chance to recover and to allow the land to be maintained.

2(2) Keeping a Horse in a Stable

The stable should offer protection against wind, rain, snow and extremes of temperature. It should be dry, light, well-ventilated and draught-free.

2(2)i OPEN STABLES AND FIELD SHELTERS

In horse breeding establishments open stables in the form of field shelters are widely used. In the German climate breeding stock can rarely be left out all the year round, but shelters may prolong the turning out period.

Open stables or field shelters are specially suitable for riding horses who cannot be exercised regularly. In theory, any breed can be kept in this way, although horses do need time to get used to this system and it is not suitable for performance horses. Outdoor stables range from the cheaply constructed field shelter to the comparatively luxurious stable with attached, drained compound. The important thing is that whatever savings are made on materials, care must be taken to ensure that the horse cannot injure himself. Hazards include boards which are too thin and through which a horse could chew, or put his foot, and projecting masonry, timber, etc. The most important points to bear in mind when planning and building an open stable or field shelter are the following:

☐ The need to obtain planning permission from the relevant authorities.

☐ The provision of automatic drinkers which do not freeze up in winter.

☐ Placing the opening of the stable on the side away from the weather.

☐ Ensuring that the roof does not reach the ground.

☐ The provision of a waterproof floor where necessary.

☐ Allowing adequate space for storing forage and straw.

2(2)ii ENCLOSED STABLES

Keeping horses in enclosed stables is the most wide-spread system of horse management in Germany. Below are a few criteria which have a decisive effect on the quality of the stabling:

Temperature, which depends on the outside temperature, to which it should be relative; 8 to 15°C is the most desirable.

Humidity A moisture content in the air of up to 50 per cent has a positive effect on performance and function; over 75 per cent has a negative effect. A healthy stable climate must always contain less than 80 per cent humidity.

Air space, which depends on the size and weight of the horse, as well as the work he is doing. These figures provide a rough guide:
   Horses, 28 to 40m^3
   Ponies up to 148cm (about 14·2hh), 20 to 27m^3
   Ponies up to 120cm (about 12hh), 15 to 20m^3

Light As a general rule not less than 1m^2 of window per horse.

Artificial lighting Ideally the boxes should be evenly lit with a light similar to natural daylight.
NB Regulations for electrical installations in damp places must be followed.

Height of stable As a general rule twice the height of the horse at the withers should apply.

Ceiling Wooden ceilings are good because they can absorb moisture if necessary.

Floor Should be tough, dry, not too hard, not cold, and above all not slippery. Brick wood blocks and roughened asphalt are recommended. Maximum slope, 2 per cent.

Gangway Minimum width 2·5m, or 3m between two rows of stables.

25

Ventilation

Ventilation is one of the most difficult problems to solve, because every stable is different in its requirements. The problem is obviously most critical when the stables are all indoors ('American barn') as is mostly the case in Germany. The location, shape and construction of the building have an enormous influence on the environment in the stables and on their ventilation. Although horses need a lot of fresh air, they are extremely sensitive to draughts.

Natural ventilation is provided by windows, doors and ventilation 'extractor' tubes. It is dependent on the natural forces of warmth, humidity, air pressure and wind. This type of ventilation, too, must be carefully planned, because it is not very adjustable. If the difference between the temperature in the stables and the outside temperature is less than 5°C, there is no airflow. 'Extractor' tubes must be at least 4m high to be able to 'draw'. Natural ventilation is not efficient in the warm season of the year.

Mechanical ventilation consists of the use of ventilators. Mechanical ventilation must be resorted to when natural ventilation is not sufficient. It is the most reliable form of ventilation because it is largely independent of outside influences. Mechanical ventilation works irrespective of whether there is overpressure, vacuum or equal pressure and is the complete ventilation system, with air intake and extraction balanced against each other. With this system the ventilation can also be regulated and adjusted. Because the random installation of ventilators never achieves the desired effect, it is absolutely essential to engage a specialist in equine environments to plan the ventilation system and make the necessary temperature calculations. It is advisable to use an expert or an experienced firm, and to obtain a written guarantee. It must be stressed that the specialist should be called in at the planning stage; if he is consulted later, more work

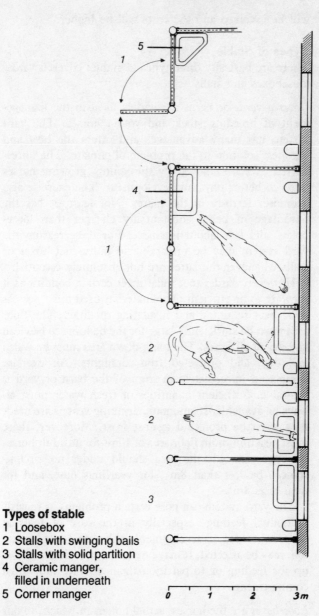

Types of stable
1 Loosebox
2 Stalls with swinging bails
3 Stalls with solid partition
4 Ceramic manger,
   filled in underneath
5 Corner manger

0	1	2	3m

will be involved and the costs will be higher.

Types of Stable

There are basically three types of stable: covered yards, looseboxes and stalls.

Covered yards or barns are widely used in the management of breeding stock and young horses. The yard system has many advantages and offers the best and cheapest solution to the problem of climate. The unrestricted exercise enjoyed by the young, growing horses leads to better physical development. The exercise also promotes fertility in the mares. Not least, it has the advantage of being substantially cheaper than looseboxes, and less labour intensive. For these reasons the yard system may be preferable to individual boxes or stalls whenever the latter are not absolutely essential.

However, yards, too, must meet certain conditions if they are to be efficient. The materials used must possess good heat retaining and insulating qualities. The floor area must be sufficiently large for the bedding to be clean and dry at all times. The lying-down area must be warm and dry, and protected from draughts. An exercise compound immediately in front of the barn or yard is desirable. Sufficient quantities of fresh water must always be available. If automatic drinking vessels are used, they must be protected against frost. Moreover, there must be a minimum floor area of $10m^2$ for an adult horse. For two-year-olds the area should under no circumstances be less than $8m^2$, for yearlings $6m^2$, and for weanlings $4m^2$.

The yard system can pose certain problems as regards individual feeding, especially in the case of foals at different stages of development, although adult horses, too, may be affected. It may be necessary to tie the horses up for feeding or to partition them off into individual compartments.

Looseboxes are the horses' actual homes in which, in our

climatic conditions, animals used for sport spend about twenty-three hours of their day. For this reason special attention should be paid to this part of the building. It is imperative that the following minimum measurements should be respected:

Box Sizes

Horses: 9m², walls 2·80 to 3·00m long

Ponies up to 148cm (about 14·2hh): 7m², walls 2·40 to 2·60m long

Ponies up to 120cm (about 12hh): 5m², walls 2·00 to 2·20m long

Height of box walls from the ground

Horses: 2·20m, of which 1·30m is filled in; 0·90m high grille

Ponies up to 148cm (about 14·2hh): 2·00m, of which 1·10m is filled in; 0·90m high grille

Ponies up to 120cm (about 12hh): 1·80m, of which 0·90m is filled in; 0·90m high grille

The rails of the grille should be 5·5cm maximum apart and should not be easily bendable. Galvanised rails are strongly recommended.

The entrances often poses problems. It should be ensured that the external doorway of a horse stable is not less than 2·5m high and of a pony stable 2m high. If there is an overhang above the external door, the height should be not less than 2·1m (horses), 1·9m (ponies up to 148cm [about 14·2hh]) or 1·7m (ponies up to 120cm [about 12hh]). The width of the doorway should be 110cm minimum. These minimum measurements apply to riding and sport horses on whom normal demands are made. For breeding stock and high performance horses, at least 10 per cent should be added to these figures. A box for a mare with a foal should be not less than 12m². Many studs prefer solid partition walls without grilles both for these boxes and for stallion boxes.

A frequent cause of accidents is an unsatisfactory fastening on the door. The fastening must in all cases

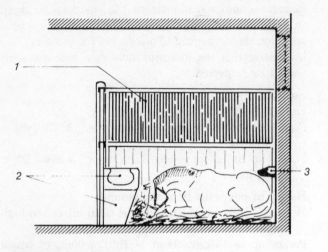

Loosebox (cross-section)
1 Partition wall with grille
2 Ceramic manger, filled in underneath
3 Automatic drinker

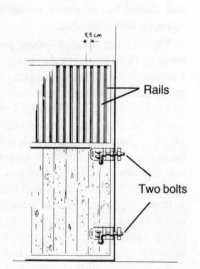

Loosebox door

serve to keep the door shut and to hold it in place at the bottom. It must prevent the horse bending the door outwards while rolling and then pulling back and injuring his leg.

Stalls were acceptable in days gone by when horses were taken out to work every day and were in their stables for only a few hours at night. Nowadays, however, stalls are only used occasionally. The length of each stall should be 3m: in those which are too short there is the risk that the horse's hind legs may come behind the end of the partition. The width of the stall should be 1·6m. In the case of fixed partitions, which are always to be recommended, the width of the stall should be greater. In the case of movable partitions, consisting of swinging bails, the stall need not be so wide, because the horses' legs go under the partition when they lie down. This sort of partition was once the norm in temporary quarters. Since there is a particularly high risk of injury as a result of disputes with the neighbouring horse, the rear end of the bail should be covered with plaited straw or straw-filled sacks. It is also particularly important that the bails can be released quickly if the horse kicks and gets a leg over the top.

Bedding
Bedding has created more and more problems just lately, not least in Germany for those riding establishments which are in the vicinity of towns and have limited storage space.

Straw still makes the best bedding material: it absorbs or binds the waste materials as completely as possible, provides additional heat insulation and protects the horse from injury. Rye or wheat straw are the best. Good barley straw also meets these requirements. 10 to 15kg of bedding per horse per day must be allocated. Peat is also suitable because it is highly absorbent (it absorbs gases as well as liquids). Although wood shavings and wood wool

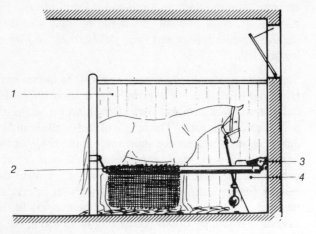

Stalls
1 Partition wall
2 Swinging bail with mat
3 Automatic drinker
4 Ceramic manger, filled in underneath

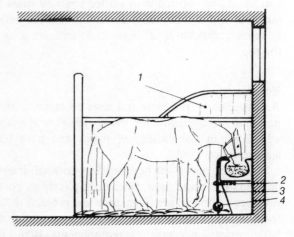

Stalls with fixed partitions
1 Fixed partition with screen
2 Tie-ring anchored in the masonry
3 Tie-rope
4 Log

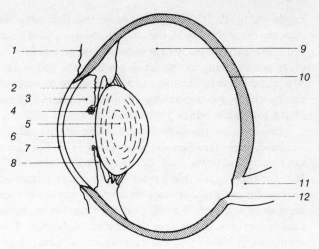

The eye in cross-section

1	Conjunctiva	7	Cornea
2	Posterior chamber	8	Iris
3	Anterior chamber	9	Cavity of the eyeball,
4	Corpora nigre		vitreous humour
	('soot balls')	10	Retina
5	Lens	11	Optic nerve
6	Pupil	12	Optic disc

and pain, and the organs of taste, smell, sight, hearing and balance, are all sense organs. Sensitivity to taste and smell is extraordinarily highly developed in the horse. The two are closely connected, with the sense of smell predominating. Hearing is also sensitive, and the organs of hearing and sight seem, likewise, to be interconnected.

Hearing with both ears is important for a horse to identify where a sound is coming from. Because the ears are a short distance apart, the sound does not reach both ear drums at the same time. This time lag makes for unconscious identification of the location of the sound. Closely connected physically with the organ of hearing is the organ of balance.

The eyeball is protected against pressure injuries and impact against blunt objects by an ample cushion of fat inside the orbit. If this cushion of fat is a thin one, the eyes are more sunken in their orbits. Above the orbit is the supraorbital fossa, which may become very hollow in older horses owing to the break-down of the pad of fat. When the horse is chewing, an up and down movement can be seen in this region, caused by the coronoid process of the lower jaw which protrudes into it.

The orbits are positioned more or less on the side of the head, their axes forming an angle of 115°. This does not correspond to the angle of the eye axes, which is 90°. It is for this reason that horses cannot define shapes as well as, for example, predacious animals, whose eye axes meet at an angle of 20 to 50°, but they can for the same reason survey a larger area of their surroundings. The arrangement of the eyes, and their horizontal, oval pupils, give the horse a field of vision of nearly 360°. The scope of adjustment to bright light and intense darkness is greater in the horse than in man, yet the time taken to adjust to sudden changes in lighting (for instance, when jumping under floodlights) seems to be longer. Colours are seen by horses with a different intensity than they are by man, yellow and green colour ranges being seen with greater intensity than blue and red. Also the horse's ability to perceive movement is far superior to that of man. The smallest briefest movements can be seen, which accounts for many cases of shying in which a rider is unable to identify the cause.

The eyelids protect the transparent cornea from external influences (eyelid reflex) and keep it moist (blinking). Secretions from the lacrimal glands ('tears') are provided for this latter purpose. Superfluous 'tears' collect in the inner corner of the eye and are taken away by the naso-lacrimal duct, which discharges into the lower corner of the nostril through a clearly visible opening. Inside the eyeball are the aqueous and vitreous humours, the anterior and posterior chambers of the eye, the lens and the cavity of the eyeball. The cornea is visibly stretched over the pigmented iris in front of the lens.

Through the process of contraction or dilation, the horizontal, oval opening in the middle (pupil) regulates the amount of light allowed in. On the edge of the pupil are peppercorn-sized bodies (*corpora nigra*). The time taken to adapt to sudden changes in light conditions (for example in indoor competitions, jumping under flood-lights) seems to be longer in the horse than in man.

The lens is a glassy, transparent, compact organ. By changing its curvature it can alter the angle of refraction of the light. This enables the horse to focus on objects at different distances. However, the sharpness of detail does not equal that obtained by man. The cavity of the eyeball behind the lens contains a transparent, colour-less, jelly-like material called vitreous humour. The innermost coat of the eyeball is the light-sensitive retina, the nerve fibre layer of which is thicker in the horse than in any other domestic mammal. At the point where the optic nerve enters the eyeball is the optic disc (German: so-called 'blind spot') which contains no light-sensitive nerve fibres.

4. Feeding

4(1) How the Nutrients are Provided

The horse does not live on food alone: it is the constituents which are the all-important factor. Food is not
itself a nutritive substance, only a vehicle for conveying
such substances. The horse possesses anatomical equipment – the digestive organs – which enable it to gain
access to the nutrients in the food. Chemical and biological processes which take place inside these organs are
known as digestion, and comprise three areas of activity:

Releasing the nutritive raw materials from the food
Proteins, fats, carbohydrates (starches, sugars), fibre,
mineral salts, trace elements, vitamins and active ingre-
dients*.

*Breaking down or converting the nutritive raw materials into
pure nutrients*
Protein into amino acids, fat into fatty acids, carbohy-
drate into soluble sugars (grape sugar†), mineral and
trace element salts into elements (e.g. into calcium,
phosphorus, iron, copper, etc).

Converting the pure nutrients into an absorbable form
This enables the nutrients to be transported around the
body and utilised.

The diagram shows in a simplified form what the horse
looks like inside, and what happens there. The horse
takes in his food mainly with the lips and tongue. The
incisor teeth (12) are only used when food is picked

---

* Active ingredients fall into the 'nutritive raw materials' category. They may be 'taste
materials', which act on the horse's tongue and make him chew and produce saliva. Drugs also
contain active ingredients. Likewise, vitamins fall into the active ingredients category.

† A type of glucose.

1 Salivary gland
2 Oesophagus
3 Lungs
4 Stomach
5 Small intestine
6 Kidney
7 Caecum
8 Large colon
9 Ureter
10 Small colon
11 Rectum
12 Incisor teeth
13 Cheek teeth
14 Thyroid gland
15 Heart
16 Liver
17 Portal vein
18 Biliary duct
19 Pancreas
20 Urinary bladder

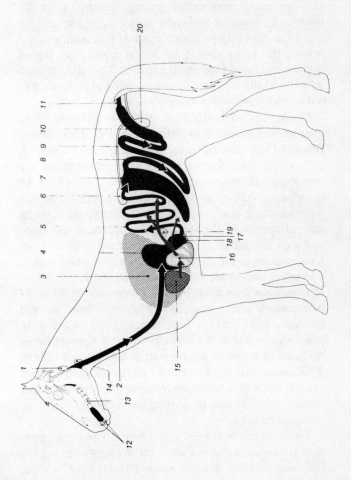

(grazing) or if solid lumps of food (beet) are eaten. In the oral cavity the food is broken up and ground by the well-developed cheek teeth (13). Chewing is a laborious but necessary task, which serves to keep the cheek teeth evenly worn (they continue growing throughout life). Without it (e.g. when something goes wrong with the chewing equipment or if insufficient chewing takes place), sharp edges and hooks form on the teeth which, in time, cause considerable feeding difficulties. In the long term, to ensure sufficient work for the jaws and, as will be mentioned again later, optimal functioning of the bowel, the horse should be fed at least 2 to 3kg of coarse-structured food (hay) per day. This also explains why the addition of hay is recommended in preference to a diet comprising only complete cubes.

During chewing, the food is well mixed with large quantities of saliva (40 to 50 litres per day). This saliva is produced and secreted by the salivary glands (1). Smooth balls of food are formed which are swallowed via the oesophagus (2) into the stomach. At the point where the oesophagus (approximately 1·5m in length) joins the stomach there is a powerful sphincter muscle. During normal activity of the stomach this sphincter can open and shut rhythmically. If there is excessive pressure or fermentation in the stomach the muscle remains closed, making it impossible for the horse to vomit.

The horse's stomach (4) has a capacity of 12 to 14 litres, which is very small in relation to its body size and its daily food intake (approximately 10 to 15kg of concentrates and bulky, fibrous foods + approximately 40 litres of water + approximately 40 litres of saliva). This means that the horse is by nature an animal which eats little and continuously. Practical horse-feeding should therefore aim at splitting the ration into as many meals as possible.

The stomach is shaped like a bean. The upper part, near the oesophageal orifice, is turned outwards and is a little antechamber. It contains digestively active bacteria.

The latter break down the starches and sugars in the food, which have already been released by chewing, into lactic acid (fermentation). This bacterial digestion is on a very small scale. However, it assumes significance when stomach conditions are disturbed and it encroaches on the main stomach. Intensive fermentation then takes place, with the formation of large quantities of lactic acid and gas. It can lead to inflammation of the mucous membrane of the stomach or even rupture of the stomach. The risk of fermentation of this type exists when the stomach is suddenly overloaded and the contents consist mainly of starchy, finely structured and pasty foods (e.g. too finely milled grain with the husks removed). A diet containing an excessive quantity of foods with a high sugar content can also predispose to this condition. This disturbance can occur, too, if a horse is put into hard work straight after a full meal.

In the substantially larger main stomach the food is piled up in layers in the order of its arrival. The increasing fullness of the stomach triggers off wave-like muscular contractions which run down the stomach wall. These contractions cause a thorough mixing of the layers of food, while throughout the process the mixture is soaked in gastric juices and the water which the horse has drunk. The gastric juices consist mainly of hydrochloric acid, which is manufactured in the top layer of the mucous membrane of the stomach and released from there into the gastric juices. Its manufacture is simultaneous with the accumulation of saliva in the oral cavity. The inner layer of the mucous membrane of the stomach has an insulating effect and prevents the stomach wall disintegrating on account of this corrosive acid, which would eat it away.

The role of hydrochloric acid in the digestive process is a broad one: it kills off bacteria which stray into the main stomach from the fore-stomach, and by so doing prevents the bacterial fermentation processes of the fore-stomach intruding into the main stomach in the way discussed previously. At the same time the food is 'disinfected'. Moreover, hydrochloric acid draws minerals and trace elements from the food and releases them completely. Finally, in conjunction with the digestive aid, pepsin (an enzyme), it is responsible for the first stage in the release of food protein materials and their breakdown into smaller protein-building blocks.

By the last stage of stomach digestion the food has become a semi-fluid material called 'chyme' and has already clearly lost its original structure. It has been reduced to very small pieces and is soft. The minerals have been fully released from the food, the breakdown of the food proteins has begun and many vitamins and active ingredients have already been released and are available in the gastric juices. Only the fibre, starches, sugars and fats are still almost in their original state. This means that the digestive process must continue. This task is taken over by the intestines, which are joined on to the stomach.

The intestinal canal of the horse is very long and consists of several differently shaped sections. The first is the small intestine (5), which is about 24m long. On the outside it is smooth, but it is full of twists and turns.

It is followed by the large, sack-like caecum (7) which is about 1m long and turned outwards. To this is attached the large colon (8), which is characterised by the many wave-like protrusions along the outside. This opens into the small colon (10) with its very deep, pocket-shaped hollows. The total length of the large and small colons is about 8m. The last section is the short, smooth rectum (11), which is about 20 to 30cm long. The total length of the intestinal canal is about 30m. It can therefore only fit into the abdominal cavity in a series of loops. In the bends and turns there is a reduction in diameter, which can easily give rise to stoppages and colic problems. This anatomical structure explains why colic is so common in horses and why it can occur in so many parts of the intestinal canal.

Intestinal digestion is started off by rhythmic contractions of the pyloric sphincter, a muscle at the exit from the stomach through which the acid chyme is released, a little at a time, into the small intestine. The first contact of the hydrocholoric acid with the wall of the small intestine causes the pancreas (19), the duct from which opens into the small intestine, to begin secreting juices which contain large quantities of sodium bicarbonate plus several digestive enzymes. About 4 litres per day are produced. The sodium bicarbonate neutralizes the acidity of the hydrochloric acid. Bile, which is produced in the liver (the horse has no gall bladder), arrives at the same time through the biliary duct (18). About 5 to 6 litres per day are produced. Apart from these substances, there is a continuous secretion of fluid, known as intestinal juices, from numerous small glands in the intestinal wall.

The next stage in the treatment of the food begins in this mixture of different fluids. The digestive enzyme diastase breaks down the carbohydrates (starches and sugars) into soluble sugars. The enzyme trypsin further splits up the protein materials, which have already been partly broken down in the stomach, into their final components, the so-called amino acids (pure food elements). The bile breaks down the fat constituents into fine particles (an emulsion), which enables the enzyme lipase to split the fat into its compounds, glycerol and fatty acids. Only the fibrous constituents come through this procedure unchanged as they are accessible only with difficulty.

They are digested, however, further on in the intestines. The caecum and the colon are especially suited to this task. They are host to a veritable zoo of microorganisms (bacteria and protozoa), whose numbers run into billions. They are not harmful but render valuable service, since they possess the special ability to break through and dissolve the tough, hard walls of the fibres. This process yields high-energy organic acids and the

73

intestinal gases. The micro-organisms feed on the protein constituents still present in the fibre. During these activities, and while constantly multiplying in number, they also produce large quantities of vitamins (vitamin K and the B vitamins). In the last sections of the intestine the micro-organisms die and are themselves subject to digestion. By this method bacterial protein is made available to the horse as a high grade protein, and bacterial vitamins are also made available. This explains why the adult horse does not need any animal protein in its diet. A healthy horse is self-sufficient in this sphere.

In the small colon the digestive processes come to an end. The intestinal contents remain in the deep 'pockets' of this section of the bowel for approximately 18 to 24 hours and, with the progressive removal of water, are turned into the characteristic balls of dung which are expelled in batches via the rectum. The movement of the contents through the intestine is brought about by continuous wave-like muscular contractions running along the intestinal walls (peristalsis). It takes the contents 40 to 60 hours to go from the stomach to the rectum, depending on the quantity and the constituents of the diet.

During the passage through the intestine, the released nutrients or their components are continuously being absorbed through the bowel wall to pass into the metabolism. This absorption takes place via an infinitely large quantity of small, finger-like processes on the intestinal wall (villi) which project into the intestinal contents like tree-roots and draw up the nutrients with water, like blotting paper.

From the villi the nutrients and the water pass into the blood vessels, which form a fine, branching network throughout the whole of the intestinal wall area. The blood vessels containing the nutrients unite in the large, well-developed portal vein (17) which enters the liver through the 'porta' and takes the nutrients to the liver (16). The liver is the most important organ in the inner body for the processing and storage of nutrients. It can be compared with a factory in which everything is sorted, registered, processed and finally so precisely prepared and graded that the nutrients leave it as finished building materials. They are then pumped directly by the heart to the 'building sites', where they can be used in accordance with special biological building plans.

The building sites are the individual cells in the body tissues. Here, from the protein-building blocks which have been delivered (amino-acids), new protein materials are constructed (e.g. flesh, muscles). The minerals and trace elements are used for building bone and for activating, and therefore controlling, important metabolic processes (e.g. muscle contractions, heart rhythm, transporting oxygen in the lungs (3) and in the blood, water balance in the tissues and reproductive processes). The vitamins and active ingredients protect against stress and wear and tear, and act as a defensive barrier against infection. The organic acids (e.g. fatty acids) and sugars are important sources of energy, to be drawn on as required for muscular activity. These metabolic processes are constituents of an overall operation which is highly complex, and in fact so complicated that many of the details are still unknown in spite of extensive research.

During the conversion and manufacturing processes inside the body, materials accrue which the body cannot use and which, if allowed to build up, lead to poisoning. These waste materials are removed when the blood passes through the kidneys (6), whose task is that of a purification plant. This organ works like a filter, keeping back the purified blood and allowing the waste materials to trickle down through the ureter (9) to the bladder (20).

Finally it must be understood that no animal is in a position fully to utilise its food and the nutrients contained in it. A certain percentage of the nutrients is always passed out in the faeces and lost. A further percentage passes out in the urine. A proportion of the nutrients must also be set aside for maintenance purposes. Only after these nutrients, which can be defined exactly by scientific tests, have been subtracted are we left with the quota which can be used for development and work (growth, muscle activity).

In practical horse-feeding the concentration of nutritive materials in the diet should be worked out so that all the nutrients are available, in the necessary quantity, for the job the horse is asked to perform. In addition, all the components of the diet should be checked for quality and combined in such a way that they cannot cause disturbances in the alimentary canal or metabolism. Only if these aspects are taken into consideration can feeding hope to fulfil the horse's nutritional requirements.

4(2) Foodstuffs

The universally acknowledged scientific theories on feeding and nutrition also apply to horses. The nutrient, mineral, trace element and vitamin content of the diet must be adequate; it must fulfil the various physiological needs and meet certain requirements as regards structure and taste.

In practice there are four main groups of foodstuffs:

1 Green foods and succulents	grass obtained by grazing; cut green feed; grass and maize silage; root vegetables
2 Forage (bulk food)	hay
3 Individual (simple) foods	oats; barley; maize; wheat*; linseed; flaked oats; bran; sugar beet pulp, etc.
4 Compound foods	mineral and special balancers, supplements and complete feeds

* Not used in British diets.

The first three food groups do not guarantee a balanced diet on their own – the latter can only be achieved by the addition of a compound feed. Average consumption of an unvaried diet of one of the following could be expected to work out as follows:

	grass, green feed	maize-silage	carrots, beets	hay	straw	cereals
protein	+++	+	+	+/++	0	+/++
energy	+/++	++	+	+	+	+++
crude fibre	+/++	++	0	+++	+++	+
woody fibre	+	++	0	+++	+++	+
calcium	+/++	+	+	+/++	+	0
phosphorus	+/++	+	+	+/++	0	++
sodium	0	0	+/++	0	0	0
trace elements	+	+	+	+	0	+
vitamins	+/++	0	+/0	0	0	+

+++ excessive supply   + insufficient supply
 ++ balanced supply   0 deficiency

Not only do the foodstuffs on this list exhibit nutritional imbalances, as the table shows, but there are also considerable variations in the content of individual samples. Green feed, silage and hay are particularly difficult to evaluate. Only in the ready-prepared compound feeds are the contents constant.

Nowadays *pasture* consists primarily of *grasses*. In the four stages of growth used as an example the contents per kg of dry matter vary as follows:

In the dry matter

	Dry matter g/kg	digestible protein g/kg	crude fibre g/kg	Mcal per kg	=approx TDN	Ca g/kg	P g/kg
very young (5 to 8cm high)	150	230	160	2.85	650	4·6	4·4

	Dry matter g/kg	digestible protein g/kg	crude fibre g/kg	Mcal per kg	= approx TDN	Ca g/kg	P g/kg
young to mature (9 to 17cm)	165	180	200	2·70	620	5·4	4·2
mature (18 to 26cm)	180	140	240	2·60	600	5·6	3·8
older to overripe (over 30cm)	220	90	280	2·40	550	5·9	3.0

The energy content of a foodstuff or of the diet as a whole is now given as *digestible energy* in Megacalories: 2.85Mcal = 2,850Kcal (Kilocalories).

The expression TDN is also used (= Total Digestible Nutrients). Foods which contain more than 15 per cent curde fibre – in particular hay and straw – are rated too favourably by TDN, which is used to measure diets that remain constant and that consist, for example, of hay + oats. (TDN is more or less equivalent to the familiar Starch Units – St.E. = Stärkeeinheiten – which are no longer in use in scientific circles.)

In all their utilizable stages of growth, *grass* and *green feed*, which should always be fed fresh, contain a considerable *excess of protein*. However, the *woody fibre* content of the young plants is insufficient. This results in gastric and intestinal catarrh (diarrhoea) and tympany (flatulence). Clover and lucern, which are substantially higher in protein than grass, are particularly problematical in this respect and not suitable for feeding on their own.

If anything the mineral content is likely to be below the levels given in the table, while the Ca:P ratio increases as the grasses in the pasture get older. A mineral supplement is usually necessary.

Silage (fermented food) is not particularly suitable for horses. However, there is one exception to this rule: *maize silage*, which is more or less uniform in quality from one year to the next (only the dry matter content varies); 25 per cent dry matter = 2.6Mcal/kg (per kg dry matter) is the most desirable. In good years the dry matter content reaches 25 to 28 per cent in Northern Germany and sometimes as much as 30 per cent in Southern Germany. In respect of the dry matter, maize silage contains substantially more energy than hay and has a favourable crude fibre content while containing less woody fibre. It can, therefore, replace both hay and cereals at once. As a guide, 10kg maize silage = 1kg hay + max. 2kg cereals/compound feed.

Beet is especially good for providing the horse with an appetising change, but it is low in nutrients and woody fibre and should only be fed within certain limits – for an adult horse a maximum of 15kg per day. If fed on a regular daily basis, 3kg is recommended as a maximum. NB if dried beat pulp is used it must always be soaked for at least twelve hours before it is fed.

The food value of *hay* is particularly difficult to judge. It depends on the botanical composition (grasses, clover, herbs) and the stage at which it is cut (heading, flowering, end of flowering), as well as on the harvesting and storage. The processes involved in mechanical hay-making (turning, baling and dropping off) inflict varying degrees of damage on the nutritious leafy parts, depending on how dry they are. Factors which have a marked effect on the food value of the hay can be detected externally, i.e. from the colour (pale, bleached, brown), the texture (leafy, stalky, coarse) and the smell (fragrant, devoid of smell, musty).

Hay is of fundamental importance in horse feeding, and should only be replaced to a limited extent by other foods. The woody fibre it contains is essential for the smooth functioning of the digestive processes.

Commercial hay is almost always of the grass type (over 80 per cent grass). Its nutritional content in respect of the same amount of dry matter is always considerably less than that of fresh grass of comparable type. The mineral content is also comparatively low, and the original high carotene content is almost completely lost, however careful the preserving process. A vitamin and mineral supplement is usually recommended to restore the balance.

Average variations in the nutritive content: hay (over 80 per cent grass)

stage at which cut	In the dry matter		
	digestible protein g/kg	Mcal per kg	= approx. TDN
full head average value quality from ... to ...	70 80 - 45	1.90	440 480 - 420
full flower average value quality from ... to ...	55 65 - 35	1·65	380 420 - 335
end of flowering average value quality from ... to ...	40 50 - 25	1·20	300 330 - 275
for comparison: mature fresh grass	140	2·40	600

As well as the differences due to the stages of growth, there are variations in quality, mainly determined by the woody fibre content and the freshness (not mouldy). For horses a medium nutritional content is sufficient, but special attention must be paid to the freshness. The colour, the smell and the presence of any mould are indicators of this.

Straw can be used together with supplements (it is deficient in nutrients and minerals) to replace hay as the woody fibre component of the diet, in instances where hay is short. If sufficient hay is difficult to obtain, a proportion can be substituted by straw. The minimum amount of hay is 1·5kg, but it is preferable to leave 3kg if possible. Even with this ratio the missing nutrients and minerals must be replaced. The feed manufacturers must be consulted so as to avoid adverse effects on the diet.

Oats are still the best cereal for horses. Their lower energy content is compensated for by a host of advantages from the point of view of digestion and nutritional physiology. Because of their husks, oats need to be chewed thoroughly and slowly. The husks keep the bowel contents loose, helping to prevent colic. The essential amino-acid content (amino-acids are indispensable components of protein) is higher than in other cereals. The fatty acids and gelling agents are dietetically valuable. In spite of their qualities, most full diets also contain barley, maize and wheat*. These cereals contain more energy (which is important for performance horses) and their quality is fairly consistent, while that of oats is not.

The weight of the oats per litre, which is easy to ascertain, provides information on the concentration of nutrients. As a guide there should be 500g/litre, which means 26 per cent husk and an energy content of 2·60Mcal. There should be an absolute minimum of green kernels, foreign bodies and dirt.

The colour of the husk depends on the type of oat and has no particular significance in relation to its food value. The important factors are ripeness and condition (freshness, lack of mould) which can also be ascertained by tasting them.

Mineral supplements are needed when any types of cereals and their derivatives, especially bran, are fed, as they contain a marked excess of phosphorus but only insignificant quantities of calcium and sodium. Experiments show that hay alone is not sufficient to restore the Ca:P:Na balance, and a mineral supplement or a balancer food containing the required amounts of Ca and Na minerals is necessary.

---

* Not used in British diet.

A wide range of *supplements, balancers and complete feeds* has been on the market for several years, making it possible for everyone to base their horse's diet on modern scientific principles. They fall into the following categories:

☐ Mineral supplements and mineral briquettes* to provide extra minerals and active ingredients.

☐ Supplements and balancers used to boost the energy, protein, mineral and active-ingredient content of the diet as a whole.

☐ Complete feeds aimed at providing all the necessary nutrients and active ingredients. Hay or straw should be added to ensure sufficient fibre in the diet. It is also recommended that the day's supply of food should be split into four feeds.

For youngstock there are the following additional categories:

☐ Milk replacement feed to be used to supplement or completely replace the dam's milk.

☐ Foal rearing feed for the first year of life.

All these compound feeds must conform to the regulations governing foodstuffs. The fact that the contents are guaranteed takes the guesswork out of deciding on the food value and the best use for the food, and ensures that the value of the contents remains consistent. The contents include nutrients which determine the protein and energy content, namely crude protein, crude fat, crude fibre, starches and sugars. Sometimes the essential amino-acids lysine and methionine are mentioned separately. The mineral substances (elements) calcium, phosphorus, sodium and magnesium are also included amongst the contents.

---

* Briquettes are mineral supplements in biscuit form. Their purpose is to provide a mineral supplement in a form which can be fed to horses who are not receiving any other kind of concentrate feed, in other words they can be fed direct and do not have to be mixed with other food.

All complete compound feeds, balancers and supplements are also fortified and contain *additives*. These are compounds of trace elements, namely salts of the elements iron, copper, zinc, manganese, iodine and cobalt as well as vitamins, flavourings, antioxidants and other substances which increase the food value or the storage life. Permitted substances and quantities are governed by EEC regulations. Racing and competitions also lay down rules regarding prohibited substances and only certain brands/types claim to be free of these.

Without appropriate supplements, either in the form of mineral/vitamin supplements or compound feeds, serious deficiencies can occur, especially in the winter. As well as the essential vitamins A, D and E, vitamins of the B complex may be needed. Also results of recent research have credited carotene, which used to be considered just a precursor of vitamin A, with a significance in its own right in the field of fertility.

The various complete foods mentioned above will supply economically and in the correct quantities the nutrients, minerals and supplements that the horse requires. It is worth considering that many of these essential substances are not accessible to the horse keeper, and that producing them and making them usable requires specialised knowledge. For example, when dealing with mineral and trace element compounds, their respective chemical and taste aspects must be taken into consideration, as must the digestive physiology of the horse, while with vitamins allowance must be made for the fact that their storage life depends on the type of food in which they are contained. When these substances are being used, the correct quantities and ratios are important: imbalances can cause physiological disturbance or even illness.

Even those substances possessing, or credited with, special nutritional, dietary or taste value, are most effective as part of a full feed supplement. Examples are skimmed milk powder, whey powder, glucose (grape sugar), linseed cake, linseed, soya bean meal, brewers yeast, grass meal, dried sugar beet pulp and molasses. (Feeding dried sugar beet and linseed as individual feeds requires special care; the sugar beet must be soaked for twelve hours and the linseed cooked.)

The selection of suitable ingredients and additives makes complete foods appetising and wholesome. They save the horse keeper the trouble, in most instances, of making up the diet himself, though in special cases it may be necessary to consult the manufacturer.

4(3) Food Storage

The amount of space required to store concentrates and forage depends on the period for which it is to be kept. When planning, it should be borne in mind that the availability of storage space can greatly affect the total cost of horse keeping. There is a big difference between the price of hay and straw bought in quantity at harvest time and then stored, and that of the same forage bought a little at a time because of lack of space. The experience of recent years shows that even if interest rates are high, income earned over the storage period does not equal the saving made by buying at harvest time. The following figures specify the amount of storage space required for a month – for longer periods they should be increased accordingly:

Storage space per horse per month based on a daily ration of 5kg oats, 6kg hay and up to 10kg straw (feed and bedding straw)

Oats   approximately $0.35m^3$
Hay   approximately $1.50m^3$
Straw   approximately $2.00m^3$

The figures relate to high-pressure baled hay and straw. Since the different types of feed must be easily accessible, a further 30 per cent must be added to cover the 'dead space'. Cubes, which are becoming increasingly popular, take up about the same amount of storage space as oats.

Where barn-type stabling is used, it is best to store the feed over the top of the stables, i.e. directly above the passageway, for the following reasons:

☐ The construction costs are considerably lower than those involved in erecting a separate building.

☐ The forage stored over the stables provides a 'natural' insulation both in winter and in summer.

☐ The foodstuffs can be passed down into the stables through hatches in the ceiling over the passageway.

☐ The mess created by carting hay and straw around the yard is avoided.

All storage areas must be well ventilated. The feed must not come into direct contact with the floor, as even hay which is dry when stored attracts moisture. A layer of dry straw on the floor provides a simple form of insulation.

In establishments with twenty or more horses a silo is recommended for the storage of oats or cubes. A supply of loose feed is very practical and, because there are no bags to be paid for, it brings considerable price savings. The manufacturer sends the feed by tanker and it is blown from the tank straight into the silo, a process which keeps the feed clean and eliminates wastage. Not only is this a space-saving way of storing feed, it also cuts out the time-consuming manual task of carrying sacks. There is no wastage of food particles through being left behind in the bottom of the sack and there are no paper sacks to be disposed of.

Indoor and outdoor silos, made of diolen, metal, or plastic reinforced with glass fibre, are available in various designs. In Germany companies belonging to the 'Horse Feeds and Feeding Methods' study circle will give free on-the-spot information to interested parties on the necessary arrangements (situation, access for the delivery vehicles, protecting against the weather, etc) and the problem of transporting food from the silo to the stable. Do-it-yourself silos and foodstores are also possible, and again member firms of the study circle will offer advice.

It is essential to check silos regularly, if possible before each delivery, and especially during the warm summer months, to make sure the food is not being contaminated or becoming lumpy owing to condensation or similar factors. Where such problems occur the silo must be thoroughly cleaned out. No silo owner should neglect this task, for he will have to foot the bill out of his own pocket for any losses incurred. Neither the silo manufacturer nor the feed supplier çan be held liable for damage resulting from storing food in á neglected silo.

4(4) Devising a Diet

Devising a diet for a horse depends on:
- ☐ The nutritional requirements of the horse.
- ☐ The compatibility and suitability of the foodstuffs.
- ☐ The cost effectiveness of the diet.

Nutritional Requirements
These are essentially dependent on the body weight and condition of the horse, as well as what is required of him or her (e.g. work, milk, growth). There are broad criteria by which the horse keeper can judge the horse's requirements; for example, the condition, the sheen and appearance of the coat, the consistency of the dung and the horse's behaviour will show whether there are any drastic faults in the diet. A great deal more information is gleaned by the horse keeper who works out the diets according to a plan (page 94) from tables showing the different requirements (pages 90-91) and composition of the various foodstuffs (pages 92-3). In these tables only the dry matter, crude fibre, crude protein, energy, calcium, phosphorus and sodium contents are given. This is because if the right quantities of these components are fed it is extremely unlikely that problems will arise. Apart from carotene and vitamin A, deficiencies of minerals, trace elements and vitamins are very rare, provided the foodstuffs are of acceptable quality.

The horse's *food intake* of dry matter is limited. As a general rule the daily intake of dry matter is between 1·5 and 2·5kg per 100kg body weight. The diet should also contain 16 – 22 per cent crude fibre in the dry matter, and a large proportion of the crude fibre must be of the woody type.

In diets containing hay, the following plan can be used (kg of food per 100kg body weight):

work load	nil		light	medium	heavy
hay (kg)	1·00 to 1·12		1·00	1·00	0·75
concentrates					
(kg)		0·50	0·75	1·00	1·25 to 1·50

If the amount of energy supplied coincides with the amount required, there should be no change in the body weight of the horse. If a loss of weight occurs, then either there is less energy in the food than has been calculated, or the horse's requirement is higher (for instance, as a result of the horse weighing more, of a heavier work load, nervousness or poor skin insulation). If there is an unexpected gain in weight, then the reverse applies.

An excess of *protein* occurs very easily, except in foals and mares with foal at foot. A certain excess can be tolerated but higher levels do not benefit the horse but place excessive strain on the liver and kidneys with a higher through-put of water. In these cases lower protein foodstuffs should be substituted. Protein quality is only important in horses up to the age of eighteen months.

The *ratio of calcium to phosphorus* is a particularly important aspect of the horse's requirement of these two minerals, and should be between 1·5 and 3 : 1 taken over the diet as a whole. Some individual foodstuffs are deficient in calcium to such an extent that it is almost impossible to make it up by swapping round the other components of the diet (pages 90-91); the best solution is a mineral lick specially designed for horses, with a calcium : phosphorus ratio of 3 : 1. The supply of sodium is almost always insufficient, so that a salt lick must

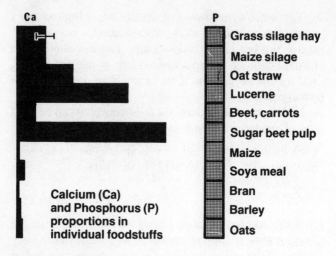

Calcium (Ca)
and Phosphorus (P)
proportions in
individual foodstuffs

Ca — P

Grass silage hay
Maize silage
Oat straw
Lucerne
Beet, carrots
Sugar beet pulp
Maize
Soya meal
Bran
Barley
Oats

always be provided.

The horse's requirement of *carotene* is about 25mg β-carotene per 100kg body weight, or 10,000 iu vit.A. The ideal seems to be to include both vitamin A and carotene in the diet. Whilst vitamin A is added to compound feeds, B-carotene, as well as being present in compound feeds, also occurs naturally, for example in grass (30 to 75mg per kg), in grass meal (100 to 400mg per kg) and in carrots (50 to 60mg per kg). The chart on page 95 shows a diet which has been worked out as an example, with a few comments added. It goes without saying that the ingredients do not always correspond exactly to the requirements. The important thing is to know how to assess these discrepancies.

The following are the particular requirements of the different groups of horses:

1. BREEDING STOCK

Barren and Maiden Mares Barren mares are 'let down' by reducing their concentrate ration by about 30 per cent. However, a good supply of minerals, trace elements and vitamins must be provided. The concentrate ration should be stepped up again at the beginning of the breeding season (when the daylight and the temperature increase). It is essential to avoid an excess of protein and imbalances in the calcium/phosphorus supply.

In-Foal Mares During early pregnancy the energy supply can be 10 to 20 per cent above the normal requirement to lessen the risk of resorption. Only from the eighth month onwards are higher levels of concentrates and mineral supplements necessary. However, contrary to popular belief, no increase in the protein level is necessary.

Lactating Mares A considerable increase in nutrients is required once milk production commences. The protein content, in particular, must be stepped up (e.g. by feeding a balancer feed for breeding stock). Foetal resorption in a mare with foal at foot may well occur as the result of discrepancies between nutrient output (milk) and input (food). However, an excess of nutrients can encourage the survival of a twin pregnancy.

Stud Stallions Outside the breeding season a stallion should be fed on a similar basis to a riding horse. About two months before the beginning of the breeding season the supply of minerals, trace elements and vitamins – in particular B-carotene – should be increased. During the season the stallion does not need more protein, as is commonly believed, but rather an increase in the energy supply. The nutrient requirement is approximately the same as that of a mare in late pregnancy.

2. HORSES USED FOR SPORTING PURPOSES

Horses used for sport need more energy and sodium for muscle activity. The requirement of the other nutrients increases only slightly. Youngsters and horses who have not worked for a long period need a temporary increase in protein, calcium and phosphorus. Increasing the

Requirements of the most important nutrients (Mcal = Megacalories = 1,000 calories, 1 Mcal = 4,186 Megajoules)

Group	Bodyweight kg	Digestible energy MJ	or Mcal	Digestible Protein g	Calcium g	Phosphorus g	Sodium g
Adult horses not working or lactating	100	19	4.5	100 ⎫	6– 8	4– 5	4– 5
	200	32	7.6	160 ⎭			
	300	43	10.2	220 ⎫	15–17	8–10	8–10
	400	54	12.9	270 ⎭			
	500	64	15.3	320 ⎫	22–25	13–15	13–15
	600	73	17.4	360 ⎭			
Adult horses in light work (½–1 hour light exercise per day)	400	54– 67	13–16	300 ⎫	17	10	14*
	500	64– 80	15–19	380 ⎭			
	600	73– 91	17–22	410 ⎭	26	16	21*
Adult horses in medium work (1–2 hours per day light exercise or ½–1 hour per day strenuous exercise)	400	67– 81	16–19	370 ⎫	18	11	18*
	500	80– 96	19–23	440 ⎭			
	600	91–109	22–26	500 ⎭	26	16	28*
Adult horses in hard work	400	18+	19+	405+ ⎫	18	12	24*
	500	96+	23+	480 ⎭			
	600	109+	26+	545 ⎭	27	17	36*

	Weight					14	10	5
Heavily in-foal mares (11th month) with no additional expenditure of energy	100	24	5.7	160		14	10	5
	200	40	9.5	260				
	300	54	12.9	350		29	19	11
	400	67	16.0	440				
	500	80	19.1	520		44	29	16
	600	91	21.7	590				
	700	102	23.4	670		50	35	18
Mares with foals, no additional expenditure of energy (requirements rising with milk production from 1st-3rd month after foaling, then falling again from 3rd-5th month)	100	36– 32	8.6– 7.6	320–	250	20	16	6
	200	60– 54	14.3–12.9	530–	420			
	300	82– 73	19.5–17.7	720–	560	37	29	12
	400	101– 91	24.1–21.7	890–	700			
	500	120–108	28.7–25.8	1,060–	830	52	41	18
	600	137–123	32.7–29.4	1,210–	940			
	700	154–138	36.8–33.0	1,360–	1,060	60	45	22
	Final Weight							
Foals aged: 3–6 months	100–200	17– 29	4– 7	140–	255	12	8	2
	300–400	40– 51	9.5–12.1	365–	470	23	17	4
	500–600	60– 70	14.3–16.7	575–	675	36	25	6
7–12 months	100–200	18– 30	4.3– 7.2	120–	210	10	6	3
	300–400	42– 52	10.0–12.4	300–	380	19	13	5
	500–600	62– 72	14.8–17.2	460–	540	29	19	9
13–14 months (thereafter see under 'Management')	100–200	19– 34	4.5– 8.1	115–	195	10	7	4
	300–400	44– 58	10.5–13.8	285–	340	19	13	8
	500–600	66– 79	15.8–18.9	435–	470	31	20	12

*Higher in conjunction with heavy losses through sweating

Analysis of the most important nutrients in foodstuffs (per kg of the original substance)
(Mcal = Megacalories = 1,000 Calories, 1 Mcal = 4,186 Megajoules [MJ])

	Dry Matter %	Crude fibre g/kg	Digestible crude protein g/kg	Digestible energy MJ	Digestible energy Mcal	Calcium g/kg	Phosphorus g/kg	Sodium g/kg	Carotene mg
Meadow grass, fresh, first growth, headed and before	18.8	42	25	1.9	0.45	0.8–1.2	0.7	0.2	50–75
Beginning to middle of flowering	21	54	28	2.0	0.48	1.0–1.4	0.8	0.2	30–50
Grass silage, wilted, first cut	30–45	90–130	20–33	2.5–4.0	0.6–0.95	2.0–3.0	1.0–1.4	0.1	40–40
Maize silage, mature	30	70	15	2.9	0.7	0.8–1.0	0.6–0.8	0.1	–
Beet leaf silage	16	22	15	1.5	0.37	1.9	0.4	1–2	5.1
Meadow hay, beginning to middle of flowering	87	268	52	7.5	1.78	3.5–6.0	2.5–4.0	0.6	10–20
Meadow hay, end of flowering	87	290	50	7.2	1.72	4.5–6.0	2.0–3.0	0.5	5–10
Lucern (dried)	89	281	84	8.5	2.02	18.0	2.9	1.7	100–200
Oat straw, wheat straw	88	400	8	5.0–5.5	1.2–1.3	2.7–3.6	1.2–0.7	1–2	
Barley straw treated with ammonia	88	402	7	5.0	1.2	2.7	0.7	1.1	
Sugar beet pulp	24	13	10	3.4	0.81	0.6	0.4	0.2	
Mangolds	11	9	8	1.5	0.37	0.3	0.3	0.3	
Carrots (orange)	13	12	10	1.5	0.45	0.5	0.4	0.3	50–60
	90	181	59	13.4	3.2	8.8	1.0	2.2	
Molasses	77	0	81	11.0	2.65	4.2	0.2	5.7	
Oats	88	102	87	11.5	2.74	1.0	3.2	0.3	

Barley	88	47	83	12.9	3.1	0.6	3.5	0.3	
Wheat	88	25	85	12.6	3.0	0.6	3.4	0.1	
Maize	88	24	68	13.6	3.25	0.3	2.8	0.2	
Soya meal	88	59	427	14.6	3.5	2.8	6.4	0.3	
Bran	88	111	112	9.7	2.3	1.6	11.3	0.5	
Linseed	90	77	168	14.1	3.38	2.5	4.7	0.8	
Brewers' yeast	90	14	440	13.8	3.4	2.3	15.3	2.2	
Skimmed milk (dried)	94	1	323	14.9	3.6	13.2	10.2	5.1	
Compound feeds (commonest average values)									
Oat substitute	88	80–120	70–100	11.5	2.75	8.0–15.0	4.0–6.0	2.0	8,000–18,000 (Vit A)
Oat balancer*	88	70–120	100–160	12.5	3.0	10.0–25.0	5.0–8.0	2.0–8.0	12,000–100,000 (Vit A)
So-called 'complete feed' to be fed with straw	88	150–180	60–90	10.5	2.5	8.0–15.0	3.0–6.0	1.0–2.0	6,000–18,000 (Vit A)
Foal rearing feed	88	50–100	140–180	13.5	3.2	10.0–15.0	6.0–8.0	2.0	20,000–30,000 (Vita A)
Mineral supplement (100g)**						12.0–24.0	4.0–8.0	at least 5.0	at least 30,000 (Vit A)

* High protein, similar composition to supplementary feeds for breeding stock

** At least 500g iron per kg

Feed chart
Bodyweight: _____ Work category: _____

Ingredients	kg	Dry matter g	Digestible crude protein g	Digestible energy MJ or Mcal	Calcium g	Phosphorus g	Sodium g	Carotene (mg) and vit A (iu)	Crude Fibre g

Feed chart

Bodyweight: 500kg   Work category: Medium

Ingredients	kg	Dry matter g	Digestible crude protein g	Digestible energy MJ or Mcal	Calcium g	Phosphorus g	Sodium g	Carotene (mg) and vit A (iu)	Crude Fibre g
Requirement			440	80–96 or 19–23	26	16	28*	125mg or 50,000 A	
Hay (end of flowering)	5.0	4,350	250	36 or 8.6	25	15	2.5	?	1,450
Oats	2.5	2,200	217	28.8 or 6.85	2.5	8	0.7	–	255
Horse balancer or supplementary feed	2.5	2,200	250	28.8 or 6.85	30	15	5.0	45,000	250
Total	10.0	8,750	717	93.6 or 22.3	57.5	38	14.5	45,000	1,955
Comment	1.75% of bodyweight		277g = excess of 63%	covers the requirement	Ca:P = 1.5:1 = balanced, provided levels in hay normal		Salt lick!	Carotene questionable Vit A may be barely adequate	22% of the dry matter, plenty of woody fibre

* Higher if heavy losses due to sweating

95

ration of a horse weighing approximately 500kg and carrying a 60-kg rider by, for example, 1kg oats enables the work load to be stepped up by:

walking	approximately 200 minutes
or gentle trotting	approximately 65 minutes
or fairly energetic trotting	approximately 25 minutes
or cantering	approximately 15 minutes
or heavy exertion	approximately 8 to 10 minutes

The stomach and intestines of performance horses should contain as little bulk as possible, which means that less forage should be fed; concentrated energy foods should be used in its place.

NB Forage should not be cut out of the diet altogether.

3. YOUNGSTOCK

Suckling Foals Foals should consume the so-called 'biestings' (colostrum) as soon as possible: it is high in vitamins and antibodies. Furthermore, eating the mare's dung while it is still warm serves to build up a colony of micro-organisms in the foal's large intestine which helps with the digestion of solid foods later on. Parasites are not passed on through the warm dung, though this does happen through older dung (eating older dung may be the symptom of an incorrect diet).

By the time the foal is about four weeks old the supply of nutrients provided by the mare's milk is no longer sufficient. The foal then either tries to obtain more nutrients from its dam's feed trough and by grazing, or receives so-called foal starter feed (supplementary feed for foals) and crushed oats in its own foal trough, which should be inaccessible to the mare (creep feed system). This method is strongly recommended, at least just before weaning. It is of considerable help in overcoming the stress of weaning.

For rearing orphaned foals, so-called 'foal milk' is available from feed manufacturers. This is also useful if the mare's milk yield is poor. However, attempts should first be made to boost the mare's milk yield by feeding are not so absorbent, they are useful in certain circumstances.

The results of experiments in keeping horses without any bedding, as is done with other kinds of animals, cannot so far be said to be satisfactory.

Stable Fittings

Incorrect mounting of stable fittings has caused many serious, often even fatal injuries. The risk is lessened if the fittings are mounted correctly.

The manger and drinking vessel, which should both be of a design which is easy to clean and disinfect, should be mounted on a level with the animal's shoulder joint. There should be no protruding edges or corners. Corner mangers are preferable to rectangular mangers because they have no sharp corners. The drinker should be diagonally opposite the manger. Food hatches are becoming more and more widespread. If they are used, they must not be more than 20cm high.

Feeding forage straight off the ground is being practised more and more. The once common practice of fitting racks up above the manger is not recommended because of the risk of damage to the back and of irritation of the conjunctivae of the eyes by falling particles of dust and food. Mounting the rack low down only serves to increase the risk of injury.

An important part of any stables is the tack room, and other store rooms, which are used for the storage and upkeep of saddlery, equipment and stable tools. Forks, shovels, brooms and wheelbarrows not in immediate use are a source of danger when left in a gangway.

The feed room is discussed in Chapter 4, 'Feeding'.

Further suggestions for the construction of stables, indoor schools and entire riding establishments can be found in the Deutsche Reiterliche Vereinigung's 'Orientierungshilfen für die Plannung and den Bau von Reitanlagen und Reitwegen', 'Hints for the Planning and

Construction of Riding Schools and Bridlepaths',
another FN-Verlag publication.

3. Anatomy and Physiology

*The theory of conformation and of the normal
vital functions of the body.*

3(1) Skin and Hoof

Together with the coat as an outer covering, the *skin*
represents the envelope which protects the body against
the many different external influences. It protects the
system against mechanical, chemical and physical influences and against ingress by parasites, bacteria and virus.
It is in a permanent state of tension, as can be seen by the
way the lips of incised wounds spread open.

Skin is completely waterproof, thus protecting the
body from drying out. The skin also acts as a regulator
for blood pressure and as an organ for storing blood. For
the purpose of keeping the *body temperature* constant it is
provided with hairs, sweat glands and sebaceous glands
as well as blood vessels. The main function of these is
vital heat regulation. If the body temperature drops
below 30°C or rises above 43·5°C, the system cannot
survive. For this reason the skin is provided with a much
denser network of blood vessels than would be necessary
just to nourish it, their additional purpose being heat
regulation. The amount of blood passing through the
vessels, and so the heat loss, is controlled by the central
nervous system through dilation or contraction of the
vessels.

The *normal body temperature* of an adult horse, at rest,
is 37·5° to 38°C, and of a foal 37·5° to 38·5°C. The skin
temperature varies over the different parts of the body
from 18° to 32°C.

During heavy physical exertion the body temperature
can rise to 41°C. The veins in the skin are then greatly
dilated and stand out clearly. The venous blood is cooled
and taken back inside the body. On the limbs the veins
run parallel with the arteries for long stretches. The

blood at body temperature coming outwards along the arteries in the limbs is cooled by the returning venous blood. This is also the case in a horse at rest without a weight on its back. The temperature in the leg region is therefore always lower than on the body. In extreme cold the skin temperature on the extremities falls to as little as a few degrees above zero. This is an effective protection against heat loss since the difference in temperature between the skin and the surrounding atmosphere becomes smaller.

The protection of the tissues against the effects of cold is achieved by rhythmically occurring dilations of the blood vessels – the skin temperature can rise temporarily by 10 to 20°C. In high ambient temperatures evaporation from the body surface in the form of sweat is the most effective way of losing heat. Horses sweat especially heavily on their flanks and in the shoulder and neck areas, and considerable quantities of sodium, potassium and protein can be lost in the sweat.

The horse adjusts to seasonal changes of temperature by *changing his coat* in the spring and growing it in the autumn. When the coat is wet through, its insulatory qualities are considerably reduced. The sebaceous glands secrete a layer of grease on to the hairs and skin to make them water-repellent.

The skin's function as a sense organ is made possible by receptors which are sensitive to temperature, pressure, tension and pain. The degree of *sensitivity* of the skin varies according to the location. On the horse the lip region is particularly sensitive.

Unlike cattle, horses rarely pick up foreign bodies with their food. A fine, brush-like row of feeler hairs about 1mm long on the edge of the top and bottom lips enables the horse to distinguish between an oat grain and a piece of gravel. By using this row of hairs the horse can also pick up a single grain of corn from a flat manger without licking. Clinical proof of sensitivity to temperature, pressure and touch is difficult to establish in the horse, since stimuli which do not cause pain are frequently ignored. On the other hand, many stimuli cause a reflex twitching of the skin muscles (e.g. a fly on the skin), though it is impossible to tell whether the horse is actually conscious of such stimuli.

The horse's *coat* is made up of the top coat hairs, which determine the colour; the shorter woolly undercoat hairs, which lie between them; the long elastic hairs of the mane, forelock and tail, and the stiff tactile or feeler hairs, which are distributed singly around the mouth, nostrils and eyes. The coat hairs are evenly distributed over the whole surface of the body. The direction of the hair and any whorls remain constant throughout the life of the horse.

The *colour* of the hairs is dependent on the pigment content (nil = white hair; low = yellow; medium = red; high = brown; very high = black). The colour of the hair need not correspond to the colour of the skin. The skin of a grey horse is dark, in contrast to the albino, which is devoid of pigment and has a pink skin and red eyes (with a red iris).

The following are made of a special type of skin: the *ergot* at the back of the fetlock; the *chestnut* on the inside foreleg above the knee and the inside of the hind leg below the hock, and the foot. The foot can be divided into several sections: coronary band, coronet, wall of the foot, sole, frog and bulbs. Apart from the actual foot capsule, the pedal bone, navicular bone and that part of the short pastern bone (os coronae) which lies within the capsule are counted as part of the foot.

In spite of its hardness the foot capsule is not totally rigid: it possesses a certain elasticity. The horse does not stand with his pedal bone in the foot capsule as if it were a shoe: the pedal bone could more accurately be said to be suspended from the wall of the foot by the dovetailing of its sensitive laminae with those of the wall. The sensitive laminae, of which there are about 600 in each foot, are non-horny plates 1 to 4mm in height. Around the edges of each lamina are up to 200 secondary laminae, or lamellae. The spaces in between the sensitive laminae are occupied by the horny laminae of the foot capsule. They are identical in shape, and fill the spaces exactly. In this way the pedal bone is connected to the inside wall of the foot capsule. Each time weight is placed on it or taken off it, the elastic foot capsule alters its shape. This is the natural expansion and contraction of the foot, or '*foot mechanism*'.

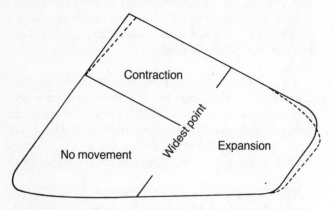

The natural expansion and contraction of the foot or 'foot mechanism'

When weight is placed on it the foot spreads at the heels, the upward arch of the sole is flattened out and the coronet sinks, owing to the pull on the layer of sensitive laminae, while the lower half of the front section of the wall hardly alters its shape at all.

Lameness always results if the foot's natural expansion and contraction is prevented. Putting nails in the shoe behind the widest point of the foot prevents this expansion and contraction and the forces that build up are so great that the nails sheer off in the holes.

The primary purpose of the shoe is to prevent excessive wear of the horns, since only about 1cm of horn grows down from the coronary band each month. Wear occurs, however, even in the shod foot, because the heels rub against the foot surface of the shoe when weight is placed on the foot, causing the horn to wear at this point. So-called 'friction grooves' form on the shoe. When the shoes are changed the toes must always be shortened more than the heels.

The plantar cushion, a wedge-shaped spongy structure made out of elastic fibres, contributes to the elasticity of the foot. It lies at the back, wedged between the horny sole and the deep flexor tendon. The inner and outer lateral cartilages, which rest on the wings of the pedal bone and encase the plantar cushion, also act as shock absorbers when weight is placed on the limb.

The plantar cushion, the lateral cartilages, the suspension of the pedal bone in the hoof capsule, the layers of cartilage in the joints and the angles of the joints are all designed to *relieve concussion* when weight is placed on the limb.

The *horn is of different types*: that of the coronary band, frog and bulbs is soft and elastic; that of the sole and the wall is hard. The *colour of the horn* is yellow to white, black, or striped. The horn (keratine) consists of a very tough protein with a high sulphur content (approximately 5 per cent).

The *wall of the foot* consists of three layers:
☐ The very thin periople, which is secreted by the perioplic ring around the top of the coronary band.
☐ The very thick horny wall.
☐ The interdigitating layer, consisting of the horny laminae.

The *periople* consists of a husk-like horn which, especially at the coronary band, swells slightly on absorbing water and takes on a whitish, opaque appearance (it can be seen in horses turned out in wet grass). In riding horses this layer is destroyed by deep sand or manure, or by incorrect or exaggerated foot care. The wall of the foot then takes on a brittle, crumbly appearance.

The thick *horny wall* consists of a stronger, hard,

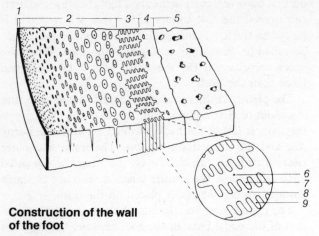

**Construction of the wall
of the foot**

1 Periople
2 Horny wall
3 Interdigitating layer
   (sensitive and horny
   laminae)
4 Sensitive tissue
5 Pedal bone

6 Sensitive laminae
7 Sensitive lamellae or
   secondary laminae
8 Horny laminae
9 Horny lamellae or
   secondary laminae

pigmented outer layer and a thinner, soft, colourless inner layer. The always colourless *interdigitating layer* is the innermost layer and consists of the horny laminae of the wall and the non-horny sensitive laminae, the two being interlocked. This colourless layer gives rise to the *white line*, a band of soft horn which runs round the base of the foot and the heels and forms the bond of union between the sole and the wall. It is particularly easy for small stones to become lodged in this area. When the foot is shod the nails are driven in along the white line. The *rate of growth* is about 8 to 10mm per month. New horn growing down from the coronet reaches the ground at the toe within twelve months, at the quarters in six to eight months and at the heels in four to five months. The horn of the sole and frog is replaced within two months.

Differences Between a Normal Forefoot and a Normal Hind Foot

When the foot is viewed from the side the ratio of the length of the toe to the length of the heel is 3 : 1 in the shallow forefeet and 2 : 1 in the deeper hind feet. The toe of the forefoot forms an angle of 45 to 50° with the ground, and that of the hind foot 50 to 55°, i.e. the slope of the hind foot is steeper than that of the forefoot.

Viewed from the front, the forefoot is wider than the corresponding hind foot. Viewed from below, the front half of the bearing surface of the forefoot is round; the widest point of the foot lies just behind the centre, and the sole is slightly concave. The bearing surface of the hind foot is more oval in shape; the widest point is at the intersection between the last two-thirds; the convexity of the sole is greater, the frog is better developed and the heels are further apart than those of the fore foot. When viewed from the front, the inner wall of both the fore and the hind foot will often be seen to be slightly more upright than the outer.

Deviations from the normally shaped fore and hind feet are narrow feet and wide feet (when viewed from the front); excessively sloping and upright feet (when viewed from the side); half narrow/half wide feet, and diagonal feet (when viewed from below).

Narrow Feet

The quarters of the feet are upright; the bearing surface is only slightly bigger than the coronet; the foot as a whole is deeper; the sole is concave; the frog is poorly developed and the bearing surface oval in shape.

Wide Feet

There is a pronounced slope to the quarters; the bearing surface is considerably wider than the coronet; the foot as a whole is shallower; the sole is flat; the frog is well-developed and the bearing surface circular in shape.

41

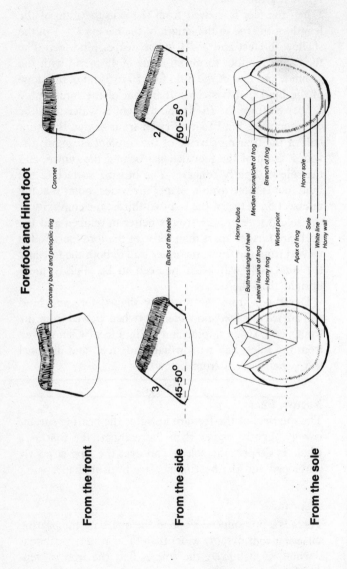

Forefoot and Hind foot

From the front

Coronary band and perioplic ring
Coronet

From the side

Bulbs of the heels

50-55°
45-50°

From the sole

Horny bulbs
Buttress/angle of heel
Median lacuna/cleft of frog
Lateral lacuna of frog
Branch of frog
Horny frog
Horny sole
Apex of frog
Widest point
Sole
White line
Horny wall

Excessively Sloping Feet

The angle of the forefoot is less than 45°, that of the hind foot less than 50° and the ratio of the length of the wall at the toe to the length at the heel is greater than in the normal foot.

Upright Feet

The angle of the forefoot is more than 50°, that of the hind foot more than 55° and the ratio of the length of the wall at the toe to the length at the heel is smaller than in the normal foot.

If the angle of the toe and the heel to the ground is almost 90° the term 'boxy foot' is used (German 'buck foot', 'ram's foot').

Half Narrow/Half Wide Feet

One half of the foot has the characteristics of a narrow foot, the other half those of a wide foot. An unbroken line can be drawn through the widest point of the whole.

Diagonal Feet

Diagonally opposite sections of foot (see diagram below)

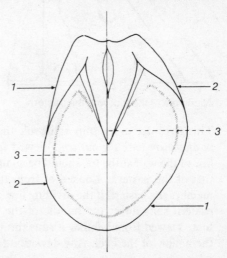

Diagonal foot
1 Narrow
2 Side
3 Widest point

match up. The lines through the widest point of each half do not meet in the middle.

The shape of the horse's foot is partly determined by breeding (heavy horses have wide feet, light horses have narrow feet). However, it is also influenced by ground conditions (hard, dry ground encourages the development of narrow feet, while heavier, wetter ground encourages the development of wide feet) as well as by the use to which the horse is put and the conformation of the limbs.

If an imaginary line is drawn through the bones of the foot and pastern, either from the side or from the front or back, it should be straight (see diagram below). The coronet and the pastern are then at right angles to each other, thus ensuring the correct distribution of weight.

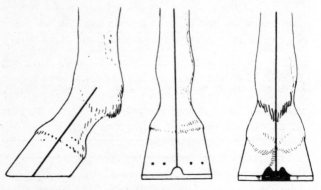

Alignment of the foot with the pastern

This gives rise to the important rule that the *foot must be in alignment with the pastern*. Viewed from the side, the line of the wall at the toe should be an unbroken line with that of the pastern. Looked at from the front, the foot matches the pastern if the dividing line down through the pastern runs down the middle of the front wall of the foot. Viewed from behind, it runs through the middle of the hollow of the heel. Any deviation from this rule due to faulty conformation, neglected or incorrectly trimmed feet, faulty shoeing or leaving the shoes on too long will lead to chronic lameness.

3(2) Skeleton and Musculature

The skeleton serves as a firm framework for the body, movement being made possible by movable connections, i.e. the joints. In the development of a vertebrate, the skeleton starts off as cartilage. In the horse, ossification takes place very early in the development, the first signs of ossification being apparent in a foetus measuring only 7·4cm from head to tail. In ungulates, the *skeleton matures* relatively *early* so that the development of the foal at birth corresponds to that of man at puberty.

Only a few hours after birth the foal can stand and run about. The *longitudinal growth* of the bones takes place in the *growth plates* provided by nature for this purpose. These are discs of cartilage running transversely across the bones. At birth they are about 4mm thick. They are located on the ends of the bones and are extremely delicate. Once they have ossified the bones cannot grow any longer. In the lower limbs this closing of the growth plates takes place at only six months of age. It is because the growth in these regions takes place so early that foals have such disproportionately long limbs.

The spine has finished growing in length by the end of the fourth year of life. Castration while the horse is young delays the closing of the growth plates and so makes the horse grow taller. An increase in height at the withers often occurs after the growth plates on the limbs have closed and is due to the ossification of the cartilage tips of the spinous processes of the withers. The saddle area develops from this.

Bone itself is not a dead organ: it is very well supplied with blood, and bone marrow is concerned with the manufacture of blood. The substance of the bone undergoes a continuous process of reconstruction. Its capacity

Anatomy and Physiology

The skeleton

1	Occipital bone	26	Fetlock joint
2	Temperomandibular joint	27	Long pastern bone/os suffraginis
3	Orbit	28	Pastern joint
4	Facial crest	29	Short pastern bone/os coronae
5	Nasal bone	30	Coffin joint/pedal joint
6	Incisors	31	Coffin bone/pedal bone
7	Canine teeth/tushes	32	Navicular bone/distal sesamoid bone
8	Cheek teeth	33	Proximal sesamoid bone
9	Lower jaw/mandible	34	Pisiform bone
10	1st cervical vertebra/atlas	35a	8th rib (8 sternal or true ribs)
11	Cervical vertebrae (7)	35b	9th-18th ribs (false/asternal/Ger. 'breathing' ribs)
12	Thoracic vertebrae (18)	36	Hip bone/tuber sacrale
13	Lumbar vertebrae (6)	37	Tuber coxae
14	Sacral vertebrae (5), sacrum	38	Ilium
15	Coccygeal vertebrae (18-21)	39	Pubic bone
16	Scapula/shoulder blade	40	Ischium with tuber ischii
17	Shoulder joint	41	Hip joint
18	Humerus	42	Femur
19a	Sternum	43	Patella
19b	Sternum	44	Stifle joint
20	Elbow joint	45	Tibia
21	Olecranon process	46	Fibula
22	Forearm	47	Fibular tarsal bone
22a	Radius	48	Hock
22b	Ulna	49	Hind cannon bone/metatarsal
23	Carpal joint/fore knee		
24	Splint bones		
25	Cannon bone/metacarpal		

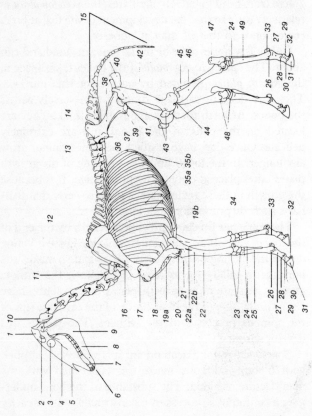

46

Points of the horse

1	Poll
2	Ears
3	Forelock
4	Forehead
5	Eyes
6	Facial crest
7	Nose
8	Nostrils
9	Upper lip
10	Lower lip
11	Corner of the mouth
12	Chin
13	Chin groove
14	Cheek
15	Jaw
16	Jugular groove
17	Gullet
18	Point of shoulder
19	Shoulder
20a	Breast
20b	Brisket
20c	Chest
21	Arm
22	Forearm
23	Fore knee
24	Cannon
25	Fetlock
26	Pastern
27	Coronet
28	Foot (quarters)
29	Foot (toe)
30	Foot (heels)
31	Bulbs
32	Ergot tuft
33	Chestnut
34	Point of elbow
35	Parotid gland
36	Crest
37	Base of neck
38	Withers
39	Back
40	Loins
41	Croup
42	Point of hip
43	Dock
44	Point of buttock
45	Buttock
46	Thigh
47	Second thigh/gaskin
48	Point of hock
49	Hock
50	Rear cannon/ shannon
51	Belly
52	Flank
53	Sheath
54	Stifle

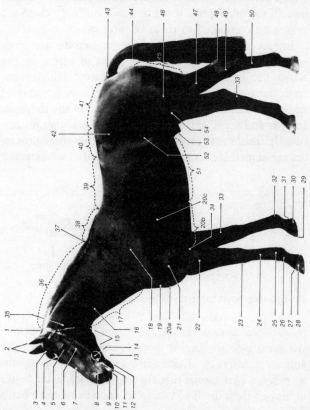

for regenerating, and adapting biologically to changing stresses, is enormous. Decalcification of the bone and a thinning of the bone lamellae can be detected by X-ray after only fourteen days. In the construction of the hollow bones of the limbs, maximum efficiency is achieved with a minimum of material. The bone lamellae inside the tubular long bones correspond to the directions in which stress (pressure and traction) acts on the bone.

The axial skeleton comprises the spinal column, the ribs and the sternum. The holes in the vertebrae are interconnected and aligned to form the spinal canal, which contains and protects the spinal cord. The horse, like all mammals, has seven *cervical vertebrae*, which are very long compared to those of most other animals.

Intervertebral discs, joints and numerous ligaments connect the vertebrae and hold them in place. In the horse the nuchal-supraspinous ligament, which runs from the occipital bone to the sacrum, is of paramount importance in the working of the back. On the thoracic, lumbar and sacral vertebrae are upward-pointing processes. Up until the fifteenth thoracic vertebra these processes are angled backwards towards the tail. The sixteenth

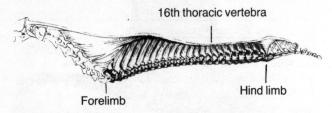

16th thoracic vertebra

Forelimb

Hind limb

Bridge-like construction of the spinal column

thoracic vertebra is vertical, and from this point back all the processes are angled towards the head. Hence the spinal column is constructed like a bridge, with the limbs as pillars. This means that the horse's back is far better equipped than the backs of other animals to carry loads of considerable size. The head and neck, supported partly by the highly elastic nuchal ligament, extend beyond the forelimbs and act like a lever arm on them. The position of head and neck and the fullness of the belly affect the position of the centre of gravity. When the horse is standing still the middle point of the mass lies approximately at the height of the sternum under the middle of the body.

The *position of the body's centre of gravity* is of the utmost importance from the point of view of the saddle and the rider's seat. Since in a standing horse the centre of gravity is nearer to the forehand, the forelimbs bear more weight than the hind. Weighing has shown that in the horse 55 per cent of the weight is on the forelimbs and 45 per cent on the hind. In a 500kg horse there is a weight of 137·5kg on each fore limb.

The fact that there is more weight over the forehand both at the halt and in movement means that the function of the latter is predominantly one of receiving and supporting the weight sent forward on to it.

The hind limbs take the form of sharply angled levers which can produce a powerful thrust for forward movement. The reason that the hind limbs work quite differently from the forelimbs (they account for 58 per cent of the total musculature of the limbs) lies in the fundamentally different way in which they are attached to the trunk. Whilst the hind legs are connected directly to the spinal column via the pelvis, and can transmit their power directly, the rib cage hangs from the shoulder blades between the forelimbs in a mobile, elastic sling made up of the ligamentomuscular *serratus ventralis* muscles.

On the fore and hind limbs there is a stay mechanism which enables the horse to remain in a standing position almost without any muscular effort. It is made up almost exclusively of tendons and ligaments. Stifle fixation is achieved with the help of the patellar mechanism. The patella is hooked behind the femoral trochlea and held

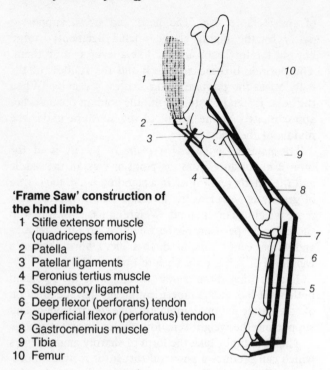

'Frame Saw' construction of the hind limb
1　Stifle extensor muscle
　　(quadriceps femoris)
2　Patella
3　Patellar ligaments
4　Peronius tertius muscle
5　Suspensory ligament
6　Deep flexor (perforans) tendon
7　Superficial flexor (perforatus) tendon
8　Gastrocnemius muscle
9　Tibia
10　Femur

there by the muscle tone of the stifle extensor muscle (*m. quadriceps femoris*), which requires a certain amount of muscular effort. Since, owing to the so-called frame saw construction, the movements of the hock and stifle are completely interdependent, the whole limb is immobilised when the stifle is fixed.

In the horse 250 paired and several unpaired muscles can be identified which, by contracting, function as flexors, extensors, adductors, abductors, rotators, tensors or constrictors. The ends of the muscles are *always connected to the bone by means of tendinous fibres* even when the fleshy part appears to be connected directly to the bone. The tendon fibre bundles contain elastic fibres which permit the tendon to lengthen by about 4 per cent

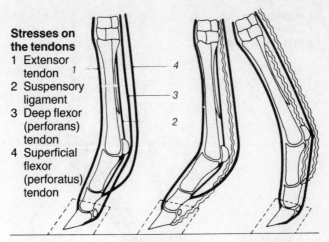

Stresses on the tendons

1 Extensor tendon
2 Suspensory ligament
3 Deep flexor (perforans) tendon
4 Superficial flexor (perforatus) tendon

Standing; all tendons stressed equally

Putting the foot down: suspensory ligament and superficial flexor tendon stressed, deep flexor tendon unstressed

Picking the foot up: deep flexor tendon stressed, suspensory ligament and superficial flexor tendon unstressed

when it is stretched. This serves as a safety device for the tendon.

Although in cross-section the muscle may be sixty times as thick as the tendon, the tensile strength of the tendon is so great that a muscle can never, under its own power, rupture its own tendon. The average tensile strength is 7 to 8kg per square millimetre. The suspensory ligament ruptures under a loading of 950 to 2,000kg, which is from four to eleven times the weight it supports when the horse is standing still.

When the foot is placed on the ground and the body weight is taken on it, the superficial flexor tendon and the suspensory ligament take the strain. When the foot is picked up this role falls to the deep flexor tendon. The suspensory ligament is attached to the sesamoid bones and comprises the main part of the suspensory apparatus. The deep flexor tendon runs over the sesamoid bones and

51

Longitudinal cross-section of lower leg and foot

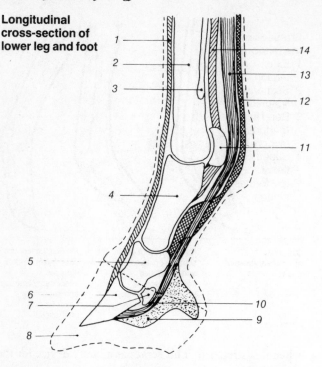

1	Extensor tendon	
2	Cannon bone	
3	Splint bone	
4	Long pastern bone	
5	Short pastern bone	
6	Pedal bone	
7	Navicular bone	
8	Hoof capsule	
9	Plantar cushion	
10	Foot pulley	
11	Sesamoid bone	
12	Superficial flexor tendon (flexor of the short pastern bone)	
13	Deep flexor tendon (flexor of the pedal bone)	
14	Suspensory ligament	

the navicular bone and is attached to the pedal bone. The deep flexor tendon, the navicular bone and the navicular bursa go to make up the *foot pulley*. The superficial flexor tendon splits at the back of the pastern, runs either side of the deep flexor tendon and attaches to the short pastern bone as flexor of the latter.

3(3) Digestive System

The functions of the digestive system are to take in food; to break it down mechanically and biologically; to bring about the absorption of the necessary materials and to eliminate the indigestible matter. The horse is a herbivore, and has six incisor and twelve cheek teeth in each jaw. There is a gap about 10cm wide between the incisors and the cheek teeth. In stallions and geldings, but rarely in mares, a canine tooth or 'tush' grows in this gap between incisors and cheek teeth. The main action of the

The mouth of an adult horse

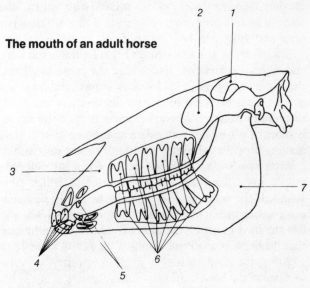

The roots of the teeth have been exposed by cutting open the sockets
1 Temporal fossa
2 Orbit
3 Upper jaw
4 Incisor teeth
5 Canine teeth/tushes (in stallions and geldings)
6 Cheek teeth
7 Lower jaw

bit (either snaffle or curb) is on that section of the edge of the jaw where there are no teeth. All the incisors and the first three cheek teeth on either side of the upper and lower jaw occur first in the form of temporary or 'milk' teeth. The change over to permanent teeth begins at two and a half and ends at four and a half years of age.

The wearing surface of the cheek teeth is oblique and slightly undulating, and because the lower jaw is narrower than the upper, horses cannot chew on both sides at once. Food is crushed by sideways chewing movements. For every mouthful of food the horse needs to chew 30 to 60 times, and he can chew 70 to 80 times per minute. During chewing, the food is mixed with saliva, the salivary glands producing on average 8·8kg of saliva per hour and 40kg per day.

The pharynx is a cross-roads between the respiratory and digestive passages. Every time the horse swallows, the respiratory passage is closed off beforehand by reflex action. This prevents food particles from entering the respiratory passage. When the airway is open the mouth is blocked off by the soft palate and the epiglottis, thus making breathing through the mouth almost impossible.

After swallowing, the food passes down the oesophagus, a muscular tube, the lower third of which runs alongside the wind pipe. At the point where the oesophagus reaches the stomach there is a sphincter which only lets the food in bit by bit. It is because of this sphincter that the horse is unable to vomit. With a capacity of 12 to 14 litres, the stomach is very small in comparison to the sections of the bowel, the total cubic capacity of the latter being about 200 litres. As a herbivore the horse has to be equipped to cope with large quantities of food. Domestication was made possible by replacing his natural diet with concentrated feeds, something which has had certain adverse effects on the horse.

The bowel, which is joined on to the stomach, is divided into the small intestine, consisting of the duodenum (approximate length 1m), the jejunum (approximately 25m) and the ileum, and into the large intestine, consisting of the caecum, the colon and the rectum. The caecum takes up a considerable proportion of the right-hand side of the abdomen.

In the intestines the food is subjected to the chemical action of secretions from the digestive organs and to the action of the bacteria and single-cell organisms. The greatly dilated large intestines are fermenting chambers in which the cellulose is split by bacteria. At the same time vitamins B and K are manufactured by bacterial action. Every day the horse defecates five to twelve times, passing 15 to 23kg of faeces, with a water content of 75 per cent. The excretion process begins twenty hours after the food enters the alimentary canal and it is only complete after four to five days.

After mixing with secretions from the liver (the horse has no gall bladder), the pancreas and the mucous membrane of the intestinal wall, the liquid contents of the small intestine become thicker in the larger intestine owing to the withdrawal of water.

3(4) Urinary and Reproductive Organs

Owing to their development, the urinary and reproductive organs belong to the same anatomical system. The urinary organs eliminate urinary waste and regulate the water balance. Every day 3,000 to 10,000 litres of blood flow through the blood vessels of the horse's kidneys and 3 to 10 litres of urine are formed. The horse's water intake depends on climatic conditions, food, milk production, exercise and habits. Water is eliminated not only through the kidneys but also through the skin, through the intestines and possibly from the udder.

The left and right *kidneys* differ in shape, position and weight. The right kidney, which is heart shaped and heavier (up to 840g), lies forward in the chest cavity, under the fifteenth to seventeenth ribs. The left kidney, which is bean shaped and smaller, is situated on a level

55

with the first to third lumbar vertebrae. The urine excreted by the kidney is sent through the pelvis of the kidney and the ureter to the urinary bladder. When empty, the elastic *urinary bladder* lies inside the pelvis; when very full it may extend as far as the navel region.

The *urine* of the horse family is mucous to gelatinous in consistency (this is due to the secretions from the mucous glands in the pelvis of the kidneys and in the ureter). The colour of fresh urine varies from pale yellow to light brown. After being exposed to the atmosphere for a while it turns darker. Understandably, the water intake is of the utmost importance in determining the quantity of urine passed. Depending on the water intake, which is calculated at 4 to 8 litres per 100kg bodyweight per day and up to 20 litres per 100kg for lactating mares, the amount of urine passed is 3 to 10 litres per day. The horse urinates five to seven times daily.

The *reproductive organs of the mare* consist of two ovaries, the womb and the vagina. In the ovaries, fertile eggs develop in fluid-filled follicles. When the follicle reaches a diameter of 4 to 5cm it bursts (rupture of the follicle, ovulation). The fertile egg goes into the Fallopian tube. A blood clot forms in the space occupied by the ruptured follicle. Special cells then grow into the clot and form the so-called yellow body.

If the egg is not fertilized, it dies in twenty-four hours. Ovulation takes place at the end of the five- to seven-day long *oestrus* or *heat*. The yellow body produces a hormone which prepares the womb for the possible arrival of a fertilized egg. After about fourteen to twenty-one days the yellow body dies. A new oestrus begins, with a new follicle developing and rupturing. If the egg cell, which is about the size of a grain of sand, is fertilized by a sperm cell, the fertilized egg cell settles into the wall of the womb. Rapid cell growth and differentiation into specialised types ensues. On the twentieth day after fertilization the foal is already formed in miniature.

A foal which is born before the 300th day of gestation

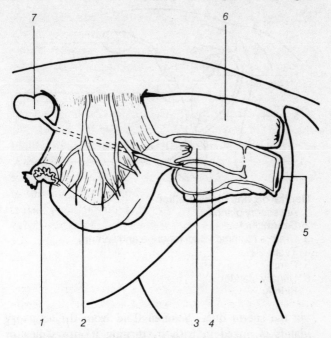

Genital organs of the mare
1 Ovary
2 Uterus/womb   5 Vulva
3 Vagina   6 Rectum
4 Urinary bladder   7 Kidney

is unable to survive because many of the organs, particularly the lungs, are not mature. However, a foal born between the 300th and the 325th day has a chance of survival. These foals (premature births) have a low birth weight and need special attention. Foals born after the 325th day count as full term. The *average gestation period* can be taken as 336 to 340 days.

The *genital organs of the stallion* consist of the testes, the epididymis, the accessory glands and the penis. The testes are responsible for the production of the male sex cells (spermatozoa). The sperm are stored in the attached epididymis. In ejaculation the sperm reach the urethra

57

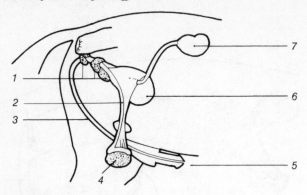

Genital organs of the stallion
1 Accessory glands
2 Sperm duct
3 Urethra (common duct for urine and semen)
4 Testis
5 Penis
6 Urinary bladder
7 Kidney

via the sperm duct. Seminal fluid from the accessory glands is mixed in with it, turning it into semen or 'ejaculate'. The average volume involved in one ejaculation is 50 to 70ml, containing about 700,000,000 sperm (100 million per ml). During mating the thread-like, motile spermatozoa enter the uterus via the cervix. They are hundreds of times smaller than the egg cells. The sperm remain fertile for about two days in the uterus and Fallopian tubes.

3(5) Respiratory System

The respiratory system is responsible for the continuous supply of oxygen; for combining the oxygen with the blood and for taking the carbon dioxide out of the blood and carrying it away. Gaseous exchange takes place in the vesicles of the lungs. On its way to these, the air is cleansed, moistened and warmed. The air enters through the nostrils and goes into the nasal cavity, which is divided by the turbinated bones into numerous compartments. It then passes through the larynx, trachea, bronchi and bronchioles into the vesicles or alveoli of the lungs. There is also a scent organ in the lower surface of the inside of the nose.

In adult horses the *respiratory rate* of the resting animal is eight to sixteen per minute. It can rise to 80 to 100 per minute as a result of energetic exercise. The average volume of the air inspired by the horse at rest is 6 litres, which gives an average volume of 63 litres per minute; during exercise this volume can rise to 300 litres.

Inspiration occurs through the contraction of certain muscles in the chest wall and diaphragm, which causes the chest cavity to expand. Since the lungs are slightly elastic and are drawn to the chest wall by the vacuum which exists between the pleura covering them and the pleura which line the chest, the resulting drop in air pressure due to the expansion causes the lungs to inflate.

In contrast with the process of inspiration, the contraction of the chest cavity which occurs in expiration is an almost passive operation, resulting from the relaxation of the muscles used in inspiration and the contraction of the elastic fibres in the lung tissues. The expiratory muscles in the chest wall only come into action in very heavy breathing. In laboured breathing the abdominal muscles may also be involved. By contracting in time with the breathing they cause an increase in pressure in the abdominal cavity which pushes the diaphragm further forward into the chest cavity. The pressure of the diaphragm squeezes the air out of the lungs. The entire breathing mechanism is controlled by the respiratory centre, which is situated at the point where the spinal cord enters the brain.

Respiratory safety reflexes are snorting, sneezing and coughing. Snorting and sneezing serve to remove foreign bodies or secretions from the nasal mucous membranes. The coughing reflex is triggered off by the presence of foreign bodies or mucus in even the narrowest ramifications of the larynx or trachea.

Only a fine dividing line exists between the respiratory and circulatory systems, since changes in the oxygen and carbon dioxide content in the blood are registered in both the respiratory and circulatory centres.

3(6) Circulatory System

The circulatory system consists of the *blood system*, the *lymphatic system* and the organs which manufacture and break down the blood cells. In the blood system the blood circulates by being pushed around by rhythmical *muscular contractions of the heart*, which acts like a dual pressure– and suction-pump.

The heart, consisting of two ventricles and two auricles or atria, is the motor which drives the blood. Ventricles and auricles are partitioned off from each other by separating walls and valve-like flaps. From the left ventricle the oxygenated blood is pumped out along the aorta to every organ in the body. Then, high in carbon dioxide, the blood returns from the organs via the venae cavae into the right auricle, from whence it passes into the right ventricle. From the right ventricle the blood is pumped along the pulmonary artery into the minute vessels of the alveoli, where the carbon dioxide is given up and exchanged for oxygen. The oxygenated blood then flows back through the pulmonary veins to the left auricle and on into the left ventricle, where the circulatory process begins again.

In the horse there are enormous variations in the size of the heart (1·3 to 4·2kg), depending on the breed. The smallest relative heart size of only 0·6 per cent of the bodyweight is that of the coldbloods. In Thoroughbreds the relative weight of the heart rises to over 1 per cent. In fit horses both the relative and the absolute heart weights increase. The rate of the heartbeat at rest is in the region of 28 to 40 beats per minute (for comparison the heart rate of the elephant is 25 to 30 and the canary 1,000).

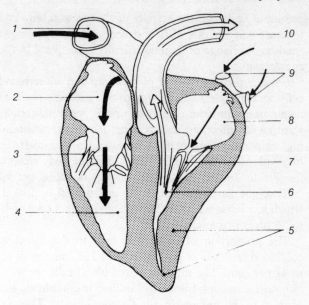

The heart in cross-section, from the right side

1 Anterior vena cava	6 Left ventricle
2 Right atrium/auricle	7 Heart valves
3 Heart valves	8 Left atrium/auricle
4 Right ventricle	9 Pulmonary veins
5 Heart muscle	10 Aorta

During physical exertion the rate rises: in racehorses and racing trotters rates of 220 have been recorded on the racetrack.

As a rule the rates of young animals are higher than those of older ones, the average rate in foals being about 80. A horse weighing 500kg has an average volume of blood passing through the heart at each beat of 850ml. This means that, with a heart rate of 34 at rest, 29 litres pass through per minute. The work done by the heart during heavy exertion can be imagined.

The vessels which distribute the blood around the body split up into smaller and smaller branches. The

61

pulse can be felt in the arteries of the jaw and tail. The pressure and the rate of flow decrease as the vessels get smaller. Exchange of materials finally takes place in the capillaries.

Blood, which consists of plasma, red and white blood cells and platelets, has numerous functions such as respiration, nutrition, carrying away waste materials, warding off infection, transporting hormones, maintaining temperature and many other uses. In mammals the total volume of blood is 1/14 to 1/13 of the body weight, i.e. 7·1 to 7·6 per cent. The amount of blood per kg bodyweight has been calculated as from 60 to 100ml, which in a horse weighing 500kg amounts to a total of 40 to 50 litres of blood.

The proportion of red blood cells in the blood of coldblood horses is 33 per cent and in Thoroughbreds up to 42 per cent. The number of red blood cells per mm^3 also varies, ranging from 5 to 7 million in coldbloods and from 8 to 11 million in fit Thoroughbreds. The red corpuscles are responsible for carrying oxygen from the vesicles of the lungs to the tissues, and carbon dioxide in the opposite direction. Their total surface area is approximately 14,000 m^2, Their number depends on the age, sex (mares have about 10 per cent more), level of performance, breed, altitude and feeding.

In the horse the *spleen* can store 20 per cent of the total volume of blood in a concentrated form and immediately release it again into the blood stream when required. The lifespan of the red blood cells is limited to 100 days. They are broken down in the spleen, the bone marrow and the liver. The white blood cells, which amount to 1 to 2 per cent of the blood cells, serve as a defence against infection. The blood platelets (200,000 to 800,000 mm^3) play a positive part in blood clot formation, which takes a long time in the horse (twelve minutes, as opposed to two to three minutes in the dog). The blood group systems vary in the horse from ten to nineteen.

The *lymphatics* constitute a second network of vessels

alongside the blood vessels. There is a constant seepage of fluid from the blood vessels through the tissues of the body. This fluid is drained into the lymph vessels and returned to the bloodstream. The lymph, which also carries with it infective agents, toxins and cancer cells, is cleansed in the lymph nodes. In the horse about 1·5 to 2 litres per hour flow through the thoracic duct which takes the lymph back into the bloodstream.

3(7) Nervous System

The nervous system is the central control which co-ordinates the various organs with their different functions. The central nervous system, comprising the brain and spinal cord, receives impulses from the receptive sense organs and sends impulses to the periphery, triggering off appropriate reactions.

The spinal cord of a horse weighing 500kg is 180 to 200cm long and weighs 250 to 300kg. The size and weight of the brain not only depend on the stage of development but are also correlated with the body size of the different kinds of animal. The absolute weight of the brain in a horse weighing 540kg is 680g, and in a mouse weighing 12·4g, 0·4g.

The relative weight of the brain, i.e. the ratio of the weight of the brain to the weight of the body is as follows:

	weight of brain	:	weight of body
Greenland whale	1	:	25,000
horse	1	:	800
elephant	1	:	439
gorilla	1	:	48
man (weight of brain: 1,300 to 1,500g)	1	:	31
mouse	1	:	31

This means that of all the mammals listed the mouse has the largest relative brain weight. But the combination of relative and absolute brain weight is highest in man.

The ratio brain weight : spinal cord is also revealing. On average in pigs, cattle and horses it is 2 : 1 and in man 48 : 1. From these figures we may conclude that as an organ responsible for the integration and regulation of nervous activity, the brain is of far greater importance in man than in animals.

Since all the organs of the body must be co-ordinated, their activities are centrally controlled and harmonised by means of a branching information transmission system. The wide range of environmental stimuli and the internal stimuli caused by the continuous changes within the body are picked up by receptors or sense organs and transmitted by appointed nerve routes to the central nervous system. Impulses are then sent out to the organs (skeletal muscles, bowel), where they trigger off appropriate reactions. The speed at which the impulse is conducted depends on the type of nerve fibre. It varies from 1 to 2m per second in thin, unmyelinated fibres to 60 to 100m per second in thick, myelinated fibres.

There is also a part of the nervous system whose function of regulating the vital functions (digestion, respiration, metabolism, secretion, body temperature and water balance) is unconscious and outside voluntary control.

One of the elementary forms of activity of the nervous system is reflex action. Reflex actions are automatic reactions to internal or external stimuli. The horse has numerous reflexes, the most typical of which are those of the cutaneous muscles of the withers, back and abdomen, those of the tendons, coronet, ear, tail, eyelids and pupils, and the cough reflex.

3(8) The Sense Organs

The sense organs work in very close association with the nervous system. They are designed to pick up and transmit the various types of physical and chemical stimuli. The organs which detect temperature, pressure

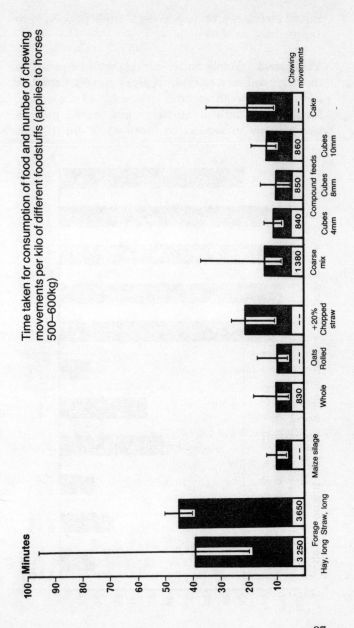

Time taken for consumption of food and number of chewing movements per kilo of different foodstuffs (applies to horses 500–600kg)

animal protein sources (e.g. skimmed milk powder, ½ to 1kg per day, or 'foal milk').

Youngstock Young horses during their first period in the stable still need an extra supply of protein. Growth is all-important, with as little as possible of the energy supply being turned into fat, which would mean a heavier body to support on limbs which are still not

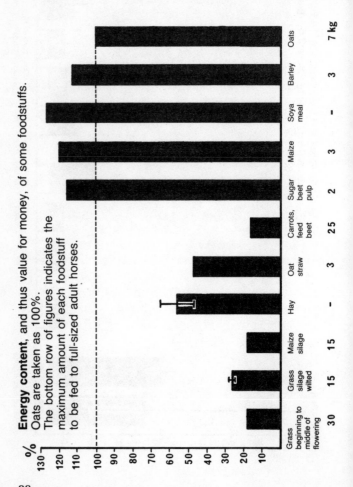

Energy content, and thus value for money, of some foodstuffs. Oats are taken as 100%. The bottom row of figures indicates the maximum amount of each foodstuff to be fed to full-sized adult horses.

completely ossified. The energy intake should also correspond to the amount of exercise. Quantities of the other nutrients should be proportionate and balanced. It is important that calcium supplementation is maintained constantly so as to prevent bone, ligament and tendon disorders.

4. PONIES

The same rules apply to ponies as to the other categories of equines. Excesses of energy food and protein are common in this category.

CAUSES OF FEEDING UPSETS

Upsets are caused by faulty feeding methods, such as using dirty mangers and automatic drinking bowls, and giving widely spaced, irregular meals. In addition, greedy feeding (eating too fast and not chewing the food properly) can lead to flatulence and colic. Lack of peace and quiet in the stable at feeding time and working the horse only an hour after it has finished eating often lead to the food being utilised less efficiently, to flatulence in the stomach and to colic. The largest meal should, therefore, be fed in the evening prior to the longest period of rest.

Laminitis can occur as a result of sudden changes of diet, or rich feeding accompanied by insufficient work, while further causes of colic include drinking excessive quantities of water while feeding (water supply next to the manger) or, in particular, drinking water that is too cold.

Watering

Drinking in sufficient quantity is just as important to the horse as eating. Drinking water should be fresh, colourless, odour-free, pure, clear, with no taste to it, and free from harmful substances. It is most wholesome at a temperature of 9 to 12°C. Water which is too cold causes chills and diarrhoea; water which is too warm is not refreshing.

The horse should drink both before and after his feed, and should always drink his fill. The average daily water requirement is between 30 and 50 litres, but it can vary according to work, the season and food. Horses who are very hot should only be allowed to drink their fill when they have dried off completely, and when respiration and pulse are back to normal. Greedy drinking can be prevented by putting a handful of hay on top of the water. In summer drinking before and after the feed is not enough. In very warm weather water must be offered more frequently. The water requirement also depends on the type of food: the drier the food and the higher the fibre content, the more water is required for digestion.

If water is provided in buckets, each horse should have his own easily recognisable bucket: this prevents the spread of infection. Automatic drinking bowls save on labour, and the horse always has water available. Unfortunately, horses often get into the habit of playing with these automatic drinkers, which results in water all over the manger, bedding and hay. This can be prevented by turning off the water supply between meals. Care must be taken to ensure that the drinkers are working properly, and they must be painstakingly cleaned out along with the manger every day.

Compatibility of Foodstuffs

The compatibility of foodstuffs is of special significance for the horse, whose system is often highly sensitive. The incompatibility of the following foodstuffs leads to certain disturbances: wheat and rye, which are low in crude fibre and high in starch, form into lumps in the stomach and cause flatulence: diets consisting only of low-protein forage cause blockages in the region of the large intestine; young green food, legumes, clover, lucerne, cabbage, apples or bread result in flatulence in the large intestine.

Mouldy food, hay and straw which have not been stored long enough, grass which has been piled up and allowed to heat, and decaying, frozen and sandy food

100

should not be fed. They can cause gastric and intestinal disorders (colic) and laminitis. Straw which is chopped too short and grass mowings can lead to obstructive colic.

The practicality of feeding sugar beet pulp should be considered carefully, since soaking it (essential in order to prevent a blockage of the oesophagus or overloading of the stomach) is labour-intensive and requires more attention to cleanliness.

The use of special foodstuffs such as brewers yeast, linseed, bran, etc, is advantageous in certain cases, for instance to promote performance or fertility, or for sick or convalescent horses.

Cost Effectiveness of the Diet

The decisive factor in horse food is the digestible energy. The price is therefore measured against the energy content, both in the case of individual foodstuffs and compound feeds (see table on page 98). However, because of the levels of certain nutrients, some foodstuffs should not be fed in unlimited quantities. Only hay can be fed ad lib. A specific food such as soya meal, even if it is the best value for money, should only be used when the protein requirement is especially high (as in the case of mares with foal at foot or weanlings).

A comparison between individual foodstuffs and complete feeds is very difficult since the latter are fortified with extra vitamins, minerals and trace elements.

5. Grooming, Foot Care and Shoeing

5(1) Grooming

The horse's health is essentially dependent on correct skin function. Daily grooming both cleanses the skin and hair of dust, dirt and waste products such as scurf and sweat, and serves as a massage, stimulating the circulation of the skin and subcutaneous fascia, as well as promoting the breathing of the skin. Grooming is not, then, just a cleaning process, but an essential for the horse's health. It plays a significant part in his well-being, performance and resistance to disease. In the natural state it is the herd companions who see to this by nibbling, and the individual horse by rolling or scratching, or in the water hole. In this context too much cleaning could be harmful, since a build-up of grease protects the horse from the elements. In the artificial environment of the stabled horse, man must take over the task of grooming.

Grooming should increase the trust between man and horse. Obviously there must be no roughness or teasing of the horse, nor must any misbehaviour on his part be tolerated. The handler should speak to the horse on entering the stall or box so as not to startle him. The horse should be patted or stroked on the neck and back. Good use should be made of the voice, which inspires confidence and has a calming effect.

5(1)i EQUIPMENT
The horse's grooming kit consists of a body brush, curry comb, dandy brush, water brush, stable rubbers, sponges, a mane comb and a hoof pick. Electric grooming machines may be viable in larger stables, since they

save time and energy, but they can lead to the spread of skin diseases if the same brush is used for every horse. Patience is needed when using a machine on a horse for the first time, as he can be easily frightened.

A thorough daily grooming session is necessary after work and following the normal cooling-down period. It should be carried out quickly and energetically. Prolonged, heavy grooming makes the horse nervous and the skin over-sensitive, and causes an undesirable increase in the amount of scurf formed. Following grooming the horse's whole body must be clean, including underneath the mane, the belly and the legs. The feet must be carefully picked out.

Ideally the horse should be taken out of his stall or box for the daily grooming session. In the first place one can see more and work better in daylight, and secondly it keeps the horse's stable clean. If there is nowhere outside where grooming can be carried out, and if the stables are of the barn type, the horse should be stood in the corridor between the boxes. Tying up the horse on both sides prevents misbehaviour. Thin, not too heavy chains or ropes should be used. They must be easy to undo at the point of attachment to the tie-ring and to the headcollar. Special quick release ('panic') clips are suitable for this. They can be released at a touch even when under tension (i.e. when the horse is pulling against them).

5(1)ii CARE OF THE COAT, EYES, MUZZLE AND DOCK

Grooming begins on the near side, working from front to back. First the coat is scuffed with the (oval) curry comb* to remove hard crusts of dirt. The curry comb is used only on the parts of the body which are covered with muscle. It is never used on parts where there is no layer

*This type of metal curry comb is in common use in Europe. It does not have 'teeth' like the square ones seen in Britain, which must never be used on the horse.

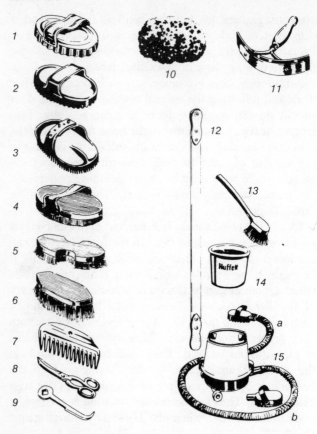

Equipment for cleaning horses

1 Metal curry comb
2 Rubber curry comb
3 Massage brush (rubber curry comb)
4 Body brush
5 Dandy brush
6 Mane brush (soft)
7 Mane comb
8 Curved-ended heel trimming scissors
9 Hoof pick with stud spanner
10 Sponge
11 Foam or sweat scraper
12 Sweat knife (sweat scraper)
13 Hoof grease brush
14 Hoof grease
15 Vacuum grooming machine
   (a) body brush for vacuum grooming machine
   (b) Rubber curry comb

of flesh, such as the head, lower limbs and hips, which should be cleaned with a brush. The curry comb must have no sharp edges. Rubber curry combs are particularly suitable especially for sensitive horses: they are effective and cannot cause injury. On the near-side front end of the horse the curry comb is held in the left hand; when cleaning the rear end it is held in the right hand. The reverse procedure is adopted on the off side.

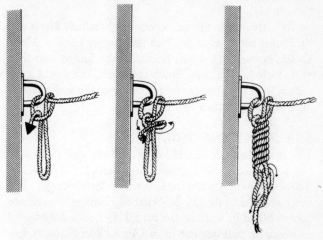

Easy-to-release knot attaching the headcollar rope to the tie ring. (In Britain, as a further safety measure, a loop of breakable string is attached to the ring, and the rope is attached to the string rather than to the ring itself).

After using the curry comb, work begins with the body brush on the near side; the brush is held in the left hand and a metal curry comb in the right. Long, smooth strokes are used to clean from the coat the dust which has been scuffed up with the curry comb. After each stroke the body brush is passed across the curry comb, which is tapped on the ground from time to time to remove the dust. Grooming the horse's head requires special care. First the headcollar is taken off and fastened around the neck, then the head is brushed carefully with the body brush. Concealed, difficult-to-clean places such as the ears, the part of the neck under the mane, inside the legs and the heels must not be neglected. To finish off, a wipe with a cloth (stable rubber) will remove the last traces of dust.

The corners of the eyes, the nostrils, the sides of the mouth, underneath the dock and the anus must be sponged out daily. Use two different sponges for the head and the dock, rinsing them out frequently and thoroughly.

On warm days the horse may be washed. However, care must be taken to dry him thoroughly all over. Heels should be well dried out, first with the fingers and then with a cloth. Washing down the back, chest and girth region with cold water strengthens the skin and protects against pressure sores and chafing.

5(1)iii MANE AND TAIL CARE

The mane and tail should be worked through daily with the fingers to remove tangles and particles of bedding. Then the mane should be laid with a damp brush. The crest and dock should be brushed. Neither brush nor comb should be used on the actual tail because they tend to break or pull out the hairs. About every two to four weeks the mane and tail should be washed with shampoo and warm water and then rinsed thoroughly.

5(1)iv PULLING, TRIMMING AND CLIPPING

The mane of the riding horse should be about 10cm long, not too thick, and should lie flat on one side of the neck. It is pulled, never cut, about every eight weeks. To pull a mane proceed as follows.

Starting at the top of the neck, grasp a few long hairs from the underneath layer of mane with one hand. Push the shorter hairs upwards against the lie of the mane with a pulling comb. Wrap the long hairs round the comb and pull them out with a jerk. Work down the whole of the mane until it is a uniform length. If the horse is

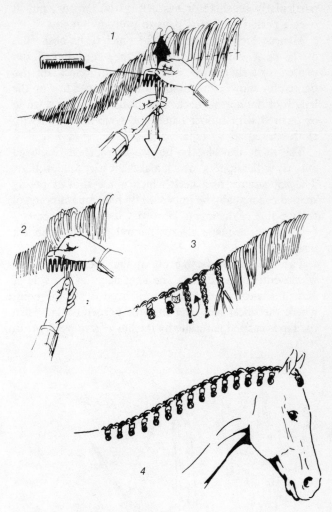

Pulling and plaiting the mane
1 and 2 Pulling the mane with a pulling comb to make it even
3 Stages in plaiting a mane
4 Plaited mane

particularly sensitive or has a very thick mane, pull it over a period of several days to prevent soreness.

Manes which do not lie flat, or which lie on both sides of the neck, can be improved if they are damped and plaited for a short time. The mane and forelock are also plaited for shows, the number of plaits depending on the length of the horse's neck. The plaits are either sewn in or secured with rubber bands and wrapped round with cloth-backed sticky tape.

The mane can also be hogged or roached (removed entirely with clippers) which makes it easier to look after. The appearance of a neck which is too thin or poorly shaped can actually be improved by judicious clipping of the top line of the mane. However, it should be remembered that the mane affords natural protection against insects.

The tail should be narrow at the dock and should widen out further down. The long hairs on the side of and underneath the dock are removed up to the point where the dock goes over into the perpendicular when the tail is carried naturally by the horse in movement. In

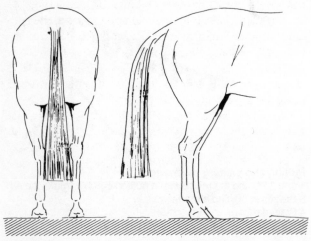

A pulled tail.

days gone by the ends of tails used to be pulled, but nowadays they are usually cut with a pair of curved-ended tail scissors or with clippers. On ponies the side hairs of the tail are not removed. The bottom of the tail is cut so that it is horizontal and about 10cm below the level of the hock when the horse is in movement. The tail of the driving horse is cut above the level of the hock. Prior to special occasions it is a good idea to dampen and plait the tail at night.

On warmblood horses the hair is trimmed off the heels to make the animal look as well-bred as possible. Trimming is carried out in a downward direction from the fetlock to the back of the pastern, using dog clippers, curved-ended heel trimming scissors or the clipping machine over the top of a comb. In this way all the hairs are shortened, without 'steps' being formed. A short, pointed, downward-facing tuft is left which directs the water past the back of the heels on to the ground. The heels are trimmed in the opposite direction, that is, upwards towards the fetlock. Having removed the horse's natural protection, it is essential to pay special attention to cleaning and drying the heels. Ponies and cold-blood horses have ergot 'tufts' or 'feathering'.

Of the long hairs found on the upper parts of the body, only the long, hard hairs which grow chiefly in winter from the ears and the ridge along the back of the lower jaw should be removed. The protective hair inside the ears and the feeler hairs on the mouth and nostrils must never be pulled out or cut off.

Clipping is beneficial for horses who grow a particularly long, thick winter coat. Such horses sweat heavily when they work, are very difficult to dry off and can, as a result, catch cold. The shorter hair of the clipped horse allows the skin to breath better, and the animal is easier to keep clean. If the horse is kept in a very cold stable or is exposed to draughts, he will need to be rugged up. Under normal circumstances in Germany, where most horses are kept in barn-type stabling, rugging up in the stable is considered to make the horse soft and to lower his resistance to chills. Summer sheets can be used as a protection against insects.

The type of clip is determined by the sort of work the horse does.

5(1)v BANDAGING, LEG PROTECTION

Bandaging protects the horse's legs from impact, kicks and blows. Bandages are recommended when working young horses, who are still unco-ordinated in their movements, and for cross-country and jumping. Care must be taken in their application, since badly fitted bandages can cause vascular congestion, pressure damage and locomotory disturbance. Grains of sand, which can get in between the bandage and the leg when riding in a manège, cause chafing and swelling. Bandages which become wet must be removed before they start to dry out, otherwise they will contract and restrict the circulation.

For exercising, woollen or elasticated bandages are required, 1·80 to 3m long and 10 to 15cm wide. Each bandage should be rolled up carefully, tightly and evenly, with the tapes inside. An unevenly or loosely rolled bandage cannot be applied properly. Any foreign bodies (sand, blades of straw, etc), must be removed from both

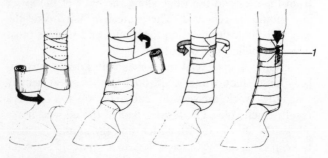

Bandaging
1 The position of the knots and the ends of the tapes between the splint bone and the tendon

the bandage and the horse's leg. When the bandage is being put on, the horse's weight must be on the foot.

The bandage is applied from the top of the cannon bone, just below the knee or hock, downwards, from right to left as far as the fetlock and then about half way back up again. It is wound at a slight angle. The pastern is not covered. The bandage must be completely flat and even, with no wrinkles and no uneven pressure on the leg at any point. If the bandage is put on properly, the leg looks the same thickness all the way down. When using the sort of bandages which are smoothed flat with the fingernail, care must be taken not to overtighten them at any point. The tapes must be knotted securely but this should not involve pulling the bandage tightly around the horse's leg. The knots must be on the outside of the leg, never pressing on the tendons. The ends of the tapes should be well secured and tucked out of the way. The danger of a bandage working loose during a ride can be prevented by putting insulating tape or bandage straps round it beforehand. Alternatively felt, leather or plastic boots of a suitable size and shape can be used to protect the horse's legs.

5(1)vi COOLING OFF

Cooling off, just like grooming, is most important for the horse's well-being and health. Neglecting this point shows a lack of consideration for the animal and is unworthy of a true horse lover and rider. Wherever possible the horse should not be returned to the stable in a sweaty condition. A sufficiently long period at walk (ten to fifteen minutes) should be provided beforehand, or the horse should be led around ('walking dry'), so that he cools off gradually. In warm weather the horse may be washed with warm water and a sponge, beginning with the legs but leaving out the loin region where the horse is particularly sensitive. The legs are first washed or hosed down. Then the water is wiped off from the top downwards with the hand. After sponging down, the wet parts of the horse's body are wiped down with the long sweat scraper (sweat knife). It is equally important to wash out all the body openings (mouth, dock, etc) thoroughly. After washing down the horse is left to dry in the sun or led around until he is dry.

The horse should not be left in a sweaty condition in cool weather either. He should be well rubbed down with a wisp made of tightly twisted straw. Old towels can then be used to finish off. When he is completely dry the horse should be groomed thoroughly to open the pores, which will be clogged with sweat and dirt, and to stimulate the circulation in the skin. Draughty stabling should be avoided.

5(2) Foot Care

The keeping and use of the horse by man deprives him of his natural living conditions: the horse's wild relations managed without foot care and shoeing. The growth and wear of the horn are supposed to balance out. The quality of the horn and the shape of the foot are supposed to be suited to the terrain.

For the work horse, riding horse and racehorse, however, conditions are completely different and unnatural. Even a horse turned out in a field is living in unnatural conditions, since he is restricted by a fence to a small area. Foot care and shoeing are therefore essential to correct the natural wear of the foot.

5(2)i CARE OF THE FOAL'S FOOT

In new-born foals there is a cushion-like, soft mass of horn (German: 'foal-cushion') covering the under surface of the foot. In a few days it dries and falls off of its own accord. The foot of a foal is essentially smaller at the ground surface than it is at the coronet. With adequate exercise it develops into a normal shaped foot. Foals have very long, flexible pasterns, which causes both the fore and hind feet to grow at a very acute angle to the ground.

Every three to four weeks foals out at grass should have their feet checked for shape, alignment with the pastern, and wear. In the winter months when the foal is stabled the feet should be shortened as necessary with the drawing knife and rasp.

5(2)ii CARE OF THE FEET OF OLDER HORSES

Unshod older horses must also have their feet trimmed with a drawing knife and rasp. Only dead, loose pieces of horn should be removed from the frog and sole. The heels should be spared. The sharp edge of the bearing surface should be rounded off slightly to help prevent the wall breaking up.

Horses should be re-shod every four to six weeks and there is no difference in the treatment of the shod and the unshod foot. Before and after work the foot should be cleaned out with a hoof pick, which should not have too sharp a point. Daily washing does not harm the foot, but it should not be overdone on the periople, which is destroyed by hard brushing or scouring with sand. The horn is absorbent and becomes more elastic when it takes up moisture. To prevent its drying out, the hoof should be greased after being washed and dried. Only salt-free, colourless grease which is not rancid should be used. The grease cannot penetrate the horn. Only the wall of the foot and not the sole should be greased. Rancid greases and old motor-oil cause serious inflammation of the coronary band, which makes the surface of the foot become cracked and scaly. Wood tar can be used to protect the sole from damp and manure. Any signs of foot rot must be treated immediately.

5(3) Shoeing

Shoeing is an important constituent of foot care. The ideal of the horse being permanently unshod is rarely possible. It is only feasible for horses who are always on soft ground and do not need to have their feet corrected (see chapter 3.1).

5(3)i SHOES

A shoe is made up of a toe, two quarters and two heels. The upper surface, which is in contact with the foot, is known as the foot surface, the lower surface as the ground surface.

The foot surface is level except for the bevel around the inner edge. The outer edge is not rounded or bevelled. In the ground surface is the 'fuller' (one-third of the thickness of the shoe in depth). In the fuller are the nail holes, four to eight in each branch. The outer and inner edges of the shoe are at right angles to the surfaces. Machine-made shoes come in the form of a foreshoe with a round toe and a hind shoe with a more pointed toe corresponding to normal shaped feet, and in different sizes to suit the horse.

The shoe is 1·5cm thick, 2·5 to 4cm wide at the toe, narrowing by about 25 per cent at the heels. The nail holes are about one-third of the width of the shoe from the outside edge.

To give the shoe a better hold it is equipped with clips projecting from the outer edge of the foot surface. Their height corresponds to the width of the shoe. The fore shoe has a single toe clip in the centre of the toe and the hind shoe has two quarter clips between the first and second nail holes.

5(3)ii SHOEING NAILS

The shoes are attached to the hoof with shoeing nails designed specially for this purpose. They are made out of very flexible, tough steel. Shoeing nails consist of a rectangular, pyramid-shaped head, a stem and a bevelled tip. The bottom part of the inner, wide side slopes into the so-called 'bevel'. On the same side as the bevel the corners of the stem are rounded off and the stem is bent slightly outwards ('taper angle'). This construction causes the nail to turn outwards into the hard wall and come out through it rather than bending inwards towards the sensitive structures of the foot. The nail should

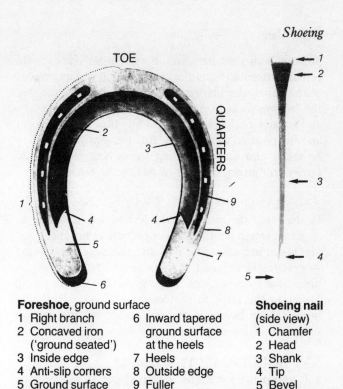

TOE

QUARTERS

Foreshoe, ground surface

1 Right branch
2 Concaved iron ('ground seated')
3 Inside edge
4 Anti-slip corners
5 Ground surface
6 Inward tapered ground surface at the heels
7 Heels
8 Outside edge
9 Fuller

Shoeing nail (side view)

1 Chamfer
2 Head
3 Shank
4 Tip
5 Bevel

therefore only be driven in when the bevel is facing the middle of the sole, and only nails in perfect condition should be used. Each nail should be carefully checked before use.

Shoeing with iron and nails has been carried out for about 1,500 years. In the last 100 years many attempts have been made to introduce new materials and techniques. Aluminium, which is lighter, and synthetic materials have made their mark as a replacement for iron, but they wear out more quickly and are difficult to work and fit.

5(3)iii ASSESSING THE LIMBS AND FEET
Before preparing and shoeing or re-shoeing the foot, the limbs and feet of the horse must be assessed while the

115

horse is both stationary and in movement. This should provide information on the conformation and movement of the limbs, the shape and quality of the foot, the way the feet are picked up and put down, the shape, length and position of the old shoes, the way they have worn out and the position of the holes. Any peculiarities can then be taken into account during subsequent visits to the farrier and attempts made to rectify the faults.

5(3)iv HANDLING THE HORSE

In the forge the horse should be handled as calmly as possible; rough treatment, inopportune punishment and loss of temper should be avoided. Titbits and reassuring words should be used to calm the horse's fear of his unfamiliar surroundings. It is a good idea to take young horses to the forge in the company of an older, quiet horse. Many horses have been ruined for life by bad treatment at the forge.

5(3)v HOLDING UP THE LIMBS★

Lifting up the forelimbs is carried out as follows: the holder walks up to the side of the horse's shoulder. He faces the opposite direction to the horse, and with the hand on the side away from the horse strokes the neck, shoulder and down the leg as far as the pastern. He grasps the pastern from the front and flexes the limb. At the same time he presses his other hand and his shoulder against the horse's shoulder to make the horse transfer his weight to the other side. He then puts the other hand around the pastern from the inside. Holding the foreleg in both hands, the holder supports it against the thigh nearest the horse. His shoulder lies against the horse's shoulder. The leg must be put down slowly and carefully.

To lift the hind limbs the holder strokes the croup and

★On the Continent a helper is usually required to hold the horse's feet for the blacksmith.

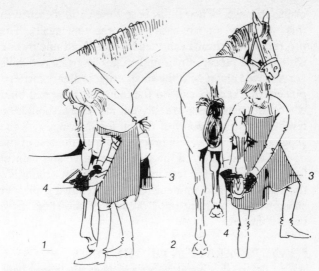

Holding up the limbs during shoeing
1 Foreleg, 2 Hind leg, 3 Apron, 4 Gloves

down the limb to the pastern with the hand on the side away from the horse. He uses the pressure of his other hand and shoulder against the hip to make the horse transfer his body weight to the other side. The helper then grasps the hind leg from the outside and lifts it by flexing the hock. Both hands encircle the fetlock from the inside and the outside. The hind leg is drawn out to the rear so that the fetlock rests on the holder's thigh.

5(3)vi REMOVING THE OLD SHOES

The first stage in removing the shoe always consists in lifting the clenches individually with the buffer, whilst taking care not to damage the wall of the foot. The clenches are bent upwards by light taps with the mallet on the buffer, which is placed underneath the clenches. Next, the shoe is loosened by driving the buffer carefully between it and the foot in the heel region. It is levered slowly away, care being taken not to break the wall or

117

bruise the sole. When it has been raised and loosened in this way it is tapped back on to the foot again. The protruding nail heads can then be pulled out one by one with special pincers ('nail pullers'). The front two nails are removed along with the shoe, using ordinary farriers' pincers. Broken off nails in the foot can cause nail bind when the new nails are driven in. They should be removed with the point of the buffer. Normally all the shoes are removed before proceeding with the rest of the operation. However, in the case of sensitive and painful feet (for example, flat feet and feet affected by laminitis), the foot is re-shod immediately after removing the old shoe, without waiting until the rest of the shoes have been removed.

5(3)vii PREPARATION OF THE FOOT

As a rule, re-shoeing is necessary when the shoes have been on for six weeks. In the case of wide feet, as the horn grows the shoe becomes too narrow; in sharply angled feet it becomes too short. The following conditions should be fulfilled in preparing the foot:

- ☐ The line of the foot should coincide with the line of the pastern (toe/pastern axis).
- ☐ The foot should be its natural size, with the dead material from the sole and frog removed.
- ☐ The bearing surface should be level. It should consist of the wall, the white line and a rim of sole horn corresponding in width to the thickness of the wall, and having a weight-bearing capacity which is as great as possible.

The first stage in the preparation consists in clearing away any crumbly pieces of sole, which cannot bear weight, and the loose pieces of frog. This is done with a drawing knife. The frog is left as wide and strong as possible. An 'exploratory cut' is made into the toe until firm horn is reached in order to see how much of the bearing edge of the wall can be cut away. The toeing knife and the mallet are used to cut round, and so shorten, the bearing edge of the wall. Care should be taken not to cut too much off the heels. The angles of the heels should not be weakened. On the fore feet the rasp is used to give an upward turn to the toe. The sharp outer edge of the wall is rounded off slightly.

Whilst the feet are being prepared, the horse should be made to place the weight on the foot at frequent intervals so that a check can be made as to whether the foot is in line with the pastern.

5(3)viii ADJUSTING, FITTING AND NAILING ON THE SHOE

The shoe is selected according to the size of the foot, and is heated in the fire until it is red hot all over. The foot surface of the shoe generally remains horizontal, although in the case of wide feet it slopes downwards from the inner to the outer edge. Behind the widest point the heel of the shoe curves round, following the line of the coronet, and then continues a little further, so that in the normal foot it protrudes outwards and backwards by about 4 to 5mm. The heels of the shoe must be clear of the lateral lacunae of the frog.

The foreshoes are bent upwards at the toe (rolled toes) which enables the foot to roll over the toe more easily. The shoe is brought to a moderate heat and the callipers are used to place it on the bearing surface of the foot. Bedding the hot shoe on to the foot should last only a short time. Afterwards it is possible to see if the bearing surface is level and the nail holes lie over the white line. After the shoe has been adjusted and fitted it is nailed on. A driving hammer is used to knock the nails through the soft horn of the white line and the harder horn of the wall. The tips of the nails protruding through the horn are immediately bent over with the hammer to prevent injury to man and horse. Nails must not be driven in behind the widest point of the foot, which would restrict the natural movement of the foot ('foot mechanism'). The nail tips are clipped off with the pincers. A special

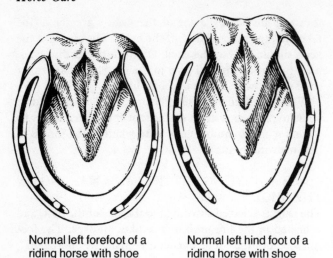

Normal left forefoot of a
riding horse with shoe

Normal left hind foot of a
riding horse with shoe

tool is used to make a bed for the clenches in the wall.
The clenches are formed by bending over the stumps of
the nails into these beds. Generally the clenches lie 2 to
3cm from the bottom of the foot. However, they can be
slightly higher, depending on the quality of the horn.
The horn should not be rasped above the clenches.

5(3)ix BRUSHING

If a horse is found to be brushing, that is, repeatedly
striking the limb which is on the ground with the
adjacent one which is moving forward, the cause and the
part of foot which is making contact must be ascertained.
Many things predispose to or cause brushing, for example, faulty conformation, shoeing and preparation of the
foot, fatigue and weakness, excitement and distress.
There is no universal remedy for these irregularities in
the action, but brushing can be prevented by raising or
lowering certain sections of the wall, shoeing with later-
ally weighted shoes (outer branch wider and heavier,
ground surface of the inner branch hollow) or with fore
brushing shoes (with the ground surface narrower by the

second nail hole) or hind brushing shoes (with the ground surface narrower at the heel end of the raised inner branch). Boots can be used as a protection against brushing.

5(3)x OVERREACHING

Another irregularity of the horse's action is overreaching, that is, striking into a forelimb with a hind foot as the latter swings forward. Overreaching seldom occurs in the walk, being commoner in extended trot, galloping and jumping.

Again, faulty conformation may be responsible, and incorrect shoeing, such as failure to use rolled toes, and the toes of the hind shoes projecting too far forward, are predisposing causes. An overreach can also be caused by chance, such as the foot suddenly sinking deep into soft ground, or through fatigue. If overreaching is caused by peculiarities in conformation, it must be corrected by special shoeing. Overreach shoes for the forefeet have a pronounced upward bend at the toe and a hollowed, sloping ground surface, and the heels of the shoes are set back under the foot and pencilled. Overreach shoes for the hind feet have a straight (square), bevelled toe.

Rubber overreach boots or 'bells' on the forefeet can be used to protect the bulbs of the heels, and boots will serve to protect the tendons.

5(3)xi PROTECTION AGAINST SLIPPING

Transverse grooves, anti-slip corners, or studs – which come in the most varied shapes and forms – in the heels of the shoes can be used to prevent slipping. Studs, whether of the screw-in or drive-in type, must always be removable. (Note: the drive-in type has a tapered stem which enables it to be driven out again, unlike the straight-stemmed 'plugs' or 'studs' which are permanent.) Calkins, either welded on or formed by bending the end of the shoe, are not recommended in view of the ever-present risk of injury. Studs must always be removed when the horse is in the stable and for travelling. They can cause bruising on the elbow (capped elbow) when the horse lies down or potentially dangerous injury to the coronet (treads).

The so-called 'grips' (toe-pieces) which can be used on the toes are the equivalent of studs on the heels. Usually they are used on harness horses working on slippery snow. Grips and studs should only be used when strictly necessary, since as well as bringing the danger of injury they make it easier for the foot to turn over sideways.

6. Ailments

This chapter deals with the most commonly occurring ailments of the horse. Particular attention has been paid to the causes of ill-health due to defective environment or to the horse being kept in unnatural conditions. This section should help prevent mistakes, since in most cases it is man who, as owner, rider or manager, is responsible for the horse's illness. Also described are the symptoms of the ailments, which will facilitate an early diagnosis. Summoning the veterinary surgeon promptly can then help prevent the condition worsening. Indications for treatment are deliberately not given, since an exact diagnosis, and the choice of a treatment from the many available, must be left to the professionals.

6(1) Skin Diseases

6(1)i WOUNDS

Injury to the skin with a break in its continuity is described as a wound. It occurs through mechanical (bruise, cut, puncture, bite), chemical (burn), thermal (burn) and electrical (electric shock, lightning strike) influences. The break in the protective skin means that bacteria can enter and cause infection of the wound. Of particular danger is *tetanus* because its causative agents are almost always present in the equine environment. Bleeding, pain and impaired function depend on the extent and position of the wound; for example severed muscles and tendons, and opened joint capsules and tendon sheaths are particularly serious.

The strength of the blood-flow is dependent on the type (arterial or venous) and the size of the severed vessel. Bright red blood and a rapid, pulsating flow are

Useful Medical Supplies, First Aid and Emergency

1. A stable's medicine cupboard should contain the following:

☐ Name, address and telephone number of the veterinary surgeon who can be contacted immediately in an emergency.

☐ Name, address and telephone number of another veterinary surgeon who can be called upon if the first is not available.

☐ A list of telephone numbers of the police, fire brigade and an emergency medical service.

☐ The vaccination certificates of all the horses in the yard so that in the case of injury the vet can ascertain whether an animal's tetanus vaccination is up to date.

☐ Bandaging material for the first-aid treatment of wounds, gauze in sterile packaging; 500g, 15 to 20cm wide cotton wool; four elasticated bandages; one tube of adhesive; one pair of scissors.

☐ A clinical thermometer.

☐ A *D.I.N.** approved first aid kit (for injured riders).

Medicines of any kind, even the commonly used purple antibiotic spray, should not be kept in stock.

2. Medicines for horses currently undergoing courses of treatment, as well as bandages and dressings, should be stored in a clean place. Boxes, tins and cupboards with tightly fitting doors or lids are most suitable, and they should be kept in clean, dust-free rooms. As a rule, tack rooms, stables and the riding instructor's office are not suitable.

* Deutsche Industrie-Norm – a German standard

3. Unused medicines are basically only fit for the dustbin. Only those which the vet says are suitable for keeping are exempt from this rule and fit to take their place in the medicine cabinet.

4. No two cases are alike. All treatment must therefore be discussed with the vet.

5. First aid for open wounds (see 6(1)i Wounds) consists of stopping the bleeding and preventing more dirt from entering. Obvious foreign bodies, which could cause further damage if left underneath the dressing, should be carefully removed with a sterile instrument (a scalded pair of tweezers). Fingers must not be poked into the wound, which must be covered as quickly as possible with sterile gauze and a bandage padded with cotton wool. In an emergency a clean cloth (freshly laundered handkerchief) may be used instead of the sterile gauze. The wound should be interfered with as little as possible, even the application of antibiotic sprays being avoided. If the position of the wound makes bandaging impossible, the gauze pad should be stuck over it with adhesive. The actual treatment must be entrusted to a vet.

6. If a horse suddenly goes off his food, colic or a fever could be the cause. His temperature must therefore be taken immediately (37·5 to 38°C is the norm).

7. If colic is suspected the vet should be called immediately.

8. When there is any doubt a specialist (vet specialising in horses) should be called.

indicative of bleeding from an artery, while a sluggish, even flow that means that the bleeding is from a vein. Bleeding often ceases spontaneously after 20 to 30 minutes. A blood loss of 25 per cent of the total (10 to 12 litres in a horse weighing 500kg) can be tolerated without the horse coming to any harm.

In the case of heavy bleeding first aid is necessary until the arrival of the vet. There are two main possibilities: A rubber strip, belt, tube, leather strap or rope is put around the limb above the wound at a point where there is plenty of muscle, and is tightened by putting a stick through it and turning (tourniquet). The limb must not be bound in this way for more than two hours because of the danger of gangrene.

A better way to halt bleeding is to use a pressure bandage. The wound is covered with a clean cloth (handkerchief, table napkin, towel) and a bandage is tied tightly round it. In difficult positions hand pressure is used. First-aid treatment of wounds by the layman pending the vet's arrival should be limited to these measures. Cauterising and the application of iodine to fresh wounds should be avoided, since both cause damage to the cells on the surface of the wound and thus favour infection.

The definitive care and treatment of wounds and the control of healing must be left to a vet.

6(1)ii CELLULITIS

Wound infections lead, particularly on the hindlegs, to disfiguring swelling caused by the purulent inflammation of the underneath layer of skin (dermis). This is known as cellulitis. The limb feels hot and is painful to the touch. There is lameness and an increase in body temperature. Cellulitis can be caused by seemingly insignificant wounds such as superficial brushing wounds, little abrasions on feet affected with chorioptic (symbiotic) mange, treads, thrush and puncture wounds. The swelling must be reduced as quickly as possible by immediate veterinary treatment: the longer it persists the greater the danger of build-up of fibrous tissue. The thickening then becomes permanent. The course of the disease is usually benign. In many cases the swelling has disappeared within a fortnight.

6(1)iii ECZEMA

The term eczema is used to describe an inflammation of the surface layer of skin accompanied by irritation and often hair loss. The causes are very numerous: sweating; dirt; prolonged exposure to wet; scrubbing; friction from saddle or harness; strong liniments; secretions from wounds; direct exposure to the sun; skin parasites; digestive problems; certain food plants and medicines. The weeping eczema in the hollow of the pastern is known as *cracked heel* and the scaly form at the back of the knee joint as *mallenders*. In summer a scaly, crusty form *sweat eczema (summer rash)* can be found underneath the saddle on horses who are made to sweat profusely.

Treatment must aim first and foremost at eliminating the causes.

6(1)iv ACNE AND FURUNCLES

The term *acne* is used to describe the purulent inflammation of the hair follicles and sebaceous glands, and *furunculosis* (boils) the purulent inflammation which develops from this and spreads outwards. Both forms are caused by the invasion of pyogenic organisms under favourable conditions, such as pressure, combined with inadequate skin care and a heavy build-up of sweat. The eruptions, which are about the size of a pin-head, burst and leave behind a small pit and a hairless spot. Since this recurring condition shows strong symptoms in the summer and dies down in the winter it is known in Germany as *summer mange*.

6(1)v NETTLE RASH (URTICARIA)

Swellings of the skin which appear suddenly and disappear again soon afterwards, and are distributed over the whole of the body, are known as nettle rash. It occurs in connection with infections, colic, allergies (to medicines, insect bites and skin irritants) and also when the horse is excited. Usually it is harmless and quickly goes down again.

6(1)vi GALLS

These occur due to a badly fitting saddle (sore back) or harness (harness galls); a rubbing girth (girth galls); lying on hard ground, or slipping rugs. Swelling, bald patches and sensitivity to the touch are the first symptoms, which should always be taken seriously. The cause must be eliminated without delay. A few weeks after the galls have healed white hairs grow over the spot.

6(1)vii FUNGAL INFECTIONS

The commonly occurring fungal infections of the horse are, as a rule, infectious. These diseases can be transmitted from the horse to man and vice versa as well as caught from other species. The thread-like microscopic fungi grow on the skin, in the hair follicles and in the hair itself. Infection is spread through direct contact or via grooming tools, saddles, numnahs or bedding. The symptoms take different forms. Even the irritation is sometimes completely absent. The lesions may appear either as round, bald patches on different parts of the body, with broken-off hairs around the edges, or as little tubercles and pustules.

6(1)viii TRICHORRHEXIS NODOSA

Trichorrhexis nodosa ('lumps on the hair') is an infectious fungal disease of the hair. Infection is spread through the horse rubbing his tail against infected stable walls or via grooming utensils. It can also be spread to man. The body hair, as well as the mane and tail, are

affected. On close examination individual hairs in different places are seen to be thickened by the presence of
tubercles along them and are broken-off, split and frayed
at the ends.

6(1)ix WARTS

Warts are horny, tumour-like growths on the surface of
the skin. They can occur individually or over the whole
of the body. The most commonly affected regions are the
corners of the mouth, the eyelids, the ears (headshy) and
under the saddle and girth. Treatment is then vital. One
possible cause is a virus. After surgical removal the warts
often return. There is one particular variety which affects
horses at grass. It is caused by a virus and is therefore
infectious and is characterized by the formation on the
lips, ears and cheeks, round the eyes, and also on the
flanks and the insides of the thighs, of a typical pointed
type of wart. Often several horses are affected in the same
field. These virus warts may disappear after a few
months without treatment.

6(2) Foot Ailments

6(2)i FLAT FEET

The term *flat feet* is used to describe exceptionally wide
feet. At the sides the walls meet the ground at an
exaggeratedly acute angle. The sole is on a level with the
bearing surface. The horn of the sole is very thin and
correspondingly sensitive. The wall breaks away very
easily.

6(2)ii CONVEX SOLES

In *convex soles*, a condition which can develop from *flat
feet*, the sole bulges outwards towards the ground. The
outer edge of the pedal bone curves upwards like the
brim of a hat. The horse goes short or is markedly lame,
depending on the sensitivity of the sole and the type of

ground. The horse can be used on soft ground if shod with sole protection and quarter clips.

6(2)iii CONTRACTED FEET

The term *contracted feet* is used to describe a narrowing of the horn capsule in determined areas.

Contracted Heels

The narrowing of the horn capsule takes place on one or both sides in the rear portion of the foot. We distinguish between contracted heels in a narrow foot and those in an acutely sloping or wide foot. When the heels of a narrow foot are contracted there is extensive wasting of the frog, usually in conjunction with thrush. The walls of the foot at the heels are drawn distinctly inwards. The wasting of the frog is due to lack of massage caused by the ground being too soft. Thrush, insufficient exercise, narrow feet, leaving the shoes on too long, and hard going are predisposing causes.

In wide and acutely sloping feet the walls at the heel are oblique and underset, and so not able to bear much weight. The heels are therefore pinched inwards owing to the weight of the body on them, and they, the frog and the horn of the sole are almost always highly developed. Incorrect foot preparation, such as excessive lowering and paring of the heel buttresses, and leaving the toes too long, tends to encourage this condition. When the contraction occurs in a narrow foot the wasting of the frog must first be attended to. Good results are obtained by using a bar shoe. A pad made of a not too firm material, with no pressure on the wall of the foot in the heel region, can be used with a bar shoe. Cutting vertical or diagonal grooves is pointless; not only does it not bring about the desired widening, it also causes pinching and bruising of the inner sensitive laminae.

When the contraction occurs in wide feet the aim is to transfer the excess pressure from the heels to the front half of the foot by raising the heels.

Feet Contracted at the Coronet
The contraction is just below the coronet, usually only at the heels. This distortion occurs in horses with wide feet following a sudden change of going from soft to hard. A return to soft ground, and shoeing with leather pads for better shock absorption, will alleviate the problem.

Contracted Soles
In contracted soles there is marked concavity of the sole, the foot becomes shorter from front to rear, and the toe appears to curl under like a claw. The sole is sensitive in front of the apex of the frog. For this reason horses with contracted soles are characteristically very lame on soft ground. An 'H'-shaped shoe gives good results. The front of the toe and the heels are not covered by the shoe, and the wide bar level with the apex of the frog joins the side pieces together and protects the sole from pressure from the ground.

Contraction of the Bearing Surface
Another form of contracted feet is contraction of the bearing surface. The diameter of the hoof is smaller at the ground surface than at the coronet. This condition occurs in young horses who have been brought up in conditions which did not permit sufficient exercise. The foot retains the same shape as that of the new-born foal, that is, smaller at the ground surface than at the coronet. Only regular corrective foot care and plentiful exercise on soft ground can prevent or improve this condition.

6(2)iv SPLITS IN THE WALL OF THE FOOT, SANDCRACKS
Splits are vertical cracks in the wall of the foot. Depending on their position they are either toe, quarter, heel or heel-buttress splits. Depending on their length they may be coronet, lower-wall or full-length splits; and, according to their depth, either superficial ('wind-cracks') or deep splits. They are caused by anything

which results in uneven loading of the foot. Since horn never grows back together again once it has been separated, the answer lies in waiting for healthy horn to grow down naturally. Treatment includes ensuring that the split does not lengthen (remove the cause and burn or cut grooves parallel to the coronet). In the case of quarter or heel splits, plastic packing (hoof repair) material is used and the foot is shod with a bar shoe and quarter clips in such a way that the split does not come into contact with the top of the shoe (this section of the edge of the wall is said to 'float' or 'hover'). For deep splits, which go right through the wall, surgery is necessary.

6(2)v CLEFTS

The term *cleft* is used to describe a defect in the wall of the foot running at right angles to the direction of the horn tubes, i.e. horizontally. It may extend inwards as far as the sensitive tissue of the foot. It occurs as the result of a tread. Particularly with deep clefts, purulent inflammation of the sensitive tissue must be averted until the cleft grows down, and so out.

6(2)vi HORN TUMOUR (KERATOMA)

Horn tumour is a conical-shaped bulge in the horn on the inside wall of the hoof, extending from the coronet to the ground surface. If the condition affects the lower part only it is known as a 'horn callous' or 'horn bump'. Horn tumour can lead to chronic inflammation of the sensitive tissue and to the formation of a groove in the pedal bone. It occurs as a result of a tread, nail bind or sandcrack. In many cases it does not cause lameness. Where lameness is present, surgery is necessary, followed by packing with hoof repair material and shoeing with a bar shoe and two quarter clips.

6(2)vii SEEDY TOE, SEPARATIONS

The separation of the horn of the sole from the horn of the wall is known either as a separation or as seedy toe.

The condition is commonest in broad feet. A dark groove gradually appears where sand and small stones have become embedded in the white-line region. If the sensitive tissues become inflamed, lameness develops. Through frequent washing or wet weather conditions the softening of the horn may worsen. Regular corrective foot care and shoeing soon result in an improvement.

6(2)viii CAVITATION

In cavitation a cavity forms under the wall as a result of heavy concussion. This cavity easily becomes infected. The hollow parts of the wall must be cut out and shoeing follow as for surgically treated horn tumour.

6(2)ix THRUSH, FOOT ROT

Decay in the cleft of the frog (thrush) and in the sole, wall and white line (foot rot) are often found in horses with neglected feet in wet bedding, and in those who receive insufficient exercise on soft ground. The frog disintegrates into loose shreds and pockets and is filled with an evil-smelling substance. The decay is caused by bacteria which are ever present in the ground and which do not require oxygen. The decay can spread to the bulbs of the foot and cause them to become detached. On the wall of the foot so-called 'thrush rings' are formed.

As a preventative measure in wet ground conditions, besides constant checks on the condition of the sole and daily cleaning of the feet, painting the sole with vegetable tar is recommended. However, vegetable (Stockholm) tar is unsuitable as a treatment for this condition because it favours the culture of the anaerobic bacteria. Treatment is with 4 per cent iodoform ether (4g iodoform in 100ml ether) after first removing completely all the loose shreds of horn, and packing the cleft of the frog with cotton wool. The commonly used blue vitriol has water drawing properties which lead to the drying out of the horn and loss of elasticity.

6(2)x INFLAMMATION OF THE SENSITIVE TISSUE

Without Infection

Non-purulent inflammations of the sensitive tissue occur as a result of strains, pinching, crushing, contusions or burns (caused by holding the hot shoe on too long when bedding it on a foot which has been cut back excessively). There is no recorded case of frost bite in an undamaged hoof capsule. The painful area can be located by squeezing with pincers or tapping with a hammer. A stronger pulse can be felt in the arteries leading to the toe. Removal of the cause (faulty shoeing), box-rest and casting-bandages* on the foot may bring about rapid improvement. In the case of bruised soles caused by stony ground the horse can be shod with a leather pad completely covering the sole. The gap between the sole and the leather pad may be stopped with tow soaked in vegetable tar to prevent thrush and foot rot. If the bruising of the sole is accompanied by bleeding, a few weeks later, when the sole is pared, red spots ('stone galls') appear in the horn. Treatment of these 'stone galls' is not usually necessary. An actual blood blister may remain which may become infected in the angles of the heels (corn).

With Infection (Foot Abscess)

Purulent inflammation of the sensitive tissue results from infection through nail-bind, puncture wounds, 'stone galls'/corns, sandcrack, horn cleft, etc. There is pronounced lameness and a strong pulse in the arteries leading to the toe, and the horse flinches when the foot is squeezed with the pincers. The bacteria gain entry to the sensitive tissue through hair-line cracks in the horn of the sole and cause infection and abscess formation. However, the pus cannot escape through these fine cracks. It spreads across the sole area and may go upwards,

---

* Bandages which set hard to form a rigid casting around the foot.

134

destroying part of the coronary band and breaking out at the coronet. In order to prevent this damage, a foot abscess must be opened up promptly through the sole. The spot can be recognized by its greyish-black colour when the sole is pared. Pressure builds up in the abscess and it is greyish-black and foul-smelling owing to the sulphur content of the horn. A funnel-shape should be cut round the abscess, and counter-pressure used to prevent the prolapse of the sensitive tissue. The formation of new horn begins in a few days. A foot bandage or a shoe with a removable plate ('lid shoe') must be fitted to protect the area.

Puncture Wounds

The term *puncture wound* is used to describe the piercing of the sole by a sharp object. Depending on the position and depth of the wound, the sensitive laminae, the pedal bone, the plantar cushion, the deep flexor tendon or navicular bone, or the bursa between the two, or the pedal joint may be affected. Veterinary treatment is necessary in each case.

Nail Bind

Injuries to the sensitive tissue or pedal bone caused by the nails during shoeing are known as nail binds. A distinction is made between a prick, where the nail involved is immediately removed again, a true nail bind, in which the nail remains, and an indirect nail bind (nail burn, nail pressure, 'close nail'), in which the sensitive structures are only pinched by the nail. If the horse has been pricked by the nail he will flinch violently as the nail is being driven in. Usually there is no harm done and it heals by itself. In true nail bind there is immediate lameness after shoeing. The nail must be removed immediately. An abscess may develop in the foot in the next few days. In indirect nail bind the lameness does not develop until several days later. The pulse in the arteries

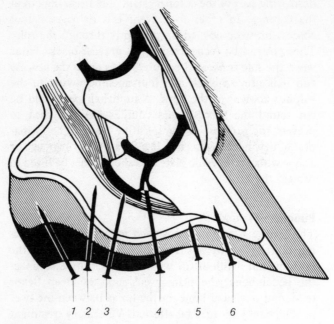

Possible sites of puncture wounds

1 Horny frog, lateral cartilage
2 Plantar cushion
3 Deep flexor tendon, bursa, navicular bone
4 Pedal joint (coffin joint)
5 Sensitive laminae
6 Pedal bone

leading to the toe is increased. Tapping or withdrawal of the offending nail is painful.

Laminitis, Founder

The terms laminitis or founder are used to describe a protracted, non-purulent inflammation of the sensitive laminae of the foot which may occur in all the feet but is usually more pronounced in the forefeet.

The condition develops within a few hours. The horse stands with the forefeet stretched forwards and the hind

136

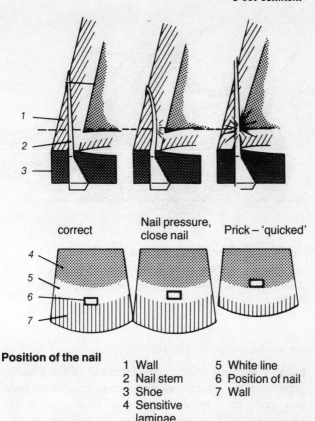

correct | Nail pressure, close nail | Prick – 'quicked'

Position of the nail

1 Wall
2 Nail stem
3 Shoe
4 Sensitive laminae
5 White line
6 Position of nail
7 Wall

legs placed under the body. He moves with pottering steps. The weight is taken not on the toes but on the heels and bulbs of the feet. In severe cases the horse cannot be moved from the spot. There is heat in the feet and they are sensitive when tapped. The pulse in the arteries to the toe is greatly increased and bounding. Fever may develop. The course of the disease varies. It may clear up in 4 to 14 days.

However, the inflammation of the sensitive laminae may lead to the loosening and detachment of the tissue layer which connects the sensitive laminae to the pedal

137

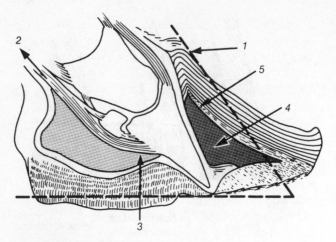

Laminitis with rotation of the pedal bone

1 Original shape of foot
2 Pull of tendon
3 Pressure from plantar
  cushion

4 Horny scar tissue
5 Separation of wall

bone. The result of this separation and of the counter-pressure of the plantar cushion is the rotation of the pedal bone in the hoof capsule. The coronet sinks inwards. The tip of the pedal bone presses against the sole. Severe cases may entail the penetration of the tip of the pedal bone through the sole, purulent inflammation of the pedal bone, complete detachment of the hoof capsule, protracted pneumonia and general infection, resulting in death.

If rotation of the pedal bone takes place, a 'laminitis foot' develops, with horizontal rings all down it, dishing of the wall at the front of the foot a few centimetres below the coronet, thickening of the white line due to the formation of horny scar tissue, and high heels. The horse projects the feet forward in movement and walks on the heels.

The causes of laminitis are numerous and varied. It may be caused by over-exertion (traumatic laminitis) on hard, stony, frozen, dry or uneven ground; riding for very long distances; prolonged standing on a hard stable floor (stable laminitis); long rail journeys; or prolonged standing on three legs in cases of severe lameness (pressure laminitis). Coldblood horses, soft, lazy types of horse and horses with acutely angled or flat feet are especially prone to laminitis.

Another cause is incorrect feeding (nutrition laminitis), for example the feeding of barley, rye, wheat, maize and molasses. Laminitis can also occur as a result of overfeeding, especially in ponies, or after colic. A further cause is consuming poisonous substances (toxic laminitis) such as aloes; tartar emetic; acacia bark, lady's smock (*cardamine pratensis*), castor oil seeds; liniments containing petroleum; crude oil; vaseline oil, or certain long acting cortisones. It may also occur as a complication of various infectious diseases or retention of the afterbirth at foaling.

When laminitis is diagnosed a veterinary surgeon must be consulted immediately. It is essential to identify and remove the cause. Moreover, the rotation of the pedal bone must be prevented. The horse should be placed in a stable with a soft floor (deep litter straw, peat, tan or sand). If the horse is shod, the shoes should be left on for the time being. Casting-bandages on all four feet can be very useful. The drugs used in treatment are very varied and depend upon the cause. Where rotation of the pedal bone has already occurred, or in order to prevent it, laminitis shoeing can be performed. In this the sole is made to bear more weight by packing it with hoof repair material. The condition tends to recur, and horses with laminitic feet need constant attention and correction to them.

6(2)xi HOOF CANCER, FROG CANCER
Hoof or frog cancer is an excrescence of sensitive tissue at

a point where the horn is missing. The term cancer, which dates from 1805, is misleading, because this is not a malignant tumour. The main factor is the absence of horn. The excrescence of sensitive tissue is to be seen as a result of this. Since hoof cancer is commoner in cold-bloods than warmbloods, the condition is seldom seen nowadays. The cause is still unclear. Surgical treatment is necessary and the foot must be dressed with numerous pressure bandages until it has healed.

6(2)xii OVERREACH, BRUISED HEEL, TREAD

Open wounds on the coronet or bulbs of the heel are known as treads and overreaches, respectively. Bruises on the back part of the foot are known as bruised heels. Overreaches on the forelimbs result from the forward reaching of the hind foot, though similar wounds on the hind feet may occur as a result of being over-ridden by the horse behind.

Treads are usually self-inflicted wounds, the opposite foot being to blame. They may be serious if caused by studs. This sort of injury is especially common when a horse is travelling, and studs should always be removed at such times. Treads should always be treated by a veterinary surgeon since they may lead to sandcrack, clefts or horn tumour.

6(2)xiii SIDEBONES

In horses with poor conformation, or as a result of incorrect shoeing, the flexible lateral cartilages may gradually ossify if the horse is worked on hard ground. There is not usually any lameness. Reversal of the ossification process is not possible. If the horse is lame, soft going and leather strips under the shoes may enable him to return to work.

6(2)xiv NAVICULAR DISEASE

The navicular region (foot pulley) consists of the navicular bone, the part of the deep flexor tendon which passes over it and the bursa which lies between the tendon and the bone (see *Anatomy*).

In navicular disease, that is chronic inflammation of the navicular region, all the parts of the region are affected. In the living horse, only changes in the actual bone can be detected, and that by use of X-rays. Navicular disease occurs, mainly in the forefeet, in all types of horses as well as in mules and donkeys. Riding horses are the commonest victims. Too narrow conformation of the foot and/or a backward broken toe/pastern axis predispose to its development. Hereditary predisposition may be a contributory cause. Because it develops gradually, and often simultaneously, in both forefeet the disease frequently goes undetected in the early stages. Lameness is almost imperceptible on soft going. On hard ground the horse's gait is short and stilted. In advanced cases the horse is lame on the more painful leg, which is pointed forward when the horse is at rest. If the pain is equal in both limbs they may be stretched forward alternately.

The excessive pressure on the deep flexor tendon during any movement leads to significant changes in the shape of the navicular bone, which can then be detected by X-ray. There can be no reversal or healing of these changes. In minor cases, where the smooth surface of the navicular bone has not yet been damaged, prolonged rest and corrective shoeing with a shoe with raised heels and a pronounced upward curve to the toe (rolled toe) can bring about improvement. Drugs have been used with success in some cases to help the disease. Lasting pain relief can be obtained surgically by neurectomy (denerving), and other surgical procedures have been reported as successful.

6.3 Diseases and Injuries of the Bones and Joints

6(3)i BREAKS (FRACTURES) AND CRACKS OF THE BONE

A bone fracture used always to be a death sentence to a horse. Nowadays new, and sometimes expensive, methods of treatment, justified by the value of the horse, make complete recovery possible in certain cases, though a horse can only be considered to be fully recovered if after the fracture it returns to its original job (for instance as a riding horse or a racehorse). Most fractures involve a joint and, after the fracture has healed, damage to the joint remains which causes chronic lameness. If incomplete recovery of this kind can be predicted from X-rays, treatment is usually undertaken only in the case of valuable brood mares or stallions.

The prognosis is particularly unfavourable in the case of fractures involving a joint or accompanied by a wound (owing to the great risk of infection in horses); fractures in highly strung horses and old horses, and fractures of the upper limb (because of the impossibility of immobilizing them). Fractures occur when the bone's strength and elasticity – the latter declines with age – are insufficient to cope with the load placed upon it (either once or repeatedly). Any bone can break or crack. The symptoms of a fracture are pronounced lameness; pain when the limb is rotated and the bony grating sound (crepitus) which accompanies this; abnormal movement, and swelling due to the rush of blood to the area.

X-rays will give information on the line of the fracture. If a bone fracture is to heal, the broken ends must be exactly aligned and kept immobile for a long time (at least four weeks). The immobilization of the fracture area can be achieved either by special bandages (e.g. forming a plaster cast) or by surgical means (e.g. screws, plates and pins). The causes of, and availability of treatment for some of the more common fractures are discussed on the following pages.

Fractures of the pedal bone can occur through a horse striking the hoof against the side of a ditch or against an unyielding object; through raising the foot, dropping it and striking the wall of the toe against hard ground, and through mis-steps, nail bind or penetration of the foot by the quarter clips in the case of a slipped shoe. Since the pedal bone is enclosed in the hoof capsule, there is usually only a very slight displacement of the ends of the fracture. Although the fracture often runs through the joint surface, full recovery is possible after two to three months' box rest if the foot can be enclosed in a rigid plastic case, so that the natural expansion and contraction which occurs with each step (the hoof mechanism) is prevented.

Fractures of the long pastern bone (os suffraginis) occur most commonly in conjunction with fractures of the pedal bone. The construction of the fetlock joint (the ridge on the cannon bone fits exactly into the centre groove at the top of the pastern bone) is such that only flexion and extension are possible. The typical long pastern bone fracture occurs when the ridge is twisted in the groove while the stress is at its greatest, as in landing after a jump. Recovery in six to eight weeks is possible if screws are used.

Fractures of the sesamoid bones do occur in riding horses but they are most common in racehorses and trotters. They occur because of the excessive strain placed on the suspensory ligament when the body weight is taken on the foot at the moment it is set down. When both sesamoid bones are fractured the fetlock is lowered excessively, so that the back of it may touch the ground, as in the case of rupture of the tendon. The prognosis is poor. When fragments have broken off recovery is possible if the fragments are removed surgically.

Fractures of the splint bones occur either as the result of an external force such as a blow or, in riding or racehorses undergoing intensive training, due to tiredness. The lower, unsecured ends of the splint bones are pushed outwards at each strike by the sides of the suspensory ligament. In unfavourable circumstances (periostitis, inflammation of the tendon) the bottom third is fractured. Recovery is possible if the broken off section is surgically removed.

Fractures of the cannon bone are seen most commonly in foals and yearlings following a kick. The fracture, which may be either horizontal or diagonal, can be immobilized by the use of a plate screwed on to the bone. Healing is often severely complicated by infected skin wounds accompanying the injury. The plate must be surgically removed a few months after the bone has healed.

Fractures of the humerus and femur cannot usually be successfully immobilized and are therefore not reparable.

Fractures of the pelvis occur as a result of falls, slipping on hard ground, running into or banging the hips against doorways and corners, or due to rough handling during a difficult birth. If the edges of the fracture are not excessively displaced, recovery is possible after a few months' box rest. If the line of the fracture runs through the hip joint, chronic lameness will result.

Fractures of the lower jaw occur as the result of a blow, a fall, or the jaw being caught in a headcollar chain or the bars of a stable partition. There are many ways in which the fractures can be repaired by surgery.

Fractures of the neck vertebrae occur as a result of falls in which the head is bent in or the horse rolls over with his neck stretched out; somersaults; running into something, or getting the hindfoot caught in the headcollar or headcollar rope. The symptoms take the form either of staggering, collapsing and an inability to rise, or of holding the head and neck crookedly. Direct treatment of the fracture is not usually feasible.

6(3)ii PERIOSTITIS

Apart from on the joint surfaces, every bone is surrounded by a membrane or periosteum, which is well supplied with blood. Mechanical irritation in the form of pressure, a blow, bruising or a strain leads to a painful inflammation of the periosteum. If the condition persists over a long period there is a tendency towards ossification.

Periostitis occurs as the result of pressure from the noseband across the horse's nose, caused by the action of the bit on the lower jaw, or through the alternating push and pull on the fore cannon bone (the so-called *splints*). Although injury was once thought to be a cause, it is in fact extremely rare.

Splints always occur between the splint bone and the cannon bone, but depending on their exact position they are classified as three types: side, rear and deep. The splint bones are joined to the cannon bone by transverse ligaments. The upper part of the splint bones form the side parts of the joint surface of the knee or carpal joint.

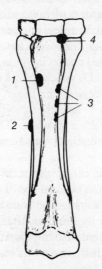

Position of splints
1 Rear
2 Side
3 Rear
4 Deep

When the stress on the knee is uneven, for example in the lateral movements, there is increased pressure on one splint bone. This results in a strain of the ligaments and ossification at the point where the ligament joins on to the periosteum. Whereas side splints are to be regarded more as an aesthetic blemish, rear and deep splints interfere with the suspensory and check ligaments and cause chronic and incurable lameness.

6(3)iii PURULENT INFLAMMATION OF THE BONE

In a purulent general infection, in open fractures, puncture wounds and infected tooth sockets, purulent infections of the periosteum or of the bone itself may occur. The outcome can be fatal. Often treatment is successful only in the early stages.

6(3)iv BONE CONDITIONS ARISING FROM METABOLIC OR CIRCULATORY DISORDERS

There is a further group of bone conditions which are caused by nutritional disorders or circulatory disorders in the bone. Among the disorders caused by problems of nutrition is *rickets*; this occurs in young horses owing to a deficiency of vitamin D, which results in a disturbance of the calcification process in the bones.

In young animals before the growth process is complete – that is before the cartilage of which the growth plates are made has ossified – a *separation* of the *growth plates* can arise.

After long periods off work, or in conjunction with circulatory disorders, a marked loss of calcium salts from the bone may be observed. The bone loses hardness and is therefore more easily broken. After lay-offs of two to three months it is essential to build up the work gradually over a period of at least two to three weeks.

6(3)v CONTUSIONS, SPRAINS AND DISLOCATIONS OF JOINTS

Contusions and *sprains* occur due to a powerful external force such as a blow; banging against or dropping down on to something; tipping sideways, or twisting round. They can be accompanied by cartilage injuries, damage to the underlying bone surface and tears to the joint capsule and ligaments. The injured joint is painful. The prognosis depends on the degree of damage sustained. Keeping the limb still is essential for recovery.

Dislocation refers to a change in position of the joint surfaces from that entailed in normal movement. Dislocations may or may not right themselves spontaneously. In the latter case a recurrence is to be expected. The commonest form of dislocation in the horse is the upward luxation of the patella. It occurs as a result of kicking out violently, slipping, falling, or standing up, and is caused by over-extension of one of the patellar ligaments. The hind leg is suddenly stretched out, with the hock and stifle joints straight, and is immovable. The condition can often be corrected by making the horse step backwards and downhill; otherwise the vet should be called in. The correction may involve anaesthetics or surgery.

6(3)vi INFLAMMATION OF THE JOINT (ARTHRITIS)

Inflammation can affect any joint for various reasons, for example, contusions, sprains, dislocations and misplaced or prolonged stress. The joint capsule bulges at the points where it lies underneath the skin (articular windgalls) owing to an increase in the amount of synovial fluid. These enlargements are most obvious on the fetlock joint and the hock (bog spavin). The swelling often remains after the inflammation has subsided. The joint is warm and lameness is slight to medium.

147

Purulent inflammation is often found in general infections when the causative organisms invade the joints, as with joint evil in foals, and after injury to the joint, such as penetration by a pitchfork. In purulent inflammation of the joint there is pronounced lameness. The condition should be treated immediately since if the infection spreads, a potentially fatal general infection may ensue. Purulent or chronic inflammation of the joint, which involves damage to the cartilage and disfigurement of the joint, comes within the province of *arthrosis*.

6(3)vii ARTHROSIS

True arthrosis is a result of defective cartilage cell nutrition in conjunction with mechanical stress. The lack of nourishment leads to extensive erosion of the surfaces of the cartilage. This is followed by the formation of swellings on the edges of the joints. Arthroses in horses are commonest on the foot joints (pedal joint, pastern joint and fetlock joint) as *ringbone*; on the less flexible part of the hock as *spavin*, and on the knee joint.

Once it has formed, the arthrosis is a non-inflammatory condition, though at certain stages inflammatory complications can arise. The onset of the condition is gradual. The gait is stilted and the horse tires more quickly than usual. Sometimes it is months or years before a clearly marked lameness develops. The horse usually finds flexion tests very painful and these are an effective means of pinpointing or exaggerating any lameness.

Changes in the bone and cartilage caused by an arthrosis are irreparable. The final stage in the disease is total ankylosis of the joint. In one form of the disease, osteo-chondrosis dissecans (commonly known as OCD), a piece of cartilage breaks off, resulting in loose particles in the joint, which are known in German as 'joint mice'. These can be removed by surgery.

6(4) Conditions Relating to Tendons, Ligaments, Tendon Sheaths and False Bursae

6(4)i INFLAMMATION OF TENDONS AND LIGAMENTS

This occurs owing to excessive strain and overstretching caused while trotting, galloping, jumping, falling or overreaching. It is common in racehorses. The tendons most commonly affected are the flexors (deep and superficial) and the suspensory ligament. It occurs only occasionally in the extensor tendons. In exceptional cases tendon inflammation may be caused by parasites.

Symptoms of tendon inflammation are supporting leg lameness accompanied by heat and thickening of the flexor tendons which are sensitive to pressure. Longstanding cases are also referred to as 'bowed tendons'. Treatment of acute cases consists of box rest, bandaging, strong liniments, firing or surgery. After the acute stage is past carefully regulated exercise should be undertaken. Months off work are necessary for recovery. The lameness may disappear relatively quickly. However, the scar tissue is not capable of taking any strain for some considerable time. Since attention is seldom paid to this point, most horses suffer a recurrence when returned to work. The contraction of the scar can result in a 'toe-dancer stance', in which the horse walks on his toes with the heels raised.

6(4)ii RUPTURE OF TENDONS AND LIGAMENTS

A tendon or ligament rupture can be total or partial. Causes are excessive strain on the tendon due to powerful traction, trotting, galloping and jumping. Ruptures to ligaments result in abnormal movement or position of the joint. Ruptures of the superficial flexor tendon or suspensory ligament can be recognised by an exaggerated lowering of the fetlock ('breakdown').

The prognosis is unfavourable. Treatment consists of bandaging, liniments and firing. Suturing the ruptured tendon is not possible owing to the enormous strain it has to bear. To help prevent the fetlock dropping, the horse is fitted with a rest shoe with extended heels connected by a raised bridge. Partial ruptures resemble inflamed tendons in both symptoms and progression.

6(4)iii INFLAMMATION OF THE TENDON SHEATH

Tendon sheaths are envelopes which are kept slippery on the inside by a mucous fluid which allows the tendons that run through them to slide more easily. When inflammation occurs production of this fluid is increased. The surrounding ligaments and periosteum may also be affected.

Non-purulent inflammations of the tendon sheath are caused by mechanical influences such as blows, strain, bruising, etc, or in young horses by overweight due to overfeeding. Purulent inflammations are caused by injury (e.g. penetration by a pitchfork) or occur in conjunction with general infections (e.g. strangles). Chronic inflammation of the joint sheath of the flexor tendons, recognisable by a filled, swollen bulge just above the sesamoid bones, is known as a windgall. A more precise description would be 'tendinous windgall' to distinguish it from the bursal enlargement on the fetlock joint which is also known as a windgall. Inflammation of the extensor tendon sheath on the carpal joint is known by riders as 'jumper's knee', because it occurs as a result of the knee striking against a jump. In fact, the use of the word 'knee' to describe the carpal joint is in itself a misnomer.

In many cases inflammation of the tendon sheath without lameness is simply an aesthetic blemish. Potentially risky methods of treatment should not be undertaken in such cases.

6(4)iv INFLAMMATION OF THE FALSE BURSAE (HYGROMA)

False bursae act as cushions at points where the skin passes over bony projections. Inflammation of false bursae occurs as a result of considerable pressure on one occasion or repeated minor irritation. Boil-like enlargements of the bursae appear, for example on the front of the fetlock as the result of a blow; on the elbows as the result of pressure from calkins or studs when lying down (capped elbow); on the point of the hock as a result of kicking the hind leg against something (capped hock); or on the withers as a result of pressure from saddle or harness. When applying treatment it is important to remove the underlying cause.

6(5) Conditions Relating to the Muscles

Ruptured muscles (partial or total) can occur anywhere in the body. Apart from great pain and swelling, there is loss of function corresponding to the muscle involved. In heavily pregnant mares the rectus abdominis muscle can rupture at the edge of the pelvis (ruptured belly). In other forms of rupture, too, the cause is tremendous strain, which can occur when the horse slips with his legs stretched out to the rear, when he kicks violently, when a limb is pulled up with a rope, when a hind leg is caught in the headcollar or rope, and so on. The increased blood flow which causes the swelling accompanying the rupture mostly disappears after seven to ten days. When the muscle concerned lies near the surface a dent can then be seen and felt between the two ruptured ends. Healing takes the form of scar-tissue formation and shrinkage. When the two ruptured ends lie somewhat apart the muscle may end up longer. Treatment consists in resting the muscle. Healing takes four to eight weeks. Surgical repair is rarely successful.

Atrophy of the muscle may occur as a result of inactivity,

151

pressure, cellular degeneration or paralysis. Recognisable symptoms appear within fourteen days.

Muscular atrophy due to lack of exercise, or insufficient exercise, affects all the muscles. In cases of severe lameness or complete lack of use of a diseased or injured leg, pronounced atrophy of the muscles of this leg occurs.

Cellular degeneration is caused by inflammation of the muscle, injury and contusion, or a defective blood supply. Damage to the nerves controlling the muscles, plus inflammation, rupture, contusion and poisoning, lead to a marked, rapid shrinkage of the muscle group concerned. Treatment can then only be successful if the cause can be removed.

Inflammation of the muscle, myositis, occurs as a result of excessive muscular exertion during a short but strenuous work-out, riding long distances, or over-strenuous race-track training. The horse stands stiffly in his box and avoids all movement. His muscles are tense, his breathing accelerated, he sweats and there are muscle tremors. Recovery may take several weeks. Box rest, warm blankets and rubbing down with spirit of camphor will serve as a back-up to the healing process.

Myohaemoglobinuria, paralytic myoglobinuria, azoturia are terms used to describe degeneration of the muscles, the onset of which is extremely sudden. The condition may occur after one to three days' box rest accompanied by rich feeding. However, rich feeding on its own or excessive muscular exertion, for instance during long distance rides, drives or eventing, without the necessary fittening, can trigger off the condition. It occurs during exercise following a rest. The horse sweats profusely, trembles, staggers with his hind legs, and has great difficulty in moving.

If the condition is suspected the horse should if possible be led immediately into his stable before he collapses. The vet must be called at once. The muscles of the animal's croup will be tense, and once he is on the ground he will try repeatedly to get up, managing effectively to raise his forehand but not his hindlegs.

When urine is passed it may range in colour from coffee to black. This coloration is derived from a colouring matter in the muscles 'which passes, from the cells that break down, into the urine. This is not a kidney disease, and the German expression 'kidney founder' is a misnomer.

In mild cases if treatment is begun immediately, recovery takes only a few days. However, there may be a wasting of the muscles which will take many months to come right. If the animal lies down and cannot get up again death will follow in a few days. The condition can be avoided by daily exercise at least at a walk and adjusting the diet to correspond with the amount of work done.

6(6) Digestive Disorders

6(6)i TEETH

The saying 'Don't-look a gift house in the mouth' is firstly a reference to the fact that a horse's age can be assessed by looking at its teeth, and secondly a reference to the high incidence of dental disease in horses. It is assumed that a gift horse is neither young nor healthy and free from defect.

Owing to the anatomical construction of the cheek teeth, most stabled horses develop sharp edges on their teeth. The wearing surfaces of the upper and lower rows of cheek teeth slope from the inside to the outside. The wearing surfaces do not lie directly on top of each other, since in the first place the upper jaw is wider than the lower, and in the second place the teeth in the upper jaw are wider than those in the lower jaw.

In incomplete, sideways mouth movements the outer edges of the cheek teeth in the upper jaw and the inside edges of the teeth in the lower jaw do not wear down.

Razor sharp edges of rock hard enamel develop, which can cause considerable injury and pain both to the mucous membrane lining the cheeks and to the tongue. Regular checking of the teeth every six months is advisable. If ever the horse experiences difficulty or problems in chewing or eating, the teeth must be examined and treatment given immediately.

Eating slowly, dropping half eaten lumps of food out of the mouth (quidding), rolling the food round in the mouth, salivation ('slobbering'), emaciation and digestive upsets are symptoms to be taken seriously. It is wrong to make it easier for the horse to chew by grinding the food up smaller. The even wear of the teeth should be encouraged by giving the jaw plenty of work. Plentiful hay should therefore be given to encourage intensive grinding movements.

Chewing on one side due to sharp-edged teeth, inflammation of the temperomandibular joint, or fractures of the lower jaw lead to the formation of a *shear mouth*. The cheek teeth on one side are not used and slide sideways past each other like a pair of shears. The cause must be removed promptly, because severe cases of shear mouth are incurable.

An uneven, step-like formation of the row of tooth surfaces, with some higher than others, is known as a *step mouth*. The cause lies in differing degrees of hardness which cause irregular wear. It occurs especially if individual teeth are diseased or faulty and also if a tooth is missing. The raised tooth must be lowered to the same level as the others.

Smooth teeth are a sign of old age in a horse. The original rough, undulating surface of the molars becomes flat because the substance of the tooth is too soft. Hay and coarse food can no longer be chewed efficiently. The horse rolls the food about in his mouth. Unchewed and undigested oat grains are found in the droppings. The condition is incurable and the horse must be fed soft food and crushed oats.

The congenital condition wherein the upper jaw is shorter than the lower is known as *undershot* (German: *pike mouth*); when the lower jaw is shorter, it is called a *parrot mouth* (German: *carp mouth*). Owing to the difference in the jaw length, the rows of incisor teeth do not lie directly above each other. Since they are not in wear, the incisors may become abnormally long and cause considerable problems in chewing.

In crib-biting, either in the form of chewing fixed objects, or when accompanied by windsucking, wear of the front surfaces of the incisors occurs.

Tooth decay, scale and fractured teeth can occur in horses just as they can in humans. The incisors and the first three check teeth grow to begin with as milk teeth, and are later replaced by permanent teeth. Problems involving the replacement of the milk teeth by the permanent teeth lead to loss of appetite. Between the ages of two and a half and three and a half years the horse's first three cheek teeth are replaced. The milk tooth sits like a cap over the top of the permanent tooth. If this cap is not cast naturally, the bone in the region of the tooth root buckles forward, and may even break through the gum. An abscess develops, and the cap must then be removed.

6(6)ii LOWER JAW

Contusions on that part of the lower jaw which is devoid of teeth are known as *bruised bars*. They are caused by the use of a severe bit and by the rider pulling up sharply, and occur in horses who are over-impetuous or who have tongue problems. The mouth is then more prone to damage owing to inflammation of the skin and periosteum of the bars.

Dislocation of the lower jaw may occur as a result of getting the jaw stuck in the partition grille of the stable or in the headcollar chain. The mouth will not shut properly, the jaws will not move, the horse is unable to pick up his feed and his tongue hangs out. The eyes protrude from their sockets. Relocation must take place under anaesthetic.

Inflammation of the temperomandibular joint is encountered most often in older horses. The horse chews carefully, there is wastage of the masseter muscle and swelling and pain in the region of the joint.

6(6)iii TONGUE

Tongue wounds may occur about 10cm from the tip of the tongue as the result of the action of the bit. The tip of the tongue lying between the incisors may also be bitten off as the result of a fall. An infected wound can lead to a swelling which may prevent the horse from swallowing his food. Occasionally the tip of the tongue has to be amputated. Up to 10cm can be removed without interfering with the horse's food intake.

Sticking the tongue out, that is letting the tongue hang either out of the corners of the mouth or between the incisor teeth, is not the result of illness or disease. It can pose a considerable problem when the horse is being ridden.

Fracture of the tongue bone often occurs in conjunction with fracture of the lower jaw owing to an accident or as the result of a violent pull on the tongue. The tongue hangs out and cannot be moved. The horse has to be fed artificially. Recovery is rare.

6(6)iv CHOKING

Choking occurs as a result of the lodging of a foreign body, such as a piece of beet, apple or potato, in the gullet; through the narrowing of the gullet itself; through restriction caused by greatly enlarged lymph nodes, or – and this is unfortunately still the commonest cause – through feeding unsoaked sugar beet pulp.

The equine oesophagus is a 150-cm long narrow muscular tube which takes about twelve seconds to massage the food down into the stomach. Dry food that is mixed with insufficient saliva and which, therefore, does not slide down easily – as was the case in the days when chaff was fed – leads to a thickening of the musculature and a narrowing of the internal diameter.

Unsoaked sugar beet does not slide well, is stopped by a muscle spasm and then begins to swell owing to the action of the saliva. Because the horse continues to eat, the whole of the gullet is very soon completely filled and blocked like a *Mettwurst* sausage. There is a continuous flow of saliva mixed with food particles from both nostrils. On inspiration it can easily be carried to the lungs. This may result in pneumonia. The horse must be treated immediately by a veterinary surgeon.

6(6)v COLIC

Under the heading 'colic' are included all the painful symptoms which arise in the stomach and intestines owing to changes brought about by disease. The causes of colic are very varied, and the symptoms are either mild – such as loss of appetite, a tucked-up appearance, apathy, frequent lying down, yawning, displaying *Flehmen's* posture*, looking round at the belly, swishing the tail, frequent passing of urine and kicking at the belly – or severe – such as marked restlessness, sweating, an anxious expression, pawing the ground, or the animal throwing itself to the ground and rolling frenziedly. In *any* case of colic the vet must be called immediately.

Overloading of the Stomach

Possible causes of overloading the stomach are food which is hard to digest; fermenting food (cut clover,

---

* An involuntary curling of the upper lip, which often occurs when a stallion smells a mare in heat, but which is a response triggered by other smells, too.

wilting grass, maize and bread); working immediately after feeding; overfeeding (access to an open oatbin), and intestinal blockage (through reflux of the intestinal contents into the stomach). Because of the small capacity of the stomach and the horse's inability to vomit, there is a possibility that the stomach may rupture, in which case death is inevitable. The stomach must be emptied immediately by a vet. This may be an extremely difficult task.

Obstruction, Impaction
An excessive build-up of food material in one section of the intestine is known as an intestinal impaction. It may occur in any section of the intestine. It is caused by an excessive intake of indigestible food matter, such as straw bedding, and tooth problems. Insufficient exercise encourages this condition.

Obstruction may also occur as a result of stricture, deformities, growths or greatly enlarged lymph nodes. Interference with bowel movement and blood supply due to migrating worm larvae can also cause or predispose to obstructions.

Treatment should aim not only at softening the impaction, relaxing the spasm or stimulating bowel movement, but also at identifying and removing the cause: attention should be paid to the teeth, to a change of diet or to worming.

Sand Colic
Sand colic can occur if soil is eaten along with the food. In the case of horses at grass there is the danger that considerable quantities of soil will be consumed in early spring and the middle of the summer when the ground is dry and the horse tears out the roots and eats them along with the grass. The soil is deposited in the large intestine and several days may pass before colic symptoms arise. Sudden death is possible due to rupture of the colon.

158

Tympany

Fermenting food can cause an excessive build-up of gas in the intestine. Clover, kale, beet, legumes, wilting grass, bad bread, etc, are inclined to ferment. Tympany can also be caused by the horse gulping in air while windsucking or crib-biting. If bowel movement ceases or there is a stoppage, this will also cause tympany within a very short time. The colic may be severe. Treatment must always depend on the cause.

Spasm of the Intestine (Spasmodic Colic)

Spasm of the intestine is a common form of colic, but the exact cause of the intermittent spasms is unclear. Some horses are prone to attacks, especially when the weather changes. Chills and feed-associated problems have also been blamed. The attacks are severe, of brief duration and repeated. Often, by the time the vet arrives the symptoms have disappeared. However, the irritation of the bowel may cause a displacement, resulting in strangulation.

Blockage of the Bowel Arteries

The bowel is interlaced with a branching system of blood vessels, because it is from the bowel that the nutrients are absorbed and carried around the body. Blood clots or pieces broken off them cause a blockage of the arteries and thus cause considerable interference with the blood supply in that part of the bowel. The blood clots are caused by worm larvae further up, in the wall of the cranial mesenteric artery. If the blood supply to a large section of the bowel is lost, bowel movement ceases. The outcome can be fatal. Interference to the blood supply of small sections of bowel can be compensated by the enlargement of adjacent blood vessels. Depending on the degree of interference, the colic symptoms can be mild or severe. Diagnosis of the condition may be difficult.

Twists, Displacement and Strangulation

There are many possible causes of a twist or strangulation. Intestinal calculi, hair balls or the accumulation of large quantities of worms, for example after worm treatment, can all cause a displacement of the bowel leading to a twist or strangulation.

Changes in the position of the bowel, such as rotation on the vertical axis (volvulus), looping accompanied by twisting, kinking, strangulation by ligaments, intussusception (telescoping) and strangulation in a narrow opening, always lead to a severe, uninterrupted and unabating attack of colic. The displacement causes considerable interference with the blood supply to the bowel. The thin-walled veins are pressed together, interfering with the blood flow and leading to a stoppage (stasis). The bowel movements cease completely and the bowel contents begin to ferment. The walls of the stomach and intestine become inflamed. In certain cases death can be prevented by promptly instigated surgical intervention, consisting of the removal of the strangulated portions of the intestine. However, it is not always possible to save the animal.

Conclusion If a horse shows colic symptoms, a vet must always be called immediately. Any delay is inexcusable.

6(6)vi LIVER DISEASES

Feeding bad or mouldy food, lupins, poisonous plants in the hay, seed corn which has been treated, and food which has been in contact with rat poison or weedkiller can lead to a degeneration of the liver cells (cirrhosis). It can also occur after infection, after general and localized circulatory disorders and following a prolonged attack of obstructive colic.

The horse goes off his feed and the faeces are muddy yellow in colour and foul smelling. In severe cases there is dizziness and staggering (German: 'liver staggers'). In liver disease an increase in the amount of bile in the blood leads to jaundice (a yellow discoloration of the mucous membranes). Degeneration of the liver can be a serious, often fatal condition.

6(7) Disorders of the Urinary and Reproductive Organs

The urine of the horse is normally light yellow to yellowish-brown in colour – it grows darker on exposure to the air – and is very slimy (mucous) in texture. Colouring in the urine derives from the admixture of blood resulting from a fractured pelvis and damage to the kidneys or bladder, or of muscle-colouring material in azoturia. It is not caused by kidney disease. The use of certain medicines can also cause discoloration of the urine.

Frequent attempts at urination are displayed by in-season mares or where there is irritation of the bladder and urethra. Adopting a position similar to that used in urination occurs in colic as a result of a blockage in the large intestine. The blocked section of the intestine presses on the bladder. Pain during urination takes the form of restlessness, walking up and down, swishing the tail, stamping the feet, and looking round when there is inflammation of the ureter and bladder.

Inflammation (nephritis) and degeneration of the kidneys occur in conjunction with infectious diseases, suppuration somewhere in the body, obstructions, bowel inflammation and poisoning. The residual materials of digestion, which should be eliminated through the kidneys, accumulate in the blood (uraemia). The horse grows dull and listless, and a foul smell comes from the mouth. The horse may die within a few days or linger on for months.

Urinary calculi (stones) form in the pelvis of the kidney or in the bladder and are made up of deposits of calcium carbonate. As long as the stones are small and do not wedge in the urethra or ureter there are no particular signs of illness. Large bladder stones cause retention of urine, bleeding and cystitis (inflammation of the bladder). They can be felt by a vet in rectal examination and can be removed surgically.

Urethral calculi are small urinary calculi which have formed in the bladder and have been washed out and then become lodged in the urethra of the stallion or gelding. Pain is intense. Urine either cannot be passed at all or trickles out. The stones must be removed surgically. However, more such stones can form at any time.

Paralysis of the bladder results in the horse being unable to pass or retain urine at will. First of all the bladder fills and expands. When it becomes too full, the urine comes out of its own accord. This paralysis is the result of spinal disorders (vertebral fractures, damage to the spinal cord, tumours). It may be accompanied by paralysis of the anus, rectum and tail.

Reproductive Disorders in the Stallion

The fertility rate for horses in the warmblood industry is about 70 per cent and in the Thoroughbred industry about 80 per cent. If a stallion's fertility rate is 20 to 30 per cent below this norm, subfertility of the stallion is to be suspected.

Some stallions lack libido owing to a hormonal disorder. They show no interest in the mare. There are also stallions who cover the mare without ejaculating. The handler must check that ejaculation has taken place.

Another cause of low fertility in the stallion is poor quality semen. The quality is determined by the number of living sperm, their mobility and their appearance. Infections of the urethra and sex glands cause total or partial infertility. They are usually transmitted while covering. This is another reason why mares should undergo swab tests, before covering, for the detection of bacteria.

Reproductive Disorders in the Mare

Infertility in the mare, i.e. the inability to conceive, is a major problem in any form of horse breeding. An essential prerequisite for fertilization is ovulation. The seasonally correlated sexual activity peaks in the period from April to August. Since the breeding season has been brought forward by human intervention to the beginning of the year, many mares remain infertile for this reason alone. Because the gestation period is very long and the uterus needs a certain time to recover, it is not natural to every mare to foal each year.

Many mares who remain barren after foaling show signs of uterine infection. The lifespan of the sperm is shortened and the chance of conception is therefore lowered. Inflammation of the lining of the womb, the cervix and the vagina causes the discharge of a muco-purulent matter from the vagina. The discharge is to be found on the inside of the thighs and hocks·and on the tail. The symptoms are most marked when the mare is in season (oestrus). However, many infected mares can only be identified by swabbing (vaginal and cervical) and culturing, by a vet. Faulty conformation of the vulva, which allows air to enter to the vagina, can render a mare susceptible to infection. Surgery can improve the shape, thus allowing it to close more effectively.

Immediately after foaling the danger of infection due to the entry of air is especially great. The mare should be left undisturbed: raising dust from hay and straw, and sweeping the gangway between the stables, must be avoided at all costs. The spread of infection from one mare to another via the stallion at covering is also common. Dusty conditions in the covering yard, for example a ground covering of wood shavings, increases the risk of infection while covering. For this reason, washed, damp sand is more suitable.

Hormonal disorders, tumours in the ovary, blocked fallopian tubes and failure of the follicle to ripen are further causes of infertility.

Covering Accidents

It is usual to hobble the mare in order to protect the stallion from kicks. If there is insufficient padding, the hobbles will chafe the pasterns. During covering the mare may receive injuries to the neck and withers from the stallion's teeth, while the mare's tail hairs may cut into the stallion's glans penis, damaging the mucous membrane. Occasionally, in a turbulent mating, the penis may be excessively twisted.

A large stallion may pierce the vagina of a small mare. If a mare is bleeding from the vagina after mating, or shows a marked listlessness in the hours which follow, a vet should be called immediately. Covering injuries of this type can be fatal.

6(8) Disorders of the Respiratory System

6(8)i BLEEDING FROM THE NOSE (EPISTAXIS)

Bleeding from the nose can have numerous causes, such as a fall; a blow; a fracture of the nose; injury to the mucous membrane caused by a probe; foreign bodies; ulcers; neoplasms; poisoning, infectious diseases, etc.

High blood pressure caused by strenuous exercise in high performance horses (eventers, hunters, racehorses) can cause nose bleeding due to the bursting of blood vessels in the nasal mucous membrane. Bleeding in the lungs also results in the discharge of blood from the nose.

Nose bleeding in Thoroughbreds is recognized as being hereditary. It occurs repeatedly and spontaneously in the stable or when the horse is being ridden. The cause is thought to be a reduced resistance of the blood vessels. Treatment is not usually necessary since the bleeding ceases if the horse is stopped and rested immediately. If it occurs frequently and spontaneously when the horse is in its stable, the cause should be investigated.

6(8)ii INFLAMMATION OF THE SINUS (SINUSITIS)

Above the roots of the cheek teeth are the multi-chamber, membrane-lined sinuses, which are connected with the nasal cavity. Infectious inflammations of the upper respiratory tract spread to the mucous membrane of the sinuses. This is especially so in strangles. Dental disorders, such as fractured teeth, purulent inflammation of tooth roots or neoplasms, can also give rise to inflammation of the sinuses.

When inflammation occurs the openings to the sinus swell and the resulting pus can only escape slowly. Since usually only one sinus is affected, the discharge is on one side only. The bone may also be affected. Treatment often lasts for months.

6(8)iii INFLAMMATION OF THE GUTTURAL POUCHES

Infections of the throat, especially strangles, are the cause of inflammation of the mucous membrane of the guttural pouches. In strangles there is abscess formation in the lymph nodes in the wall of the guttural pouch, and rupture into the guttural pouch. Usually the condition affects one side only. When the head is lowered there is a gradual discharge of yellow pus from one nostril. The pus which remains in the guttural pouch may become hard and crumbly and a chronic infection may ensue. Sometimes there is difficulty in swallowing and a one-sided swelling in the region of the salivary gland. Liniments, draining the guttural pouches, or surgery are required.

6(8)iv INFLAMMATION OF THE NASAL AND LARYNGEAL MUCOUS MEMBRANE

This occurs in conjunction with colds due to viral or bacterial infections. The most obvious symptoms are the frequent, painful paroxysms of coughing. Coughing is triggered off by pressure on the larynx or swallowing food. The membrane is reddened, swollen and covered in ulcerations. There is a discharge of watery mucus from the nose. The body temperature may be raised for a few days. Box rest in a dust-free environment is needed for recovery (care should be taken when bedding down and sweeping, and food should be moistened), otherwise the condition can last for months.

6(8)v LARYNGEAL PARALYSIS

The larynx and vocal cords protrude into the airway, making it narrower at that point. The width can be altered by the muscles in the larynx. If these muscles are paralysed, the left half (in the majority of cases) of the larynx drops into the airway. The vocal cord is then no longer taut and appears paralysed. In fast paces a roaring, whistling noise is heard. In the trot, canter and gallop, owing to the extra strain, breathing difficulties arise, characterised by flared nostrils, heavy sweating, laboured breathing and signs of suffocation. The neigh is hoarse and expressionless. The exact diagnosis of 'laryngeal paralysis' can only be established by a veterinary surgeon through special examination of the larynx (endoscopy, laryngoscopy).

The cause of laryngeal paralysis is damage to the nerves which control the muscles. The damage can be caused by overstretching the neck, poisonous substances, ('mutter peas' or lead) or in connection with strangles and inflammation of the mucous membrane of the upper respiratory tract. There has always been speculation that the condition could be hereditary, but not all authorities accept this. However, a connection does seem to have been established between the size of the horse in relation to the length of its neck, and the incidence of the disease. Another suspected cause is the peculiar anatomical position of the left nerve, which runs around the arch of the aorta. Especially in fit horses, where the heart muscle has increased in size and dropped slightly in the chest, it is thought that the pulsing of the blood vessel might damage the nerve.

Usually surgery is required to correct the interference with the breathing. If the mucous membrane is stripped from the pouches between the vocal cords and the laryngeal wall, the vocal cord adheres to the wall as the wound scars over. New surgical measures work on the principle of reinforcing the slack, paralysed muscle with a piece of elastic. Fitting a metal tube in the windpipe to facilitate inspiration is rarely practised nowadays.

6(8)vi BRONCHITIS (inflammation of the bronchial mucous membrane)

The airways to the lung are lined with a mucous membrane. Colds complicated by a bacterial or viral infection of the membrane, as well as breathing in dust, mould spores or particles of insufficiently chewed food, are the causes of bronchitis. A hypersensitive reaction (allergy) to certain substances (e.g. pollen) can also be a cause.

Chronic bronchitis is often the result of neglecting an insignificant fresh inflammation of the mucous membrane and returning the horse to work too soon. The membrane becomes swollen and covered with thick, sticky mucus, which causes irritation and hence coughing. In the smaller bronchial tubes the swelling of the mucous membrane causes significant breathing difficulties. Because there is no rise in temperature, chronic bronchitis gives rise to little disturbance of the general state of health. The coughing is highly distressed and dry. Treatment and recovery can take weeks or months. During this period the horse must not be worked, or pulmonary emphysema may result.

6(8)vii PULMONARY EMPHYSEMA

The cause of pulmonary emphysema is almost always bronchitis. However, the airways can also be narrowed through an allergic reaction.

Great strength is needed on inspiration in order to

draw the air through the narrowed bronchioles into the air vesicles. However, there is insufficient strength in the expiration process to squeeze all the air back out of the vesicles. The airways are narrowed by the swelling and the presence of mucous. The air vesicles become more and more full of air and are overstrained. The elastic walls of the vesicles do not have the power to aid the expiratory effort by squeezing the air out. The over-straining of the vesicles is accelerated by lungeing, chasing the horse about or overexertion. If there is a sudden build-up of pressure in the lung, as when the horse coughs, individual air vesicles may burst. The lung area expands further and further owing to the bloating of the lungs with air.

The condition develops gradually, without a rise in temperature. It starts with a slightly laboured, prolonged expiratory effort. Later two distinct stages in expiration can be identified. After the normal expiratory effort there is a squeezing together of the belly muscles, whereby the intestines are pressed against the diaphragm, which helps push the air out of the lungs (abdominal breathing). The anus is pushed outwards when this happens. The effort involved causes extra development of the abdominal muscles. An oblique line forms across the flank (*heave line*). It stands out especially after exertion owing to the build-up of sweat. The cough is weak, short and hollow.

There is not yet a successful method of treatment for pulmonary emphysema. Turning the horse out to grass may bring about a temporary improvement. Certain medicines alleviate the symptoms for a limited period. The use of severely affected mares for stud should be avoided since the advanced stages of pregnancy tend further to impede the breathing.

6(8)viii PNEUMONIA

Inflammatory processes in the air vesicles of the lungs are known as pneumonia. The vesicles become filled with a secretion. It occurs as the result of a bacterial or viral infection of the lungs via the inspired air or the circulatory system. Severe physical exertion, travelling, draughts or bad feeding favour the development of pneumonia. All the causes of bronchitis can also lead to pneumonia. Often it occurs as a complication of strangles or joint-ill. Especially in conjunction with choking, food particles 'going the wrong way' can lead to necrotic, usually fatal pneumonia. The horse runs a high fever and is dull and off his feed. The pulse is rapid, and there is a mucous purulent discharge from both nostrils, together with paroxysms of soft coughing.

Absolute rest in well-ventilated quarters, nutritious food and veterinary treatment are necessary if the horse's life is to be saved and serious permanent damage to the lungs avoided.

6(8)ix CHEST INJURIES

Chest injuries due to kicks, falls and road accidents are usually accompanied by broken ribs. When a rib is broken the end can pierce a lung and cause severe haemorrhage. If the pleural cavity, which is under a vacuum, is opened, air accumulates in one side of the chest (pneumothorax). The lung shrivels and empties of air. Breathing and circulation are severely impaired. As a first aid measure until the arrival of the veterinarian a clean handkerchief should be pressed against the wound in the chest. Fatal consequences can be avoided in this way.

6(9) Diseases of the Circulatory System

6(9)i HEART DISORDERS

The heart is the organ responsible for the circulation of blood. Disturbance in the activity of the heart can have its origins in any part of it (heart muscle, pericardium, valves, cardiac nerve supply).

Valve failure is usually the result of an inflammation. It takes the form either of a narrowing of the orifice

169

(stenosis), or the inability of the valve to close. The most obvious symptom is breathlessness.

Heart muscle disorders result from excessive physical exertion, and also from conditions which place extra strain on the heart, such as lung, kidney and liver disorders. The affected horse is very listless and breathless, and there is sweating. Either recovery or death are possible.

The frequency and regularity of the heartbeat can be adversely affected by derangement of the cardiac nerve supply or by nerves outside the heart. Cardiac fibrillation, either in the form of occasional attacks or as an ongoing condition, can have a highly adverse effect on the horse's general health.

Irregular heartbeats which occur singly and occasionally are often without any significance.

6(9)ii DISORDERS OF THE BLOOD VESSELS

The blood supply to the individual organs is regulated according to its needs at the time by a widening or narrowing of the blood vessels. In *shock* there is a general collapse of the walls of the vessels so that vital organs (brain, spinal cord) receive insufficient blood. Shock can be caused by blood loss, considerable violence (a fall) or mental trauma (fright). The symptoms of shock are a cold body surface, cold sweat, dilated pupils, muscle tremor, extreme listlessness and decreased consciousness. Absolute rest and warm clothing are needed immediately and until the vet arrives.

Worm larvae cause a *dilation* of the anterior mesenteric artery. The roughened surface of the wall leads to the formation of blood clots, which break loose and can cause a blockage of the bowel arteries (colic). However, the artery can be dilated to such an extent that the wall bursts, causing internal haemorrhaging. Blockage of blood vessels (*thrombosis*) occurs also in the region of the pelvic girdle, ilium and femur. Here, too, worm larvae are mainly responsible. Whereas usually when the horse is at rest there are no symptoms, in movement there is lameness, which starts off as slight and gradually increases until it is very severe. It disappears again after a short rest. In severe cases of thrombosis the horse may even collapse.

Treatment is rarely successful. Over a period of months the horse may recover of its own accord, owing to an increase in the size of the surrounding blood vessels and the shrinkage of the clot.

6(10) Disorders of the Nervous System

6(10)i BRAIN DISEASE

Brain disease is characterised by considerable disturbance of consciousness or evidence of failure of one of the twelve nerves leading out of the brain. Sudden *circulatory disturbances* are characterised by a decrease in consciousness, the degree of which corresponds to the blood starvation. There is no response to stimuli, such as a blow or poke. The causes of starvation may be severe blood loss or shock. Direct exposure to the sun (*sunstroke*) or other forms of overheating (*heat stress*) can affect the brain. It occurs in horses carrying a lot of condition, on hot or sultry days. Listlessness, giddiness, falling, heavy sweating over the whole body and the rising of the body temperature above 42°C are potentially fatal symptoms. Shade, rest and immediate cooling by hosing with cold water may save the horse.

Concussion occurs as a result of a fall, kick or collision. Symptoms, such as bewilderment, giddiness, inability to stand, unconsciousness, twitching of the eyes and muscular convulsions, appear immediately. Absolute rest for several days is necessary even in the case of an accident that produces no apparent ill-effects.

Encephalitis and meningitis are caused by infections carried in the blood or lymph. The disease begins with the

171

horse showing bewilderment, standing motionless in one spot and placing the legs in unnatural positions. Also, now and then, there is restlessness, nervousness and frenzied behaviour. Signs that the nerves from the brain are involved are twitching of the eyes, gnashing of the teeth, paralysis of the lips, ears, tongue and jaws, staring eyes and dilated pupils.

Recovery is rare. Death may follow in a few days. If the horse survives, he is frequently left with paralysis or convulsions, which will soon cause his death.

Hydrocephalus is a condition in which the amount of fluid in the brain cavity increases as the result of something preventing its escape. The symptoms develop very gradually. The quiet behaviour, which is the first sign to appear, may even be welcomed. Later symptoms include standing motionless, eating slowly, interruptions in chewing (with the hay hanging out of the mouth), prolonged wandering about the box, unnatural positions of the legs, and clumsy and intractable behaviour under the rider. Reining back can only be achieved by force.

This incurable disease increases in severity over a period of months and years until the horse becomes completely unusable.

6(10)ii SPINAL CORD

In disorders of the spinal cord there is no disturbance of consciousness. Sensory and locomotory disturbances extend over wide areas of the body.

Compression of the spinal cord occurs as the result of a fall or the horse getting cast. It is especially common in the neck region due to an overflexion of the vertebrae. The spinal cord is crushed in the spinal canal when the spine is bent round. Bony growths into the spinal canal resulting from arthrosis of the vertebrae can also bring permanent pressure to bear on the spinal cord.

Locomotory disturbances of varying degrees, depending on the degree of compression, arise immediately after the fall or over the course of weeks. Severe compression of the cord in the region of the first six cervical vertebrae may result in death due to paralysis of the diaphragm (breathing paralysis). Severe compression in other areas leads to fracture of the cord and inability to stand due to paralysis.

Even in mild cases, after months of box rest, the horse does not usually recover.

6(10)iii PARALYSIS

Paralysis of the tail, the bladder and the rectum occur as a result of a nerve disorder in the end section of the spinal canal. There is often no sign of damage, such as that caused by a fall, from the outside. The tail hangs limp and devoid of sensation between the hind legs. Normal defecation is absent. The anus hangs open and the faeces may fall out one ball at a time. The bladder either dribbles continuously or empties in a sudden burst, especially when the horse moves. The condition is usually incurable, though it is not an immediate threat to life. With suitable treatment (evacuation of the rectum and bladder, prevention of inflammation in the rectum or bladder) the horse can be kept alive for months.

Disorders of individual nerves cause sensory and locomotory disturbances extending only over the area served by the nerve concerned.

Facial nerve paralysis occurs as a result of compression of the nerve by the headcollar (especially on the left side, caused by the headcollar buckle) or when lying down (colic). The lips on one side are paralysed. Such paralysis results in difficulties in feeding and drinking. The partial closure of the nostril on the affected side can cause breathing difficulties. Food should be liquid or pulpy. If there is no improvement in fourteen days, the prognosis for recovery is poor.

Radial nerve paralysis is characterised by loss of function of the extensor muscles of the forelimb from the shoulder joint down. The limb hangs flexed and limp and cannot be drawn forwards and extended. Suspected causes are compression of the nerve due to a kick or fall, or lying on hard, uneven ground. Usually an improvement is obvious after only hours or days.

Paralysis of the suprascapular nerve occurs as a result of hitting the shoulder against doors, fences, uprights and the corners of buildings. There is loss of function in two muscles which lie on the outside of the shoulder-blade and act as ligaments on the outside of the shoulder joint. As well as lameness being present, the shoulder falls outwards each time weight is placed on it. Over a period of a fortnight there is considerable atrophy of the muscle. Recovery may take place in two or three months.

6(11) Disorders of the Sense Organs

6(11)i EAR FISTULA (TEMPORAL ONDONTOMA)
An ear fistula is a lentil-sized opening on the front edge of the ear with grey mucus discharging from it. It occurs in yearlings and two-year-olds. It extends right down into the ear, and is caused by residual embryonic tissue. This deformity must be corrected surgically.

6(11)ii LACERATIONS OF THE EYELIDS
These injuries are caused by protruding nails and hooks. Immediate treatment by a veterinary surgeon is always necessary. Prompt and meticulous alignment and stitching of the edges of the wound will prevent displacement of the lid, an increase in the gap between the top and bottom lid and permanent disfigurement of the eye. An eyelid which turns inward owing to scarring can be a permanent source of irritation to the cornea.

6(11)iii CONJUNCTIVITIS

There are many possible causes of conjunctivitis. Foreign bodies such as cereal awns, pieces of straw, sand, hairs, dust and pollen play a major part. Usually only one side is affected, as is the case also with external violence (blows). Other sources of irritation, which usually affect both sides, are an atmosphere heavily laden with ammonia, lime dust, smoke, a cold, burning, and ultra-violet light. Conjunctivitis can also occur in conjunction with an infection, such as strangles and infectious catarrh in the upper respiratory tract. It also occurs in conjunction with periodic ophthalmia.

Conjunctivitis caused by flies can be observed in horses at grass from the beginning of June to the beginning of October. The flies have a predilection for the areas around the corners of the eyes. Inflammation develops as a result of stings (horse flies), egg deposits or the migration of certain worm larvae into the conjunctival sacs. A shortage of vitamin A can encourage the condition. There is a discharge of mucus from the eye and pronounced swelling and redness of the conjunctivae, accompanied by photophobia and sensitivity. First the cause must always be identified and removed, then the condition may be treated with oil- or water-based eyedrops or ointments. It is essential that foreign bodies be removed. It is necessary to provide a supplement of vitamin A (i.e. its precursor) with the feed (green food, carrots and grass meal).

6(11)iv BLOCKAGE OF THE NASO-LACRIMAL DUCT

The outlet for the secretions produced by the lacrimal gland is the naso-lacrimal or tear duct. Inflammation of the mucous membrane or pressure from the surrounding area can cause the duct to become blocked. Tears trickle continuously from the inner corner of the eye; as a result the hair falls out and there is purulent inflammation of the skin below the eye. Medical and surgical treatment must be used to re-open the duct.

6(11)v INJURY TO THE CORNEA

Injuries to the cornea occur as a result of running into sharp objects, blows with a whip, foreign bodies in the eye and chafing. The injury may be superficial or it may extend right into the anterior chamber of the eye. The first signs of a corneal injury are pronounced photophobia, lacrimation and sensitivity. Small, superficial wounds are often impossible to identify without a special colouring matter. An opaque area appears in the cornea around the wound, which heals gradually from the edge inwards. Greyish-white scars may be left. In deep wounds in the cornea, the aquaeus humour escapes and there is prolapse of the iris and lens. Purulent infections may ensue. The treatment of any injury to the cornea must be entrusted immediately to a veterinary surgeon.

6(11)vi CATARACT (German: GREY STAR)

A cataract can have many causes. It may be congenital, or it may occur as a sequel to inflammatory processes in the surrounding area (periodic ophthalmia) and infectious diseases (contagious pleuropneumonia, dourine and influenza). The pupil appears greyish-white. The affected eye is blind. Successful treatment of cataract in horses is rare.

6(11)vii PERIODIC OPHTHALMIA (MOON BLINDNESS)

Periodic ophthalmia is a non-purulent inflammation of the iris and choroid, and also involves the posterior chamber and the lens. It tends to recur. Although the disease has been known for centuries and is the most researched eye disease of the horse, the cause is not yet certain. It is known, however, that there is more than one cause. It occurs frequently in certain areas (marshy lowlands). Allergies, poisoning due to digestive disturbances after eating bad hay and mouldy oats, parasites and virus infections are among the suggested causes. Since sporadic cases of moon blindness have been observed in new-born foals, heredity was once considered. However, the infection has been found to have been passed on by the dam, who was also infected with the disease.

The disease strikes suddenly. Photophobia, lacrimation and sensitivity, reddened conjunctivitis and a contracted pupil are the first symptoms. Loose clots form in the anterior chamber and the cornea is cloudy. The disease usually affects one eye. Often there is only one attack, although further attacks can follow at irregular intervals (weeks or months). Usually the horse goes blind in the eye after repeated attacks. The other eye may also succumb to the disease. There is no reliable form of treatment. However, in many cases prompt, extensive treatment will prevent permanent damage.

6(12) Foaling Disorders

6(12)i MISCARRIAGE (ABORTION)

The expulsion of a non-viable foetus from the womb is known as abortion. Foals born before the 300th day of pregnancy have no chance of survival. Premature births between the 300th and 325th day may thrive with special care. Abortion may occur at any stage in the pregnancy. Early abortions may easily be overlooked by the mare's attendant owing to the small size of the foetus (approximately 20cm by the 150th day).

Causes of abortion are twin pregnancies, bacterial, fungal and viral infections, hormone deficiency and developmental abnormalities. They may also be caused by some factor in the management of the horse. About 1 per cent of all pregnancies are twin pregnancies, which in the majority of cases end in abortion or premature birth. Bacterial infections, carried in the bloodstream or gaining access through a faulty vulval seal, are frequent causes of abortion. They can trigger off a miscarriage at any stage in the pregnancy. A virus which is responsible for infections of the upper respiratory tract causes outbreaks of abortion. Most virus abortions occur after the fifth month of pregnancy. Immunity to the disease develops in the mare after she has aborted, but it is short lived.

Often, though not in every case, the foals aborted are deformed. Outside influences such as a blow, a fall, jumping and abnormal exertion can also cause abortion. The symptoms of abortion depend on the stage of pregnancy. If an early abortion occurs within the first twenty days, the mare should come back in season (oestrus). If the abortion takes place after the thirty-fifth day, the mare will not come in season again for some time owing to the commencement of hormone production.

Up until about half way through the pregnancy, abortion takes place without any warning. In the later stages of pregnancy an experienced handler will notice a slight swelling in front of the udder and of the udder itself about twelve to thirty-six hours beforehand. Occasionally there is also milk secretion. The horse is restless and lies down. The mare also 'runs milk' in a twin pregnancy when one of the twins dies. This milk production may go on for days or weeks before the abortion takes place.

After the abortion there is a discharge from the vulva. Pieces of afterbirth may hang out. Retention of the afterbirth is very common following an abortion.

Hormone treatment can be attempted in the case of a threatened abortion.

6(12)ii ARTIFICIALLY INDUCED LABOUR

Although unwanted pregnancies due to misalliances (e.g. when an unlicensed colt covers an in-season mare in the field) are relatively uncommon, the interruption or termination of a pregnancy may be desirable for various other reasons, among them the early detection of a twin conception.

Illness of the mare, such as laminitis or rupture of the abdominal wall, which becomes worse as the pregnancy progresses, is another reason for artificially inducing labour, as is a pregnancy which has gone way past its term. A prolonged pregnancy (over 360 days) does not seem to present any danger to the foal, despite its increased birth weight and excessive size. However, it can cause complications in a mare with a narrow birth canal.

The commonest reasons for inducing labour are for the sake of organisation in large studs and for convenience. Because 90 per cent of foalings take place during the night, a watch must be kept over the mare at that time. This is often very exhausting or costly, since the watch usually has to be kept for several nights.

The birth can be induced in a short time by the use of drugs. After a careful examination by a vet, which shows that the mare is ready to foal, labour can be induced after a pregnancy of at least 340 days provided the udder is well developed. However, preference should still be given to a natural birth.

6(12)iii INCORRECT PRESENTATION, POSITION AND POSTURE

The mare's pelvis forms an unyielding bony hoop through which the foal must pass during the delivery. This can only take place when the foal is in a certain presentation, position and posture. Any deviation leads to problems.

'Presentation' is the name given to the alignment of the foal's longitudinal axis relative to that of the mare. The normal presentation of the foal during delivery is head first, that is the head and forelegs are the first part to go through the pelvis.

The expression 'position' refers to the alignment of the foal's back relative to the dam's back. The only normal position is right way up, that is the backbone of the foal points towards that of the dam – the foal lies on its belly.

179

The expression 'posture' refers to the disposition of the movable parts of the foal to its body. Here again there is only one normal posture, that in which the head, neck and forelegs are stretched forwards and the hind legs are stretched backwards.

Not until the first stages of labour does the foal turn its body and stretch out its legs ready for the delivery.

Incorrect presentation, position and posture can make the passage through the pelvis impossible. Correction must be attempted with great care and skill, since when the foal is wedged in the pelvis it can die very quickly from compression of the umbilical cord. If it is not possible to save the foal, it must be dismembered within the womb in order to remove it. Caesarian section is rarely used in horses because the foal dies so quickly in the birth canal and there is a high risk of infection.

6(12)iv DEFORMITIES

Deformities which result in excessive growth of the foal (relative oversize) cause difficulties in foaling. Heredity is not the only cause of deformity. There are numerous other influences, such as the age of the mare, severe oxygen deficiency, virus infections, nutritional deficiencies (vitamins, protein), radiation, light deficiency and physical violence.

Deformities which cause difficulties in foaling are hydrocephalus, abdominal oedema, generalised oedema, crooked neck and limbs and 'double headed monsters'. Usually the mare shows no signs of ill-health. In hydrocephalus there is an accumulation of large quantities of fluid in the brain cavity so that the bones of the skull are pushed apart and present an obstacle to delivery. In generalised oedema circulatory disturbances in the foal lead to a considerable increase in girth.

A crooked neck or crooked limbs can cause considerable injury to the mare during delivery owing to the lack of flexibility in the foetus. As a rule, in the case of all the above-mentioned deformities embryotomy (dismembering) must be performed by a vet while the foal is still in the uterus.

6(12)v DAMAGE TO THE MARE DURING FOALING

In first-time and difficult foalings the violent straining of the mare during labour can easily lead to a *tear of the vulva or the perineum* (the strip of tissue joining the vagina and the rectum). This is sometimes unavoidable even if the utmost care is taken. However, its commonest cause is incorrect assistance during foaling. The main faults are pulling too early before the soft birth canal has dilated sufficiently; the use of force and in the wrong direction; jerking and failure to protect the perineum adequately.

As a rule, in a normal foaling the mare does not need any assistance in the way of pulling. If on occasions things need to be speeded up, the most that is needed is for someone with clean hands to grasp the foal by the cannon bones and help the straining along. The direction of the pull must correspond to the path through the pelvis, that is, it should be angled slightly downwards. On no account should more than two men be engaged in pulling. To protect the perineum the flat of both hands is pressed down on to the foal at the point where it passes underneath the perineum.

Small tears of the vulva or perineum are easily overlooked owing to the soiling and the fact that they do not bleed much. Provided they do not become infected, they heal by scarring. This interferes with the natural seal of the lips of the vulva, making it possible for germs to gain entry into the vagina. Infection can then spread to the uterus and cause infertility in the mare.

On the other hand, complete rupture of the perineum is easy to see. The constant soiling with faeces increases the risk of uterine infection. Once the afterbirth has come away, the natural proportions must be restored by surgery. A *fractured pelvis* can result from the mare slipping or throwing herself down, or the use of force to pull out an oversized foal.

Violent straining can cause a *prolapse of the bladder or the rectum*. Diagnosis of this condition presents no problems. The straining must be prevented while the organ is replaced, which must be done immediately. The prolapse usually causes more violent straining, which in turn makes it worse. After a few hours the rectum becomes gangrenous and the outcome is often fatal. *Prolapse of the uterus* after the birth is also possible, and potentially just as fatal.

A short time after a normal birth the placenta comes away. Sometimes it comes away with the foal. If the afterbirth is still in place after two hours there may be *retention of the afterbirth*. The vet should be called immediately, even at this early stage, since it takes only twelve hours for a potentially fatal infection and *foaling laminitis* to set in. The detachment and removal of a retained afterbirth must always be carried out by a vet. Obstinate fertility problems can occur as a result of retention of the afterbirth.

The *utmost cleanliness* should be observed at any foaling since febrile diseases can easily arise due to bacterial invasion of the vagina and uterus. Numerous different organisms are responsible. Thorough cleansing of the mare's hindquarters followed by disinfection prior to foaling, housing in a stable with plentiful clean bedding, and scrupulous cleanliness when assisting the birth will help to prevent infection.

In the later stages of pregnancy and during lactation, owing to the special demands made on the mother there is a marked tendency towards *metabolic disturbances*. These are caused by deficiencies and must be prevented by judicious feeding and management. The cause may be not only a shortage of certain substances (nutrients, minerals, vitamins), but also an imbalance of the calcium to magnesium ratio. Muscle spasms or paralysis may result.

6(13) Disorders of Foals

6(13)i MECONIUM RETENTION

While the foal is developing in the uterus a pasty, dark brown mass of faecal material collects in the bowel. This is the so-called meconium. Discharge of the meconium usually takes place in the first hours of life and is stimulated by the first milk (colostrum). Retention of the meconium does not cause much of a problem on the first day. The foal wags his tail vigorously and strains slightly. However, severe colic symptoms rapidly develop. The foal rolls and lies in unnatural positions and the belly swells up. He may still show a desire to suck. It is usually possible to remove the meconium with enemas and lubricants. The foal then recovers rapidly.

6(13)ii DIARRHOEA (SCOURING)

Diarrhoea is common in foals and has many different causes.

The milk of an in-season mare can cause diarrhoea, which usually clears up when the mare goes out of season. The diarrhoea is particularly severe when the dam is in her 'foaling heat' (the fifth to twelfth day after foaling). The foal is very bright and lively. As a rule diarrhoea caused by the mare being in season lasts only two to three days, but this type of diarrhoea can develop into a bowel infection.

Another cause is infection with the *strongyloides westeri* worm (see page 200) which coincides with the foal heat. Infection takes place through the milk. Taking too much milk in the first hours of life can cause a yellow coloured diarrhoea which does not have an evil smell. The commonest victims are strong foals with elderly dams. When diarrhoea is caused by a bowel infection the faeces are greyish-white in colour and foul-smelling. The foal is immediately rather miserable and dejected. There is a fever (over 40°C) and mild colic as a result of abdominal pain.

In older foals diarrhoea can be caused by the feeding of large quantities of red clover hay and lucerne hay; mouldy hay; licking the exudate off stone walls; prolonged licking of a salt-lick; worm infestation and consuming synthetic fertilizers. The body always suffers considerable losses of fluid and mineral salts. The condition must be taken seriously, the cause identified and treatment carried out.

6(13)iii JOINT-ILL (German: FOAL LAMENESS)

The (German) name foal lameness is a general term given to an infection which affects the whole body in the first days and weeks of life. Various bacteria are responsible. As the infection spreads through the body inflammation is set up in one or more joints. This causes the lameness and stiffness in the foal from which the disease takes its name.

The infection comes from the stable and from human assistance and handling during and after foaling. The disease would not occur in a mare foaling loose in a field. In rare cases the infection is transmitted from the mare to the foal while the latter is in the womb. Infection takes place through the mouth, nose and navel. The risk of infection is greatest during the first thirty-six hours of life. At this stage the wall of the intestine can still be penetrated by bacteria and the navel has not yet dried out. The navel should be painted with tincture of iodine immediately after delivery in order to prevent infection. The mare's udder must be washed clean. Only in exceptional circumstances should the hands be placed in the foal's mouth, and then they should be scrupulously clean. A foal's endearing tendency to suck fingers and clothes must be prevented in any circumstances.

In spite of today's intensive treatment methods, heavy losses are still incurred from joint-ill. It can occur within the first two days of life (*early joint-ill*) or from the second week to the third month (*late joint-ill*). In the early variety the foal is generally born healthy. Within twelve to thirty-six hours he rapidly becomes more and more listless; since he shows no desire to suck he becomes weak until he is quite wasted. Respiration and pulse increase from one hour to the next. The back is crooked and the head stretched out in a fashion peculiar to this disease. Diarrhoea and swelling of the joints occur later in the course of the disease. Death may occur within a few days.

In the late variety of the disease the picture is of a slow, long-drawn-out general infection. There are joint swellings, especially in the knee and hock, inflammation of tendon sheaths, and pneumonia with coughing and breathing difficulties. There is obvious lameness, stiffness and distress. The foal may die within a fortnight or linger on for some considerable time.

Preventative vaccination against joint-ill is not always successful, especially since so many different organisms are responsible. Intensive treatment by a vet may bring about recovery if the disease is diagnosed early.

6(13)iv PERVIOUS URACHUS

In new-born foals or a few days after birth it is not uncommon to see urine escaping from the navel, either in a continuous dribble or sometimes in a thin stream. The area a hand's breadth around the navel becomes soiled, the hairs stick together, the navel becomes swollen and there is a disturbance of the foal's general health.

There is a duct which runs from the bladder to the umbilical cord, and which is sealed when the cord is severed. In premature births or when the cord is broken off above the designated point, this duct remains open. In cases of meconium retention the violent straining and pressure can cause a failure of the spontaneous sealing process. There are various ways of treating pervious urachus. Although spontaneous recovery is possible, it should always be treated to prevent its developing into a general infection.

6(13)v UMBILICAL HERNIA

The tendency to develop an umbilical hernia is considered to be hereditary. In the navel region there is a hole of variable size in the abdominal wall through which the intestines protrude. The skin and the peritoneum are undamaged. The size of the hernia ranges from a finger-tip to a cabbage. The swelling is painless and the foal's general health is not affected. The contents are soft and easily pushed back into the abdominal cavity.

Especially if the hernia is large and the hole through which it protrudes is small, strangulation of the intestine may occur at any time. This gives rise to colic symptoms such as trembling, rolling, breaking out in a sweat and an increase in respiration and pulse rate. The hernia feels hard and is painful. It can no longer be pushed back into the abdominal cavity. Within a few hours the strangulated section of intestine becomes gangrenous. The condition is potentially fatal and immediate surgery is necessary.

So as to avoid the potentially fatal condition of a strangulated hernia, treatment for a hernia should begin as soon as possible. There are several methods to choose from. Spontaneous recovery should not be counted upon. Foals with this condition should not be used for stud, neither should mares who beget affected foals.

6(13)vi INGUINAL HERNIA AND SCROTAL HERNIA

In the groin region there is a slit in the abdominal wall on either side where the blood vessels of the scrotum pass through it. Some colt foals are born with these slits so large that the intestines protrude into the scrotum (scrotal hernia). In new-born foals this is no cause for anxiety. Usually this condition rectifies itself within the first five months of life. Strangulation is rare in scrotal hernias.

Inguinal hernias, on the other hand, are usually acquired. Heavy exertion while pulling, kicks, slipping and pulling heavy loads can lead to a sudden enlargement of the inguinal ring. Loops of small intestines are pushed into the slit and strangulated. Inguinal hernia is not visible from the outside. The corresponding testicle, usually the left, is drawn right up and cannot be moved. It is painful to the touch. The strangulated intestine causes severe colic symptoms. Only prompt surgery will save the horse.

6(13)vii CRYPTORCHIDISM (RIGS)

While the colt foal is developing in the uterus, the testicles must pass from the abdominal cavity into the scrotum. If one or both testicles remain in the abdominal cavity, the horse become a cryptorchid. It can be identified by the absence of one or both testicles from the scrotum. Since hormone production is unaffected, rigs can cover mares. However, the misplaced testicle is not capable of producing fertile sperm. If both testicles are misplaced, the horse is sterile. The condition is hereditary.

Rigs become difficult and bad-tempered as they grow up. The difficult operation to remove the testicles should be carried out when the horse is two years old at the latest.

6(13)viii HYPERFLEXION

Hyperflexion refers to a steep angle of the pastern and foot to the ground. The fetlock may even protrude forwards in front of the vertical ('knuckling over'). Hyperflexion occurs in new-born foals as well as in older animals. In older foals and horses the cause of the condition is tendon or joint disease. The condition develops gradually. Hyperflexion in new-born foals arises immediately after birth or within the first two days of life. The foal cannot straighten one or both forelegs in the foot region. It walks on the front of the fetlock joint or on its knees. It has to be lifted up to the mare's udder to allow it to suck. Its strength gradually declines. Infections such as joint-ill set in and cause deterioration

187

of the general health. Unless it is treated, the outcome will be fatal. The use of support- and extension-bandages right up to the elbow will correct the condition in four to six weeks.

There is so far no conclusive explanation of the cause of congenital hyperflexion. The theory that a disorder of the joints and tendons is responsible cannot be proven. It is highly likely that the cause is a congenital weakness of the extensor muscles and tendons. In most cases there is a rupture of the extensor tendon, but in spite of this the horse recovers.

6(13)ix CLUB FOOT

At birth foals generally have long, springy pasterns. As they grow up the pasterns become more upright. At two to six months they may become so upright that a club foot develops. A club foot is an upright foot with high heels. Its development is favoured by lack of exercise, being kept for a long period in a stable with deep litter and, in particularly well-developed foals, by hard ground.

At the age of six to eight months the pastern bones and cannon bone have finished growing. Up until this point there is intensive bone development in the pastern area with which the muscles and tendons cannot keep up. There is an ostensible shortening of the flexor tendons. In deep litter, as the pastern becomes more upright the toe can dig into the soft floor. Since there is no weight on the back of the foot, the tendons and muscles are not stretched to their proper length.

What happens to cause club foot in foals in the dry summer months in the fields is quite different. In the dry season the ground is very hard in places, and the grass is eaten down very short. Because of its disproportionately long legs the foal must spread or bend its legs to reach the grass. This causes excessive wear on the tip of the toes and hardly any on the heels. This, too, can cause a club foot to develop.

If a foal shows signs of developing a club foot, it must be shod with a half-moon shaped shoe ('grass tip'). In severe cases a shoe with an extended toe piece is used. With prompt treatment club foot can be eliminated by the time the horse is a year old.

6(14) Infectious Diseases

The term infectious diseases (infection) refers to the invasion of the body by pathogenic organisms which multiply and cause illness. The disease may be transmitted by insects or by contaminated food and drinking water. Man is often the culprit in the spread of disease. The infective agents gain entry into the body by natural routes (mouth, nose). As a rule they are unable to get in through undamaged skin, although they can do so through wounds. The organisms may be located in one part of the body or they may spread to the whole body via the bloodstream. There is accompanying fever which usually causes loss of appetite. Varying lengths of time may elapse from the entry of the organisms to the appearance of the first symptoms. If a large number of animals are affected, the word *epidemic* is used.

After recovery from an infection the horse may possess a resistance (immunity) which protects him from further attacks. This capacity to develop immunity is utilised to provide preventative immunisation (vaccination) against certain infections.

6(14)i CONTAGIOUS PLEUROPNEUMONIA*

Contagious pleuropneumonia is a virus disease consisting of pneumonia often accompanied by pleurisy. The disease begins suddenly with a high fever, pronounced listlessness, a rapid pulse and yellowish-red mucous membranes. On about the third day rapid shallow breathing and an amber- or rust-coloured nasal discharge indicate the presence of lung disease. There is rarely any

* This disease has now been practically eradicated in Europe.

coughing, it being suppressed owing to the pain caused by the pleurisy. Because of the long incubation period (three to five weeks), the epidemic takes a long time to spread around the yard. Infection is through contact with diseased animals or ones who recovered some time previously. Mortality can be as high as 20 per cent.

Whilst contagious pleuropneumonia used to be very common, nowadays it is rare. By prompt treatment it is possible to avert serious consequences which may make the horse unusable.

The sequel most to be feared is pulmonary emphysema resulting from damage to the lung tissue.

6(14)ii EPIDEMIC COUGH ('HOPPENGARTEN COUGH', INFLUENZA)

Epidemic cough is a virus disease which causes inflammation of the mucous membrane of the respiratory tract. There is fever for the first two to three days (39–40.5°C), swollen lymph nodes in the throat, reddening of the nasal mucous membrane and an increased clear, serous discharge from the nose. Only after a few days does a deep, hollow, often distressed cough set in. If the course of the disease is benign, this disappears in three weeks.

Usually no special treatment is necessary if the horse is allowed several weeks rest. However, the temperature should be checked daily. A recurrence of the fever indicates that bacterial infection of the lungs has set in as a complication. This can lead to severe pneumonia. There is a purulent discharge from the nose, the fever is sustained and the coughing intensified. This disease can also lead to pulmonary emphysema, especially if apparently sound horses are returned to work too soon.

The incubation period of this virus disease is only one to three days so that the whole yard can become infected within a few days. Infection is transmitted by the nasal secretion. The spread of 'Hoppengarten cough' is caused by contact with horses who have been suffering from the disease, for instance, at shows, competitions and race meetings. In this way it quickly spreads to many different establishments. Vaccination, which must be repeated frequently, is available against this disease.

6(14)iii STRANGLES

Strangles is a particularly infectious inflammation of the mucous membrane of the upper respiratory tract accompanied by suppuration in the lymph nodes. It is caused by a certain type of bacteria which cause illness only in horses and donkeys. It occurs especially in foals and weak horses.

Strangles begins with a high fever. A few days later there is a swelling of the lymph nodes in the throat and a cough. The swelling increases in size over a period of about eight days. Finally the suppurating lymph node ruptures outwards. The pus is yellow, thick, creamy and odourless. In the case of suppuration of the lymph nodes of the guttural pouches, the pus discharges first into the guttural pouch, then slowly out of the nose when the head is lowered. When the lymph nodes of the guttural pouches are affected the laryngeal nerve may be damaged. As a result of the paralysis the horse becomes a 'roarer'.

If the virus spreads to the rest of the body it causes suppuration of other lymph nodes. Suppuration of the lymph nodes in the thorax and abdominal cavity in particular can have fatal consequences. The disease is transmitted via the respiratory tract or the alimentary canal. The box, drinking water and bedding are contaminated by the nasal discharge from the affected horse and by droplets which are released when the horse coughs. Convalescent horses are still infectious for some time afterwards. Suckling foals suffering from strangles can transmit the disease via the mare's udder, and stallions can transmit strangles to mares at mating ('covering strangles').

The causative organisms of strangles have considerable

resistance to outside influences. Even when dried out they remain infective for an extraordinarily long time, and even an apparently healthy horse can carry and transmit the virus. Certain factors, such as a damp stable, over-exertion, a cold or a virus cough, favour the onset of the disease. The incubation period is four to eight days at the most. If the horse is weak for any reason, this time is shortened.

Vaccination does not always prevent the disease occurring, but once having suffered an attack, the horse enjoys several years' natural immunity. In establishments which have a lot of young horses, strangles spreads rapidly, whereas in stables of old horses it is mainly limited to a few odd cases. At the first suspicion of strangles the affected horses must be isolated immediately. Treatment must aim at getting the suppurating lymph nodes to discharge as soon as possible. Antibiotic treatment does not always achieve this aim, only serving to retard and protract the course of the disease. The stable must be disinfected constantly. Attention should be paid to the problem of the handlers transmitting the disease.

6(14)iv PURPURA HAEMORRHAGICA

Purpura haemorrhagica in the horse is a non-infectious condition, although it is caused by bacteria. It involves haemorrhages and accumulations of fluid in the skin. Often it is a sequel to strangles, contagious pleuro-pneumonia, pneumonia and serious wound infections. However, it cannot always be traced back to an earlier bacterial infection. There is damage to the walls of the blood vessels leading to the escape of blood and fluid from the vessels into the tissues. As a rule the first symptom is bleeding in the mucous membrane. Usually it takes the form of specks and flecks, but it may be in patches and streaks. Fluid accumulates underneath the skin (oedema) in the girth region, underneath the belly, on the sheath, on the head in the mouth region and in the legs. In severe cases there are monstrous disfigurations such as 'big head' (German: 'hippopotamus head') and 'big leg' (German: 'elephant leg').

The condition leads to disturbances in locomotion, feeding and urination, and to breathlessness. There is a fever, but it is not constant, sometimes being quite mild. Purpura must always be taken seriously. Simple cases clear up in fourteen days with no complications. In spite of intensive veterinary treatment the mortality rate is about 40 per cent.

6(14)v EQUINE INFECTIOUS ANAEMIA

Equine infectious anaemia is a specific, infectious disease of horses which has the same characteristics as blood poisoning. The course of the disease varies greatly, and there may or may not be clearly recognisable anaemia.

Infection is spread by communal drinking troughs, infected bedding and food, and insect bites. Horses of all ages are affected, and the disease spreads slowly among stable horses but quickly among horses at grass. On average the incubation period is about twenty days. The infection of an establishment takes place through apparently healthy horses who are carriers of the virus.

In the acute form there is a high fever, listlessness, loss of appetite, swelling of the eyelids, jaundice and a reduction in the amount of red blood corpuscles. Death occurs in a few days. In another form of infectious anaemia these symptoms are present in a milder form and persist for weeks or months. There are alternating periods with and without fever, each lasting several days. There is a marked loss of condition and either the horse grows so emaciated that it dies or the disease becomes chronic. Poor condition, bouts of fever and anaemia may persist for many months. Recovery is possible from this form, but otherwise the disease is considered incurable.

The veterinarian must report any suspicion of equine infectious anaemia to the veterinary authorities. Diagnosis can be confirmed by a special blood serum examination (Coggins test). If the result is positive, destruction of the horse is ordered.*

6(14)vi INFECTIOUS MENINGO-ENCEPHALO-MYELITIS (BORNA DISEASE)

Borna disease is an infectious, non-purulent inflammation of the brain and spinal cord which is caused by a virus. The name comes from the town of Borna in Saxony. The disease is localised in certain regions, and it is a striking feature that it only affects horses who work on the land. Sometimes the virus can remain infectious in the ground for years. The incubation period varies. Over the period of a week the horse displays fever, listlessness, yawning and dribbling. This is followed by a reduction in consciousness and a marked loss of responsiveness, accompanied by drowsiness and staggering. In other cases there may be excitability, characterised by frenzied behaviour, nervousness, restlessness, straining and grinding the teeth. Later, paralysis and locomotory disturbances occur. The mortality rate is about 80 per cent. In the provinces of Baden-Württemberg, Hessen and Bavaria, Borna disease is notifiable.

6(14)vii LOCKJAW (TETANUS)

Tetanus is a disease caused by the tetanus bacillus, which gains entry through a wound infection and causes a tonic spasm of the muscles. Tetanus bacilli occur everywhere in the horse's natural environment, for example in horse dung, dust, soil and on hay. The horse, man and the goat are particularly susceptible to tetanus. Chickens, however, are immune to it.

The organism must gain entry through damaged skin or mucous membrane (wound infection), and the majority of cases occur as a result of foot injuries (puncture wounds, treads and nail bind), barbed wire injuries and following castration. Sometimes the wounds are very small or have already healed when the disease makes its

* In Britain the disease is notifiable but destruction of the horse is not ordered.

appearance. The incubation period varies from a day to eight weeks.

The bacilli multiply at the site of infection only in the absence of air. They remain at the point of entry and it is there that they produce their toxin, which then spreads in the bloodstream to the rest of the body. The toxin lodges in the brain cells and causes generalised tetanus. The spasm of the muscles begins at the head. If the head is lifted up, the third eyelid or nicitating membrane (a fold of skin in the inner corner of the eye) comes out across the eye. The nostrils are flared. The lips are pressed hard together. Chewing is carried out very slowly and there is always interference with eating and drinking. The mouth cannot be opened. The ears become stiff and the horse adopts a sawhorse position, with the abdomen tucked up. The slightest disturbances cause increased excitability. With tetanus there is no disturbance of consciousness. In 50 to 80 per cent of cases the disease causes death through paralysis of the respiratory system.

The best protection against tetanus is *vaccination*, which must be carried out *as early as possible on all horses* (foals from three months onwards). All people who have contact with horses should also be vaccinated.

6(14)viii GLANDERS AND FARCY

Glanders is a malignant, epidemic disease of the horse family which is caused by the glanders bacillus. It is characterised by the formation of nodules and ulcers in the respiratory tract, the lungs and the skin. The infection is transmitted directly via nasal discharge and via the pus from the skin ulcers, and gains entry via the respiratory and digestive tracts. Depending on the location of the ulcers it is classified as nasal or pulmonary glanders or as *farcy* (that type producing skin lesions). The incubation period is only three to five days.

Glanders is one of the notifiable infectious diseases. All diseased or suspect horses are destroyed and the carcasses disposed of. The stable must be shut up and disinfected.

There have been no cases in Germany in recent years.*

6(14)ix DOURINE (MALADIE DU COÏT)

Dourine is a notifiable venereal disease affecting the horse family, and is transmitted by covering. It does not exist at present in Germany, but could be brought in from abroad. The incubation period varies from a week to several months. The first symptom in infected mares is a mucous to purulent discharge from the vagina. White spots develop on the vulva and udder. Raised patches occur on various parts of the body. If the disease persists, paralysis sets in, especially in the hindquarters. Treatment of this condition is possible, but affected or suspect horses may not be used for breeding again until they have been officially cleared by a vet.

6(14)x HERPES VIRUS (COITAL EXANTHEMA)

Another venereal disease is herpes,† which is caused by a virus and transmitted by covering. It is characterised by swelling and reddening of the mucous membranes accompanied by a purulent discharge and pustules. The infection is usually a benign one which clears up in two weeks. In Germany there used to be an obligation to notify this disease but this has been lifted. Affected horses must not be used for breeding for a period.

6(14)xi RABIES

Rabies is an infectious encephalitis caused by a virus, which affects all domestic animals and man. Rabies is transmitted to horses through the bite of wild animals, especially dogs or foxes. In the horse the incubation period is four to eight weeks. Infected horses show a desire to bite, and kick out at or run into obstacles. There is irritation in the bite region, loss of balance and paralysis which causes death in a few days. The disease is notifiable. Vaccination is available, and is recommended

---

* In Britain the disease is notifiable but destruction of the horse is not ordered.
† Does not occur in Britain.

for all horses who are kept at grass in areas where there is a risk of rabies.

6(15) Parasitic Diseases

6(15)i STOMACH BOTS

Bots are flies some 18mm long and thickly covered in hairs. They live for only about fourteen to twenty days, in which time they do not take in any food. After mating, the female lays in the region of 2,500 eggs, each in a protective shell and endowed with the facility to stick to hairs. They are laid on horses on the hairs of certain parts of the body: the mane, neck, sides of the chest and limbs. The larvae which hatch from the eggs burrow through the skin or mucous membrane of the mouth into the body. They migrate through the body to their particular habitat, the mucous membrane of the stomach, to which they attach themselves and continue their development. After, on average, eight to ten months they are passed out in the dung. They remain in the soil or dung as pupae for three to seven weeks, then emerge as flies.

The larvae migrating through the body and residing in the stomach membrane produce considerable inflammation of the mucous membrane of the mouth, causing difficulties in chewing and swallowing, constriction of the throat, abscesses and inflammation of the stomach and small intestine. Chronic diarrhoea and marked loss of condition are the result.

Control should start immediately after the eggs have been laid, so that the migration of the larvae is prevented. The eggs can be scraped off the hairs to which they are stuck with a sharp knife. Another method is to wash the affected ares with water (50°C) at about four-day intervals to make the larvae hatch. This tedious method of control is not much used with horses kept at grass.

The alternative is treatment with special preparations in the November to January period when the larvae should all be in the stomach.

6(15)ii ROUND WHITE WORMS (ASCARIDS)

Round white worm invasion is seen mostly in foals and yearlings. Older horses possess a good resistance to these parasites. The worms live in the small intestine, grow to a length of about 35cm and are as thick as a pencil. The sexually mature female lays up to 200,000 eggs per day. The eggs arrive in the outside world in the dung. Over a period of eight to fifteen days infective larvae develop in the eggs. The eggs are extremely resistant to drought and cold and can remain viable for several years.

The horse ingests the eggs with his food or water. The larvae hatch in the intestines, burrow through the intestinal wall and travel in the blood and lymph to the lungs. There they develop further and break into the air-filled alveoli. They migrate up the windpipe into the throat, where they are swallowed, and in this way they reach the small intestine. Here they develop over a period of twelve weeks into adult white worms.

The main damage is caused by the migrating larvae. They cause bleeding and inflammation in the lungs and thus developmental disturbance. Larvae migrating into the brain cause nervous disorders. The adult worms in the intestines cause inflammation which shows up in a capricious appetite, staring coat, colic symptoms and poor condition. The use of drugs will kill the adult worms in the intestine but not the migrating larvae. Treatment against ascarids must therefore be repeated four to six weeks later. Foals should first be treated at two to three months old.

6(15)iii RED WORMS (STRONGYLS)

The most commonly occurring and most influential parasites of the horse are red worms. These worms, which are colourless in themselves, derive their red colour from the blood they suck from the intestinal wall. According to their size and life cycle they are classified as large and small strongyls, of which in turn there are numerous sub-classifications.

Large strongyls are 15 to 45cm long and live in the caecum and large intestine. The larvae can burrow through body tissue with ease. They begin by burrowing into the blood vessels of the intestine, then migrate along the inner lining of the blood vessels, against the direction of the blood flow, to the larger arteries. This causes damage to the inner lining of the vessels and thus leads to the formation of blood clots. After a period of six months the larvae arrive back in the large intestine via the blood vessels. There they develop into adult worms, attaching themselves by their mouths to the mucous membrane of the intestines. This can cause anaemia since each worm sucks up to 0.2ml of blood per day.

The migrating larvae in the blood vessels cause fever, some loss of appetite, peritonitis and colic due to blockage of the blood vessels. Larvae straying into the spinal cord can cause paralysis in the hindquarters.

Small strongyls are 4 to 5mm long and also live in the caecum and large intestine. While developing, the larvae burrow only into the wall of the intestine. The adult worms live off the surface cells of the mucous membrane wall of the intestine. If large quantities of the worms are present, there is large-scale disturbance of the intestinal mucous membrane which can develop into ulcers.

The sexually mature females lay millions of eggs, which are passed out in the dung. Infective larvae hatch out of the eggs and spread around the area surrounding the dung. They climb up the grass stalks. Strong sunlight and drought suppress this migration. These larvae are taken in by horses grazing the meadow, and so a new generation develops. The larvae do not usually survive in the grass for more than three months.

A field which has not been grazed for a year is largely free of worms and larvae. So as to keep down the contamination of the field as much as possible, horses should be wormed twice, with a month in between, before being turned out. Droppings should be removed from the field on a weekly basis. Spreading the droppings out should be avoided, otherwise the whole field will soon be contaminated. Grazing cattle in with horses is recommended because cattle parasites hardly ever affect horses; the larvae of horse parasites are killed in the alimentary canal of cattle and vice versa.

There are numerous methods of worm control, but they are all effective only against the worms in the intestines. The larvae migrating in other parts of the body are not affected. A single worm treatment results only in the replacement of the worms killed by larvae from other parts of the body. For this reason repeated dosing is of the greatest importance, particularly in young horses.

With regular removal of droppings there is little danger of constant, repeated worm infestation in stabled horses.

6(15)iv STRONGYLOIDES WESTERI
Strongyloides westeri are parasites of the small intestine which occur only in foals. They grow to 8 to 9mm in length. The larvae burrow through the skin or gain entry with the food into the foal's body. They migrate through the lungs and then up the windpipe and throat into the small intestine. Damage is caused by the larvae in the form of pneumonia and by the worms in the intestine in the form of intermittent colic and diarrhoea. The droppings are partially blood-stained, and foul-smelling. Since the worms only take eight to nine days to develop, the condition can spread very quickly around a stud. Fatalities are possible. By the age of four to six months a natural resistance has developed which enables the body to fight off the infection and prevents further attacks.

6(15)v THREAD WORMS (OXYURIS)
Thread worms are parasites of the large intestine which occur most commonly in older horses. The females can be up to 10cm long. For their single egg-laying session

they migrate to the anus where they lay up to 60,000 eggs in a sticky fluid which quickly dries. When the horse rubs itself the eggs fall into the grazing or bedding, whence they are picked up again by the horse.

In the small intestine the larvae hatch and migrate into the large intestine where they develop into sexually mature worms in four to five months. Damage done by thread worms is slight. When the females migrate out there is marked irritation which can cause bald patches on the tail due to rubbing.

6(15)vi TAPE WORMS

Tape worms occur in horses at the point where the caecum and the small intestine meet. Depending on the variety, they vary in length from 4 to 80cm. They usually occur only in small numbers and symptoms, such as digestive disturbances, colic and diarrhoea, are rare. If tape worm infestation is diagnosed, special treatment is necessary.

6(15)vii MANGE

In the horse there are four kinds of mite which are responsible for mange in the head, rump, ear and foot regions. The microscopic mites burrow into the skin and cause pronounced itching. Rubbing causes irritation and thickening of the skin, together with crusts and oozing. The horse is restless, stamps his feet, gnaws at himself and rubs at every opportunity. Horses weakened by illness or poor feeding are particularly susceptible to mange. New treatments have almost eradicated this formerly widespread disease.

6(15)viii LICE

Another condition of underfed and weakened animals is lice, heavy infestations of which occur in the winter months only. They can be detected with the naked eye. They feed on scales of skin and on hairs, and occur mainly in the head, neck and croup. The intense itching causes constant restlessness and leads to sores and leg injuries. Treatment is always successful. Stable, equipment and saddlery must be treated at the same time.

6(15)ix TICKS
Occasionally in horses at grass, or after a ride through a wood, an isolated case of ticks crops up. Ticks bore into the skin, fill themselves up with sucked blood and then fall off again. Damage to the skin is minimal. However, certain infectious diseases can be transmitted by ticks.

7. Identification, Assessment and Description

7(1) Identification

The description of a horse or pony begins with his identification. This consists of a description of his colour and markings, the identification of any brand he might have, and an assessment of his age. Before buying any horse the purchaser should compare what he sees with the corresponding details in the foal identity document of the animal concerned. Only if they correspond exactly can he be certain that the document pertains to the horse in front of him. Many court cases could be avoided by obeying this rule.

7(1)i BODY COLOURS

The following colours are distinguished:

Chestnut (German: Fuchs [F.])
The coat hairs are red; the long hairs (mane, tail, ergot tuft) must be chestnut or light coloured and should not contain any black hairs. The following variations are recognised:
□ Chestnut (Fuchs [F.])
□ Light chestnut (Hellfuchs [Hlf.])
□ Dark (liver) chestnut (Dunkelfuchs [Df.])

Black (Rappe [R.])
The coat hair is black, as are the mane, tail and ergot tuft, with the inclusion of no other colour except for white markings.

Bay and brown (Brauner [B.])
The coat hair is bay or brown. In contrast to the chestnut, the legs and long hairs (mane, tail and ergot

tuft) are predominantly black. The following variations are recognised:

☐ Light bay (Hellbrauner [Hb.])
☐ Bay (Brauner [B.])
☐ Bay-brown (Dunkelbrauner [Db.])
☐ Bay-brown (Schwarzbrauner [Schb.])

Horses who are black in colour but have a brown tinge to their flanks and a brownish-coloured muzzle (German: 'copper muzzle') belong in the black-brown category.

Grey and roan (Schimmel [Sch.])

Greys and roans are generally born dark in colour, but carry the greying gene with them. The following variations are recognised:

☐ Chestnut roan/grey (Fuchsschimmel [Fsch.])
☐ Light chestnut roan/grey (Hellfuchsschimmel [Hlfsch.])
☐ Dark (liver) chestnut roan/grey (Dunkelfuchsschimmel [Dfsch.])
☐ Blue/black roan/grey (Rappschimmel [Rsch.])
☐ Bay roan/grey (Braunschimmel [Bsch.])
☐ Light bay roan/grey (Hellbraunschimmel [Hlbsch.])
☐ Bay-brown roan/grey (Dunkelbraunschimmel [Dbsch.])

Other colours:

Albino/cream (Albino)

Albinos are horses with white, unpigmented hair and no pigment in the skin.

Chestnut with flaxen mane and tail (Isabell)

The 'Isabell' is a chestnut but with yellow or sometimes grey or tawny coat hair. The mane and tail are always light in colour. The feet are also light coloured. A sub-division is the Palomino, which must have a golden sheen to its coat hairs, and whose mane and tail hairs must be as gleaming a white as possible.

Dun (Falbe)

The dun is a bay, but with coat hairs which range from yellow to grey, together with black legs, feet, mane and tail.

Piebald/skewbald (Schecke)

Piebalds and skewbalds have large, interconnecting patches in any colour, hence there are chestnut and white skewbalds, bay and white skewbalds, piebalds (black and white) and blue and white skewbalds.

Spot (Tiger)

The spotted horse (spot) is characterised by round or oval spots of different sizes. Spotted markings are found in all colours and are classified accordingly, as chestnut spotted, bay spotted, etc.

7(1)ii HEAD MARKINGS

For details of head markings, which are described by beginning at the forehead and working downwards, see the drawings on pages 206-7.

7(1)iii MARKINGS ON THE LIMBS

For identification purposes these are described in the order left fore, right fore, left hind, right hind (the *horse's* left and right, not the limbs as seen by a person standing in front of the horse and facing him). For details see the drawings on page 208.

7(1)iv DISTINGUISHING MARKS

This category comprises details of the mane, tail, ergot tuft, body marks, whorls, eel stripes, shoulder stripes, zebra marks on the legs, variations in colour round the eyes and scars. If a horse has no distinguishing marks, this should be stated.

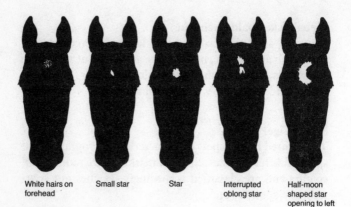

White hairs on forehead

Small star

Star

Interrupted oblong star

Half-moon shaped star opening to left

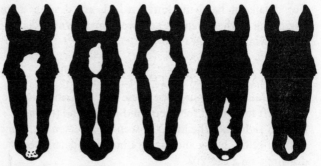

Blaze, irregular at top and spotted at base

Interrupted star and stripe, stripe narrowing half way down and then widening again

Wide blaze irregular at top, extending to left at base

Low, irregular wide blaze extending into left nostril, and white spot on upper lip

Snip

Large, bordered star

Large, long wedge-shaped star

Long stripe

Narrow stripe, widening at the top

Star and stripe conjoined with white hairs around top of star

Very large, long snip, extending into both nostrils

Interrupted star, stripe and snip, widening at base

White upper lip

Large, irregular, wedge-shaped star, tied in at the middle, and irregular snip extending into white upper lip

White face, wall eye right

207

Left fore white heels

Left fore white spot on outside coronet, right fore coronet white

Left fore white spots outside coronet, right fore coronet and heels white

Left fore white pastern, right fore irregular white pastern with black spot in front

Left fore white pastern with black spots outside coronet and white spot back of fetlock

Left fore white to half cannon rising to three-quarter cannon in front

Both forelegs irregular white to half cannon

Left fore irregular white to three-quarter forearm, right fore white to below knee

Left hind bordered white pastern, right hind white pastern

Both hind legs white to hock, rising to above hock in front

Left hind irregular white to half pastern, right hind white to half cannon irregular inside

Left hind white heels, right hind irregular white to half cannon

208

7(1)v BRAND MARKS (See page 247)

Brand marks fall into two categories: the foal brand or brand of origin, which shows which breeding district the horse comes from, and the registration brand. The foal brand or brand of origin of the German provincial studs is on the horse's left thigh. Since foals are branded before the age of six months, this brand grows with them. Brand marks which seem too small may be fakes. If a mare has been accepted for registration in the relevant stud book of her particular breed association, she bears a registration brand on the left hand side of the neck. English Thoroughbreds and trotters are not branded.

7(1)vi ASSESSING THE AGE

Estimation of the horse's age is necessary for a correct assessment of its value and usefulness. A mature horse who can be put into full work is worth more to the buyer than a young, immature horse or a horse who is too old. Unscrupulous dealers may attempt to deceive the inexperienced buyer as to the age of a horse.

Highly bred horses and the primitive breeds, especially ponies, are late maturing, and do not finish developing until they are between the ages of five and seven. The cold-blooded horses are in full possession of their strength by the time they are four years old.

The official date from which a horse's age is taken is 1 January. In non-Thoroughbred breeding in Germany all foals born between 1 January and 31 October count as being born on 1 January of that year, while those born from 1 November to 31 December are aged from 1 January of the following year. For Thoroughbreds and trotters the age is taken from 1 January of the calendar year in which they are born.

In young horses the lines of the head are soft and blend into each other, while in adult horses they are sharper, and the head seems longer and narrower. After the age of twelve the profile becomes progressively harder, and the gradual disappearance of the sub-cutaneous fat causes the

Signs to look out for when assessing age

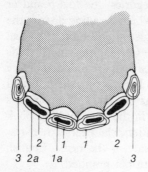

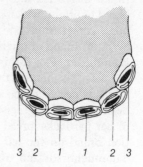

3 years

1	Central incisors (in wear)
1a	Infundibulum
2	Lateral incisors (permanent)
2a	Infundibulum
3	Corner incisors (temporary)

5 years

1 and 2 Central and laterals in wear
3 Corners coming into wear

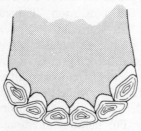

9 years
Infundibula have disappeared

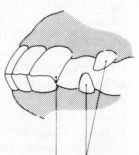

Hook

Tushes or canine teeth (in stallions and geldings)

lines of the bones to stand out more sharply, the hollows over the eyes to deepen, and the throat area to look hollow and wasted. At fourteen years, or sometimes earlier, grey hairs appear around the eyes.

The horse has six incisor teeth in the upper jaw and six in the lower jaw. Starting from the centre, these are the central, lateral and corner incisors. There are also twelve cheek teeth in each jaw, six at the front (pre-molars) and six at the back (molars). The latter only occur as permanent teeth. The canine teeth (tushes) are situated between the incisors and the cheek teeth. They seldom erupt in mares, and since they are a secondary male characteristic they are frowned upon in brood mares.

It is the eruption, shedding and wear of the (incisor) teeth in the lower jaw which serves as a guide for assessing a horse's age. The information is provided up to the age of five by the eruption and shedding of the teeth; from five and a half to eight years by the disappearance of the infundibulum ('mark') from the incisors in the lower jaw; from nine to eleven years by the disappearance of the infundibulum from the incisors in the upper jaw, and thereafter by the shape of the tables.

At birth or by the age of two weeks the temporary central incisors and the temporary premolars are present. The temporary lateral incisors usually appear after three to six weeks, and the corners at from five to nine months. The fourth cheek tooth is usually present at one year, the fifth at two years and the sixth at three and a half years. In a young horse it is easy to tell if the teething process has been accelerated in an attempt to deceive, because the sixth cheek tooth will be absent.

☐ The central incisors are changed at two and a half to three years.
☐ The lateral incisors are changed at three and a half to four years.
☐ The corner incisors are changed at four and a half to five years.

☐ The first two cheek teeth are changed at two and a half years.

☐ The third cheek teeth are changed at three and a half to four years.

Assessing the age by the wear of the incisors is a much less precise method than judging it from the eruption and changing of the teeth. The infundibula, which are dark, clearly defined depressions in the wearing surface of the incisors, are 7mm (i.e. three layers) deep in the lower jaw and 14mm (i.e. six layers) deep in the upper jaw. Since each year one layer of the tooth is worn away, it takes three years in the lower jaw and six years in the upper for the infundibula to disappear. This means that the following rules apply for assessing the age from the infundibula:

The infundibulum in the central incisors of the lower jaw disappears at six, in the laterals at seven and in the corners at eight years; in the upper jaw it disappears from the centrals at nine, the laterals at ten and the corners at eleven years. Nine-year-old horses often have a hook on the corner teeth of the upper jaw, though this hook may occur at any age once the horse has acquired all his permanent teeth. It usually disappears at ten to eleven years.

Wearing of the incisors and thus the disappearance of the infundibulum can occur at different rates depending on the hardness of the enamel and of the food the horse is given to eat, and this can make the horse look older or younger than he is. After the age of twelve, when the infundibula have disappeared, the horse's age can only be gauged approximately, by looking at the shape of the tables. At the age of approximately twelve to seventeen the tables are roundish; at approximately eighteen to twenty-four they are oval (longer from front to rear than from one side to the other), and from approximately twenty-four years onwards they are triangular.

In a young horse, when viewed from the side with the mouth closed, the incisors meet almost vertically (German: 'pincer mouth'). With increasing age (eight to seventeen years) they slope more forwards ('half pincermouth') until in old age (over seventeen years) they form an acute angle ('pointed mouth').

These guidelines apply to horses. In late-maturing ponies the eruption of the temporary incisors often takes place later. Since ponies, especially Mountain and Moorland breeds, have harder teeth than horses, they wear more slowly and so the infundibula and traces of them take longer to disappear. This should be borne in mind when assessing ponies according to the above guidelines – the age of ponies will usually be underestimated.

7(2) General Assessment

The horse should be assessed from the point of view of his suitability and value for the job he is intended to do. One should determine the general quality and not look for individual faults, which will often have no effect on performance. Often constitution and temperament have more effect on performance than individual conformation faults. We should aim to be judges of horses, not of faults, and to judge the horse as a whole. We want performance horses, not dull, mediocre ones with perfect conformation, and our idea of beauty should be the sort of conformation which is desirable and necessary for the job. The assessment of a horse in hand is only one of the additional elements of performance testing, and the results of this test are only used as a back-up to the evaluation of his actual performance.

There is no such thing as a normal horse, because different jobs favour and require different shaped horses. However, it has to be said that many horses in daily use, and competing in performance tests, either do things for which a visual appraisal would not deem them suitable or do not do that of which they appear capable.

When a horse is offered for sale, it is a good idea for the potential purchaser to arrive unexpectedly so as to observe the horse's behaviour or, especially in the case of a pony, to see him being caught in the field and saddled up in the stable.

The horse should be assessed at halt and in movement, in hand and under saddle. He should be tried under saddle not only by an experienced rider but also, if possible, by the rider for whom he is intended. The examination at halt should be carried out on level, firm ground, with the horse and the examiner on the same

Assessing a horse on a triangle

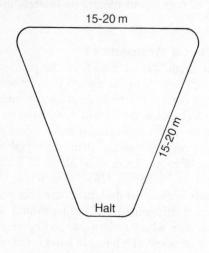

Position of assessor

level and 4 to 5m apart. The examination of the horse in movement should take place, if possible, on a triangle, which enables the observer to judge the horse from behind, from the side and from the front.

When he first looks at the horse, the examiner should get a general impression of type, harmony, constitution, condition, boldness and temperament. He must be able to see whether the horse in front of him is suitable for the job he will have to do. Only this general assessment will enable him to judge whether deviations from the 'ideal type' can be overlooked or whether they are to be considered as faults. Obvious and significant 'plus' points of temperament, body, limbs and action must be weighed against the so-called weaknesses. Finally there is the evaluation of the horse in movement, which gives the 'casting vote' as to his suitability for the work required of him. The expert will describe a horse in a few words which will sum up clearly the sort of horse he is, his most important good qualities, and his faults and therefore his suitability for the job.

Breeding stock must be judged according to the highest standards. They must be as perfect and typical examples of their breed as possible, and must possess the characteristics of their family and sex – otherwise, although they may be useful horses, they are certainly not suitable for breeding.

For riding or driving horses, and especially for horses intended for sport, it is performance which counts most. The external examination can certainly give useful information about this, but it is inner qualities such as soundness, readiness to perform, temperament, boldness, toughness, amenability to training, and whether or not the animal is a good 'doer' (utilises his food efficiently) which are the deciding factors. Valuable information on these aspects can be gleaned from the face and eyes, the carriage and behaviour, the horse's step and his reactions to what is going on around him, and also from the way he moves, which should be energetic and purposeful.

In riding horses slight variations in the proportions and individual points of conformation are desirable, depending on the job for which the horse is required. A horse who is in equilibrium is always desirable. While being examined he should stand, calm but alert, on all four legs in a harmonious position and should not need to be corrected by being pushed backwards or pulled forwards. In all his gaits he should move lightly and freely, in perfect harmony, carrying himself with impulsion and taking ground-covering and elastic strides. He should have a very good, level, kind temperament and good ability in the intended field of activity.

The harmonious riding horse should have clearly defined 'lines' and stand over a lot of ground. The basis for this is a clearly defined neck; a clearly defined, sloping shoulder with a clearly defined upper arm; distinct withers; a clearly defined back, and hind limbs made up of clearly defined levers and with the bones at favourable angles to each other.

7(2)i CONFORMATION
The Head and Neck
The head should match the body. It should be clean cut and expressive, and should be neither characterless nor coarse or shapeless. It should embody the characteristics of the breed and, most important in the case of breeding stock, of the animal's sex.

The eye is the window of the mind. It should be alert, bold and kind. A lively eye shows readiness for work, while too much white in the eye – which is often only visible at times – may be a sign of a bad temperament. A dull eye, like a dull coat, denotes ill-health. Variations in the colour of the iris (German: the unsightly 'glass eye', where the iris is whitish to light grey, and 'birch eye', where the iris is light blue, etc) are often caused by low deposits of pigment. They do not affect the horse's usefulness, but are major aesthetic blemishes. Small, sunken 'pig eyes' and large, protruding eyes (German: 'ox eyes') are unsightly, and are not usually a sign of great promise and intelligence.

Sticking the tongue out, often an inherited trait, is a serious fault in breeding stock and riding horses, especially dressage horses. Before buying a horse, always put a snaffle bridle on him and watch to see if he plays with the bit with his tongue or tries to poke it out underneath it.

Large, open nostrils, with thin, mobile edges, soft, and covered with fine hairs, are a sign of breeding and enable large quantities of air to be inhaled. The nostrils should move only slightly when the horse is at rest – over-activity may be a sign of respiratory disease, for instance broken wind.

The teeth: when assessing the head, examine the teeth to ascertain the horse's age, to assess their condition and position, and in particular to see if the mouth is under-shot or overshot (and if so, to what extent) or is in any other way abnormal.

The poll: the connection between head and neck at the poll should be flexible.

Jaws which are too narrow and a short, thick *throat* make flexion and 'bridling' difficult and are a constant source of trouble to the rider.

The neck, which is made up of seven cervical vertebrae, is thick and muscular in stallions and longer and finer in mares. In riding horses it should be well set on, sufficiently long, and carried freely and elegantly. Short necks are inharmonious and undesirable, especially in riding horses. Low-set necks make schooling more difficult and affect the animal's balance.

The Body

The withers are made up of spinous processes which slope backwards, the more they do so the better. In riding horses they should be long, high and broad, forming, in conjunction with a long, sloping shoulder, a good saddle place. Horses who are higher at the croup than the withers are often on the forehand if their lack of withers is not compensated by a well-carried, long neck.

The chest in breeding stock should be wide, deep and long so as to afford sufficient room for the internal organs. Performance horses, who are required to work at speed, may have narrower chests and flatter ribs. The important thing is that the sternum should be long, which makes the chest cavity long and thus provides plenty of room for the heart and lungs. A narrowing of the chest just behind the shoulder is undesirable.

The back: the eighteen thoracic vertebrae form the basis of the skeleton. Eight of them are attached to the sternum. The length of the back should be such that the forelegs, the back and the hind legs form a rectangle. Mares have relatively longer backs than stallions. Backs which are too short make 'Losgelassenheit'* difficult to obtain and the movements required of the riding horse too difficult. A short, straight top-line used to be popular, but nowadays a longer, slightly dipped back – that is a back with a slight dip behind the withers – is preferred. The saddle sits particularly well on this type of back, and horses who are built in this way are often excellent jumpers, with soft movements which are pleasant for the rider. Slack backs, hollow backs, high backs and roach backs are faults.

The loins: the horse has five to seven lumbar vertebrae. Some animals – frequently square-shaped, pure-bred Arabians – have five lumbar vertebrae, while others have seven, but most have six. The transverse processes, which serve as attachment points for important muscles, should be as wide and long as possible. The lumbar region should be broad and well muscled, its length proportionate to the rest of the body. A moderately long loin is not a fault, but loins which are too long make the

---

* The closest English equivalent is 'looseness'; for a detailed explanation of this term see *The Principles of Riding*.

horse less robust and – especially when they look narrow and sunken – are a sign of poor food utilization.

The croup is made up of the sacrum, which consists of five sacral vertebrae fused into one, plus the first four of the fifteen to twenty-one coccygeal vertebrae and three pelvic bones: the ilium, ischium and pubis. The croup, which is the horse's power lever, must be long, broad and well muscled. In conjunction with the hind limbs it is the source of all energy. In a performance horse the croup should slope slightly and should not be horizontal as was the aesthetic ideal in days gone by.

The tail: a handsome horse should have a well-carried tail. Horses who do not carry their tails well are usually lacking in boldness and temperament. Clamped tails are very often a sign of nervousness and tension. Tails carried to one side are very unsightly, can be a sign of a back problem and may lessen the horse's value.

The Forelimbs

The value of irreproachable forelimbs, which are the be all and end all in racehorses, must never be under-estimated in any horse, although the hind limbs, as the motor, are of great importance. The forelimbs are joined to the body by muscles and fascia. The body hangs, as it were, in a sling. The forelimbs should form a vertical line, that is, seen from the front they should be parallel, and seen from the side they should be placed neither too far under the body nor too far out to the front. A vertical line dropped from the middle of the top part of the shoulder blade should divide the forearm and cannon bone in half down their length, and touch the ground almost at the back of the bulbs of the heels.

The shoulder should be long, broad and sloping to give ground-covering, springy strides. The shoulder joint should be relatively far forward and should form a right angle with the humerus (arm), which should not be too short.

The elbow: the olecranon process – the backward and upward projection of the ulna at the elbow joint – must be as long and as laid back as possible, since it serves as an attachment for the most important extensor muscles of the forearm. Warmblood horses with their elbows tied in to their chest walls are useless for fast work. There must be enough room between the elbow and the chest to insert the flat of the hand, otherwise the freedom of movement of the forelimbs will be impaired. Horses with tied-in elbows are not safe for jumping, since if they make a mistake they can all too easily lose their feet.

The forearm (radius) should be powerfully muscled and long in relation to the cannon bone.

The knee should be large, broad and well-defined, and warmblood horses in particular should have a prominent pisiform bone. An ill-defined, narrow, smooth knee, or a leg tied in above or below the knee, is a sign of weakness.

The cannon bone (metacarpal) should be broad and short in relation to the forearm. The front of the cannon bone should not be concave in profile, and at the back the tendons must be clearly defined, clean and broad, without any sign of thickening or lumps: tendons which do not 'stand out' from the back of the cannon bone are not a good sign in a horse required to stand up to hard work.

Being slightly *over the knee* is not a fault in racehorses and competition horses, provided it is not due to wear and knuckling over of the joint. Horses who are from birth slightly over at the knee (i.e. have 'slack tendons') have a measure of elasticity in their knees and do not break down so easily as those with very straight legs or legs which are concave in profile. Horses whose forefeet are too far underneath them are not in natural balance: since the legs which support it are slanting, the forehand hangs out over them.

The cannon bone should be of sufficient size to match the rest of the body and should look harmonious. Harmony, and in particular boldness and courage ('blood') – that is the energy for performance – can never be judged by the measurement around the leg below the knee, which should be used only as a technical aid.

The fetlock should be large, clean and well defined, and neither smooth and rounded nor puffy.

The fore pasterns must be harmonious with the legs in angle and strength. Short, upright pasterns are undesirable, and constitute a serious fault in jumping horses, making them less steady on their feet, and causing premature breakdown. However, their effect can be compensated by a well-placed shoulder and humerus. Pasterns which are too long make movement more difficult, reduce speed and make the horse less steady on his feet. Boxy feet and 'bear' feet (excessively upright feet combined with excessively sloping pasterns) can usually be attributed to hereditary predisposition.

The Hind Limbs
The hindquarters are the horse's power-house, from which the power for upward movement originates. They derive their effect from the judiciously angled long bones, which make up the lever system of the hindquarters. These levers send the body forward by mechanical action, catapulting it forward in fact. The hind legs are connected to the body through *the hip joint*.

The thigh should be as powerfully muscled as possible, long, broad and oblique, so that when a stallion is viewed from the side the sheath is obscured from view. If the angles of the hind limbs are too open, developing and maintaining power at fast paces is difficult.

The stifle must be broad and powerful. The whole of the upper leg, from the thigh down through the gaskin or second thigh (German: 'the breeches') must be clad with

221

a full, well-defined powerful musculature, otherwise the horse is said to be weak in the thighs and gaskins (German: 'fox thighs'). Gaskins which are correctly positioned and long enough offer the best chance of generous strides. Short, usually upright gaskins result in short, fumbling strides.

The hock is the most important joint in the horse's body, and in horses who work at speed it is the one which is subjected to the most strain. It consists of seven bones, of which the first and second cuneiform bones are fused into one. The tibial tarsal (astragalus) and the tibia make up the joint in which the extension and flexion take place. Since the point of the hock (tuber calcis) serves as the point of attachment for the most important extensor tendon, its length and breadth are of paramount importance to the horse's ability to perform. The bigger the tuber calcis, the bigger the hock. A short, small tuber calcis which does not stand away from the rest of the hock makes for a small hock.

When looked at from the front, the side or from behind, the hock should be well defined, long, broad and as near the ground as possible. It should run smoothly into the gaskin and cannon bone. A hock which appears narrow either from the side or from behind will not stand up to heavy strain. A very angular hock joint (*sickle hock*) sprains easily. A mild degree of sickle hocks, which is a characteristic of most mountain breeds, is acceptable. Racehorses with bent hind legs are very often fast starters. The increased angle enables them to engage the hind legs more quickly under the body than a horse with straight hind legs.

On the other hand there are numerous well-known racehorses – both stayers and sprinters – as well as famous jumpers, with very straight hind legs. Dressage horses usually have normal or slightly angular hind legs, because it is very difficult for horses with straight hind legs to sit right back on their haunches.

The nearer the knee and hock are to the ground the steadier the horse will be in his movements in any kind of country. Really good horses very rarely have high-placed hocks.

Bowed legs and *cow hocks*, especially when combined with weak hocks, lead to diseased changes in the bones of the hock due to the uneven loading. The best known is *spavin*, which is an enlargement of the small bones of the hock caused by chronic periostitis. The elasticity, flexion and extension of the hock can be seriously impaired. Bumpy hocks are often the result of prominent bone structure and not spavin. When assessing a horse with work and competitions in mind, this should not cause undue concern provided the horse is not lame (spavin test).

A visible enlargement on the back of the hind leg below the hock is called a *curb*. Curbs which are hereditary or caused by external injury are usually harmless from the point of view of work. The heads of the splint bones are often mistaken for a curb.

A *capped hock* is an enlargement of the false bursa at the point of the hock, which fills with fluid. It is often due to mechanical influences, for instance hitting the hock against a wall, and is usually considered merely as an aesthetic blemish.

A *splint* may occur in the form of an enlargement on the upper outside face of the cannon bone. It is only detrimental when it is positioned so that it exercises painful pressure on the flexor tendons.

Hind cannon bone and pastern: the hind pastern should be somewhat more flexible than the fore pastern, otherwise the requirements are the same as for the forelimb. Horses with flexible, elastic hind pasterns are usually a pleasant ride. Pasterns which are too flexible make the horse slower. Horses with pasterns which are too upright wear o it more quickly and often have hard, jarring paces.

A slight outward turn of the pasterns is without consequence, but if exaggerated it impairs the energetic pushing off of the hind limbs and leads to strains and premature breakdown.

Splints and windgalls in young horses are usually a sign of soft constitution. Splints are often due to external injury (a knock or blow) to the inside or outside of the cannon bone, especially if the cause persists over a long period. They also occur as a result of uneven loading, especially on the outside of the cannon bone. Splints on the outside are usually of no consequence provided they do not interfere with a tendon. Splints on the inside of the foreleg are undesirable since they are often connected with bowed cannon bones and so with a disturbance of the static ratios.

Windgalls (bursal enlargements on the fetlocks) are more serious than bursal enlargements on the upper part of the limbs. Bursal enlargements occur either as a result of overstrain or of overfeeding, especially with protein. Hardened bursal enlargements often lead to lameness. A slight outward turn of the pasterns is without consequence, but if exaggerated it impairs the energetic pushing off of the hind limbs and leads to strains and premature breakdown.

The Foot
When assessing a horse, particular attention must be paid to the foot. The early retirement of many horses is caused by diseased or prematurely worn out feet. The shape and size of the feet, which are determined by breeding and environment, must be proportionate and in keeping with the upper body. In light horses they are small and more upright, in heavy horses larger and broader. Soft, in particular marshy ground makes for flatter, bigger, softer feet than harder, stony ground.

The foot should be made of hard, solid horn, and should not be brittle. It should be smooth, without any irregularities in the wall such as rings or cracks, etc.

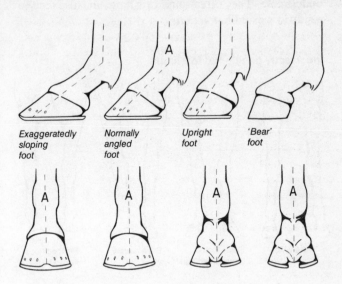

Exaggeratedly sloping foot

Normally angled foot

Upright foot

'Bear' foot

Pair of normal feet viewed from in front and behind
A = normal foot

The frog must be healthy and well developed. Low heels, especially in conjunction with upright pasterns, are a serious fault in performance horses, depriving them of the necessary spring. The foot is said to be aligned with the pastern when, viewed from in front, a line (A) drawn down through the middle of the pastern also runs through the middle of the toe, and when viewed from behind the line (A) dividing the cannon bone in half drops half way between the bulbs of the heels. When viewed from the side, the line of the pastern (A) runs parallel to the line of the toe (the toe/pastern axis is the line running down the front of the toe). Any deviation from this is abnormal, unless it is a characteristic of a particular breed. For example, Fjord ponies often have turned out toes. Turned in toes on the forelegs are undesirable. They often cause brushing, and also tend to result in a paddling action.

Incorrectly positioned forelimbs

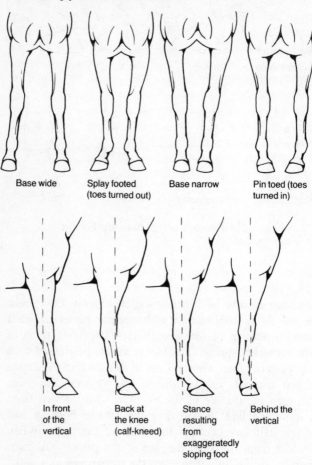

Base wide | Splay footed (toes turned out) | Base narrow | Pin toed (toes turned in)

In front of the vertical | Back at the knee (calf-kneed) | Stance resulting from exaggeratedly sloping foot | Behind the vertical

7(2)ii ACTION

A horse's action is assessed under saddle in the three gaits, walk, trot and canter, and in hand in walk and trot. Icelandic ponies are also assessed under saddle and in

226

hand both pacing and in the tölt. Carrying out this test on a triangle makes it possible to assess the horse from behind, from the side and from in front. The correctness and mechanics of the gaits are assessed, as is the horse's willingness to go forward. The horse must move straight and tread where his feet point. The action should be ground-covering, rhythmical, elastic and full of impulsion and energy. A long, flowing walk, in which the feet do not seem to stick to the ground, is the most important gait in any breed of horse. The longer the walk the better. Horses with a short walk are not suitable for any job: they are worthless. In a normal walk the hind feet should tread at least in the prints of the forefeet, and possibly beyond them (which shows a high degree of forward thrust). If the hind feet are set down distinctly behind the forefeet, the walk is too short.

The walk is made up of a diagonal sequence of footfalls. The four feet are set down at four equal intervals, i.e. left fore, right hind, right fore, left hind. Horses with a good walk often have a good canter.

The trot should be a natural, ground-covering gait without excessive knee action. A good trot full of impulsion originates in powerful hindquarters. The cadenced steps of the hind legs should reach well under the centre of gravity. In the trot the feet are set down diagonally in pairs and two regular beats are heard.

The canter: the ground-devouring, long canter stride of the well-bred warmblood horse should be in no way earthbound. The canter is a natural movement to the horse. The three individual phases (leaps) should be light and ground covering, and should follow on rhythmically (in three time).

Stringhalt (German: 'cock step') is an abnormality of the action consisting of a high, upward jerking of one of the hind legs as a result of exaggerated contraction of the hind leg muscles.

227

Size: oversized horses, especially if they are 'on the leg', should be treated with caution both as potential breeding stock and as potential riding horses. They are often unreliable in the stock they throw, and uneconomical to keep since they require large quantities of food. Performance-wise, and especially in cross-country work, they lack the stamina and cleverness of medium-sized and smaller horses built in a 'large frame'. The latter carry the rider's weight just as well as large horses and do not tire so easily even when carrying heavy weights. In spite of this, many riders prefer not only oversized horses, but those who are 'on the leg', thinking that they look better.

7(2)iii TEMPERAMENT, INTELLIGENCE AND CONSTITUTION (THE INNER QUALITIES)

The assessment of the inner qualities is an indispensable and particularly important element in the examination of a horse. It should reveal whether the horse in question is likely to fulfil the needs of the rider and trainer.

The inner qualities have a considerable effect on the animal's suitability as a riding horse and so on its value. As a result of regular performance testing, defects have now been largely eradicated from German studs. On the other hand some countries, especially in the East, are exporting horses whose inner qualities, especially temperament, are defective: by selling them abroad, no redress is to be feared. A more expensive horse from a good German stud usually works out cheaper at the end of the day than a foreign horse who has not been thoroughly tested, or who has not spent some time in the possession of or under the supervision of a recognized rider or instructor.

Vices such as biting, kicking, and jibbing in harness, which are often hereditary and crop up frequently in certain bloodlines, should be eradicated if possible. They are difficult to correct: great kindness, feel and energy is required to effect a cure, and the problems tend to recur with a change of rider.

Like faults, good qualities are also hereditary, especially a good nature (kind, honest, willing horses) and an aptitude for certain areas of activity. This means that a connoisseur of any given breed can make many predictions as to the likely qualities of a horse by studying his pedigree.

Other inner qualities which are all-important to the value of the horse and his proposed career are health, constitution, powers of recovery after heavy exertion, food utilisation (whether he is a good or a bad 'doer'), readiness to work, temperament and intelligence. The horse's attentiveness and ability to understand the rider's wishes and aids depend on the latter. Calmness and attentiveness are at least as important as an attractive appearance and good conformation.

One should beware of dull, nervous, timid horses, as well as horses with deficient health and constitution, and ungenerous horses. The modern horse must be naturally well endowed with the qualities required for riding and sport.

8. Advice on Buying a Horse

The person buying a horse must be aware of the responsibility he is taking on. Unlike, for example, when buying a car, *he is acquiring a living creature*; not only will it be at his disposal, he must also be at its disposal, providing for its upkeep, grooming and feeding, and also for the essential *exercise and care*. Only if this is fully understood and these requirements can be met should a horse be bought. The purchaser must then decide what sort of horse to buy. This will depend upon whether he wants it for competitions, leisure activities or some other purpose. It is this, together with the level of the rider's training, which will determine not only the choice of breed, type, size, etc, but also the method of purchase.

In Germany there are five ways of buying a horse, namely from a breeder; from an auction; from one of the breed association marketing centres; from a private seller, or from a dealer. There are advantages and disadvantages to each of these, depending on the sort of horse required and above all on the buyer. The latter is strongly advised to seek the advice of an experienced horse person, because once the sale is concluded there can be no redress against outwardly recognisable defects, which include 'ridability' and education.

If the buyer is seriously interested, he should take his time looking the horse over. The animal should be given a fair trial by the expert advisor, who may be a paid professional, or as far as is possible the rider himself. It is also important to check that the papers, i.e. the pedigree, and the horse correspond from the point of view of age, colour and markings. If not, the purchase should not go ahead.

A veterinary examination is recommended in all cases.

The extent of the examination is governed by the price of the horse and the purpose for which it is intended. The vendor and the purchaser should agree on a veterinary surgeon or clinic, as well as responsibility for payment, and when the examination is to take place. The horse should be examined at the earliest possible opportunity. If the purchaser and the vendor are in agreement, a contract is formulated, either verbally or in writing. The written form is recommended especially in the case of contracts which promise legal minimum requirements. In all cases at least one of the following clauses, or a combination of several, should be included.

Legally free from fault

In Germany, when nothing else is agreed, the imperial decree of 27 March 1899 applies. In this case the purchaser is only protected against the six principal defects; hydrocephalus, glanders, windsucking, roaring, periodic ophthalmia, broken wind. The decree is based on the assumption that if the fault is discovered within fourteen days of purchase it was already present at the time of purchase. The vendor is therefore held responsible if these faults are discovered within the *warranty period* of fourteen days from the date the horse is handed over. However, the purchaser must notify the vendor of the defect at the latest within the next two days – the *notification period* – but if possible immediately after discovering the defect.

The *six week limitation period* follows the warranty period. Within this period the purchaser must have lodged a complaint, or filed a petition with evidence, if no agreement has been possible with the vendor over taking the horse back or exchanging him.

If the purchaser does not respect these time limits, he no longer has any legal redress unless he can prove some devious deception on the part of the vendor. The expiry date of these periods is determined with reference to the point at which the risk is transferred from the vendor to the purchaser. With the exception of horses sent out on trial prior to purchase, and of deferred, conditional sales, the risk is transferred at the point when the purchaser takes hold of the headcollar rope or reins with the intention of taking possession of the horse, or the transporter takes the horse with the intention of loading it. However, the point at which the risk is transferred should be specified in the sale agreement, especially if the vendor is to keep the horse for a period following the completion of the sale (liability insurance).

NB If the horse dies, the notification period begins on the day of his death.

Sale with trial

With this form of agreement the sale only comes into force once the trial period has passed without complaint. During this period it is the vendor who bears the full risk, which presupposes a high degree of trust on both sides.

Sale with agreement to exchange

The purchaser can return the horse within an agreed period if he does not like him. He undertakes, if he returns this horse, to accept another from the vendor. The vendor undertakes to supply another, with price adjustment where necessary.

Deferred, conditional sale

The sale comes into force on receipt of the positive results of the pre-sale veterinary examination, the date and the extent of which should be established beforehand. The purchaser learns in a relatively short time all he needs to know about the horse's physical condition. The vendor, on the other hand, can rest assured that any defects which crop up later or did not show up at the time are no longer his responsibility.

Sale where the horse is guaranteed 'sound and free from fault'

With this sort of sale the vendor is liable for major illnesses and faults, but not for any defects which do not result in the loss of value or usefulness of the horse. If no warranty period is agreed, the purchaser must be able to prove that the defect in question was already present when the risk was transferred to him. This can lead to problems in certain cases over where to draw the line between major and minor defects.

Sale pledging certain attributes

Provided the attributes are clearly defined, this form of contract is beneficial for vendor and purchaser alike. However, it does require a certain level of knowledge on either side. The attributes pledged do not have to be limited to soundness but can be extended to include pregnancy, level of training, ability, veterinary treatment and operations, etc. There is a difference between pledging certain attributes and singing a horse's praises.

However, more and more frequently, in spite of every precaution, purchaser and vendor are unable to reach an agreement over some objection or other. Legal proceedings can be taken, but this takes time. The *Deutsche Reiterliche Vereinigung* has therefore set up an arbitration committee which can take action once the ratification of the arbitration agreement has been agreed. The advantage of this arbitration procedure is that the case is dealt with rapidly and by experts.

APPENDIX

Below are described the principal defects encountered in the horse as set out in the imperial decree of 1899:

1 Glanders (Farcy)

Glanders is a malignant, epizootic disease affecting members of the horse family and caused by the glanders bacillus. It can be transmitted to man. It is characterized by the formation of nodules and lesions in the airways, lungs and skin. Infection is directly through the nasal discharge and the purulent discharge from the skin lesions, by digestive or respiratory routes. Depending on the location of the ulcers, it is known as nasal glanders, lung glanders or skin glanders (farcy). The incubation period is only three to five days. Glanders is a notifiable epizootic disease. All infected or suspect horses are destroyed and the carcasses disposed of. The stable should be shut off and disinfected. This disease has not occurred recently in Germany. In 1977 there were some cases of glanders in Turkey.

2 Hydrocephalus

Hydrocephalus is an incurable disease of the brain. The onset is either gradual or sudden (acute attack). The horse's level of consciousness is reduced.

3 Broken wind (heaves)

Broken wind is a respiratory problem caused by a chronic, incurable diseased condition of the lungs or heart. The incurable conditions which are classed as broken wind are chronic pulmonary emphysema; chronic bronchitis; chronic pneumonia (see Chapter 6); neoplasms in the lungs; heart valve defects and other incurable heart conditions.

4 Roaring (whistling)

Roaring is a respiratory disturbance caused by a chronic, incurable condition of the larynx or trachea and characterized by a clearly audible noise. Conditions responsible are laryngeal hemiplegia (see Chapter 6); neoplasms in, and deformities of, the larynx; chronic inflammation of the larynx and stenosis of the trachea.

5 Periodic Ophthalmia (inflammation of the inner eye, moon blindness)

Periodic ophthalmia consists of inflammatory changes in

the internal organs of the eye caused by internal influences. The definition is broader than that given in Chapter six as periodic ophthalmia. For legal purposes, any inflammatory processes of the iris, lens, retina and cavity of the eyeball are included, provided they are not caused by external violence. Changes due to external influences do not count as principal defects.

6 Windsucking (crib biting)

Windsucking is a trick which is defined as an opening of the pharynx accompanied by a clearly audible noise. Crib biting, in which the horse catches hold of, for instance, the manger or the top of the stable door, is the commonest form of windsucking. The horse is seen to contract the muscles on the underside of the neck, belch and swallow air. In windsucking alone, as opposed to crib biting, the horse does not catch hold of anything, but arches its neck, jerks its head forward, making characteristic lip movements, and emits a hiccoughing noise.

There is another form of windsucking (German: *Luftschnappen, Windschnappen*) in which air is swallowed with or without a hiccoughing noise, and without the horse catching hold of anything.

9. Horse Breeding

9(1) Total horse population

The graph of the development of the horse population shows clearly the enormous fluctuations caused by the complete restructuring of the market for non-Thoroughbred horses. In Germany at the beginning of the 1950s there were more than 1.5 million horses. Within twenty years, by 1970, the horse population had reached its lowest level, with a total of a quarter of a million. After this there was continuous growth of approximately 5 per cent per year due to the almost exclusive use of the horse for sport.

In conjunction with the rise in the total horse population, an *increase in the breeding stock population* also occurred, with corresponding fluctuations. In the case of the *German Riding Horse* the graph on page 238 shows that the increase began back in 1965 and was particularly sharp in the years 1970 to 1975. This can be traced back to the high level of prices at the beginning of the 1970s. At present 57,000 warmblood mares are registered with the breed associations of the Deutsche Reiterliche Vereinigung. The growth in the brood mare population has been even more rapid for *ponies* than for riding horses.

The stallion population increased in conjunction with the brood mare population. In the 1960s there were 247 registered stallions, but by 1982 this had risen to 1,541 privately owned stallions and 528 state owned stallions. There are currently approximately 1,600 stallions of different breeds licensed and recognised by the breed associations.

Within twenty years the population had risen nearly four-fold. However, there is now a marked stagnation

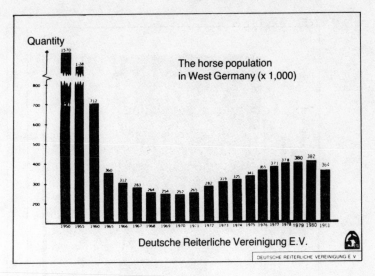

The horse population in West Germany (x 1,000)

Deutsche Reiterliche Vereinigung E.V.

due to the saturation of the market.

In a breakdown into individual pony breeds, by far the largest proportion belong to the *German Riding Pony* group (31.2 per cent), followed by the Haflinger (27.2 per cent), the Welsh (12.4 per cent) and the Icelandic (10.3 per cent).

The *coldblood industry* has been hardest hit by motorization. However, a certain residual population of coldblood breeding stock seems to have been preserved. At present there are still approximately 1,400 mares and 120 stallions (27 of whom are state-owned) in the stud books of the breed associations.

A synopsis of breeding stock population levels is given in the chart on page 240.

9(2) The organisation of the horse breeding industry

The first systematic development of horse breeding took place within the agricultural industry where, along with

237

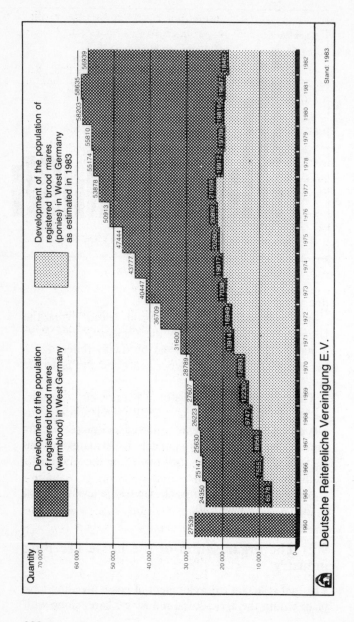

Quantity

Development of the population of registered brood mares (warmblood) in West Germany

Development of the population of registered brood mares (ponies) in West Germany as estimated in 1983

Deutsche Reiterliche Vereinigung E.V.

Stand 1983

other types of farm animal, the horse was bred for profit. This development owed much to the interest in horses for war.

When organised horse breeding first began, clubs were set up on a regional basis. In this way the first stallion co-operatives and societies evolved. Hence there were breeding stallions in the private sector as well as in the state studs. Even the responsibility for the stud books was gradually taken over by these societies. Later, it was from these that the first breed associations evolved, mostly on a provincial level.

Nowadays the breed associations are registered societies, that is, civilian bodies. They are recognised by the state and undergo regular checks. For a breed association to be recognised, it must conform to the law on animal breeding, the decree on breeders' associations and breeding enterprises, and the decree on stallion registration. The main duties of breed associations are:

☐ The identification and registration of breeding stock.
☐ Selective breeding within a strictly defined breeding programme, the practical expression of which is acceptance and registration of breeding stock in the stud book or stallion register.
☐ Assistance with marketing, usually by holding auctions, running sales centres and drawing up sales lists.

With the exception of the directorate for Thoroughbred breeding and racing, and the main association for the breeding and racing of trotters, all the breed associations are grouped together under the umbrella of the breeding section of the Deutsche Reiterliche Vereinigung. The breeding division co-ordinates the work of the breed associations and represents their interests in Germany and abroad.

A basic essential in the identification of horses which deserves mention is that the drawing up of an exact description of the colour and markings may only be carried out by a person appointed by the association.

239

	Warmbloods			Coldbloods			Ponies		
	1981	1982	±%	1981	1982	±%	1981	1982	±%
Registered mares	58,635	56,939	– 2.9	1,412	1,391	– 1.5	19,647	18,462	– 6.0
Admissions to breeding register	8,488	7,783	– 8.3	260	247	– 5.0	2,398	2,343	– 2.3
Stud stallions State owned	549	528	– 3.8	24	27	+ 12.5	27	29	+ 7.4
Privately owned	1,514	1,541	+ 1.8	70	89	+ 27.1	1,593	1,580	– 0.8
Total	2,063	2,069	+ 0.3	94	116	+ 23.4	1,620	1,609	– 0.7
Coverings By state stallions	24,499	22,018	–10.1	374	471	+ 25.9	563	506	–10.1
By privately owned stallions	23,143	22,008	– 4.9	1,010	1,196	+ 18.4	10,968	11,138	+ 1.6
Total	47,642	44,026	– 7.6	1,384	1,667	+ 20.5	11,531	11,644	+ 1.0
Registered foals	24,963	23,843	– 4.5	488	541	+ 10.9	5,926	5,987	+ 1.0
Licensed young stallions*	269	252	– 6.3	30	19	– 36.7	153	147	– 3.9

* Born 1979 and 1980

This person is also responsible for branding foals with the foal brand, which considerably increases the chance of ensuring the horse's identity. After identification and branding, a pedigree document is drawn up, although obviously this can only be done if the horse's parentage is above suspicion. The importance of the pedigree document cannot be overemphasised, because only with this is the horse entitled to be registered later on in the stud book of one of the breed associations – if it meets the minimum requirements from the point of view of external characteristics and performance. Moreover, the pedigree certificate is of primary importance in the registration of a horse for sporting purposes.

The keeping of stallions is of great importance in the organisation of the horse breeding industry, as is the collaboration between the private and state sectors in this respect. The state studs have had, in the past, considerable influence on the development of horse breeding: both East Prussian and Hanoverian horse breeding would have been unthinkable without them. This influence is now reduced.

However, the fact that horse breeding is subject to market forces in a way which no other branch of the agricultural industry is, means that, as was seen more than ever in the 1960s, the state studs represent the stabilising influence in the horse breeding industry. Maintaining the provincial studs is a promotional measure by the state, not the least important function of which is to make available quality, performance-tested stallions, which benefits both breeders and riders.

The breaking down of the different breeds of horse into distinct groups has long been a topic for discussion. After careful evaluation of all the arguments, the following divisions, based on the breed policies of the various

241

breeding zones, seems reasonable:

☐ Racehorses
  Thoroughbreds
  Trotters
☐ Riding horses
  Trakehners
  Arabians
  Regional warmbloods
☐ Ponies
☐ Coldbloods

9(3) **Racehorses**

9(3)i ENGLISH THOROUGHBRED

Into this category fall all those horses whose pedigree traces back in an unbroken line to the English ancestors listed in the first edition of the *General Stud Book*, which was published in 1793. The English Thoroughbred breed resulted from the crossing of the small, tough Galloways with oriental horses. Nowadays three Arabian stallions are considered to be the foundation sires of the Thoroughbred, namely the Byerley Turk, the Darley Arabian and the Godolphin Barb. The English Thoroughbred has been bred for racing for nearly two and a half centuries. The first record of racing results dates back to 1709, and from 1727 onwards a racing calendar was published regularly. It is racing which is the motor of the English Thoroughbred breeding industry. Of particular interest are the five Classic races for three-year-olds, namely:

☐ The 2,000 Guineas, run in April over 1 mile (1,600m) for colts and fillies (first run in 1809).
☐ The 1,000 Guineas, run in April over 1 mile (1,600m) for fillies only (1814).
☐ The Derby, run in June over 1½ miles (2,400m), for colts and fillies (1780).

☐ The Oaks, run in June over 1½ miles (2,400m), for
fillies only (1779).

☐ The St Leger, run in September over 1¾ miles
(2,900m), for colts and fillies (1776).

In Germany these Classics have the following counterparts: Henckel-Rennen, Schwarzgold-Rennen, Deutsches Derby, Preis der Diana and Deutsches St Leger.
Except for the Preis der Diana and the Deutsches St
Leger, which are respectively 300m and 700m shorter
than their English equivalents, the length and dates of
the races are the same. The first official race in Germany
was run in 1822 in Bad Doberan, Mecklenburg.

In Germany the stud book for Thoroughbreds is the
Allgemeine Deutsche Gestütbuch (ADGB), kept by the
directorate for Thoroughbred breeding and racing
(Directorium für Vollblutzucht und Rennen), which has
its headquarters in Cologne. At present there are approximately 2,000 registered mares – after the Second World
War there were only 450. This organisation is also
responsible for racing.

The Thoroughbred has always been used in warmblood breeding as an upgrading influence. There is no
question but that the riding horse breeding industry
cannot nor ever will be able to do without the Thoroughbred, whose stamina, speed and powers of recovery are
just as important for purposes of improvement as are
individual points of conformation such as shoulders and
withers. The important thing is knowing how much
Thoroughbred blood to use, since too much causes
temperament problems in warmblood breeding. On no
account must the addition of Thoroughbred blood lead to
the loss of valuable warmblood genes. In Germany at
present the use of Thoroughbred stallions on 8 to 10 per
cent of the mares is considered desirable.

9(3)ii TROTTERS

In theory the trotter owes its existence to the fact that

people need to get around quickly. Races were the natural outcome of this, and they in their turn encouraged the breeding of trotters, which evolved in various different locations.

The oldest breed of trotter is the Orlov Trotter. Count Orlov developed this breed at the end of the 18th century with the help of rigorous performance testing. He successfully used inbreeding as a means of consolidating the breed genetically. Crossing Orlov trotters with American trotters (Standardbreds) later resulted in the creation of the Russian Trotter, which is faster than the Orlov, but considerably slower than the Standardbred.

At almost the same time that the Orlov Trotter appeared, the Standardbred was created in America from very mixed origins. The Standardbred is characterised particularly by its speed over a short distance (1 mile). Also popular in America is the pacer, which is even faster than the trotter.

The third important breed is the French trotter, which originated in Normandy, from the same roots as the Anglo-Norman, by selective breeding based on trotting ability. Only a few years ago was the stud book closed so that no further Anglo-Normans could be accepted. It is worth noting that even today approximately one-third of French trotting races are conducted under saddle.

The breeding of trotters in Germany, which is based primarily on the American Standardbred, is however influenced nowadays by the French Trotter. Only minimal use is made of the trotter in warmblood breeding. One reason for this is the enormous variations in type. However, it is a known fact that the products of trotting stallions are characterised by their jumping ability, as was proven by the now almost legendary Halla, among others. The *Hauptverband für Traberzucht und -Rennen* is the body responsible for trotting racing and the keeping of the stud book. Its headquarters are in Kaarst.

9(4) Breeding Zones of the German Riding Horse (Deutsches Reitpferd)

Evolution – present day breeding policies

There has always been a great tradition of horse breeding in Germany. At the beginning of this century there were still four outlets for the stock produced: the army, industry, agriculture and sport. Not only did these outlets make different demands on the horse breeder, but each group also required different types of horse. The army required various types, from the light, fast, man-oeuvrable Hussar's horse, bred primarily by the East Prussians, to the powerful, steadfast artillery pole-horses, who came mainly from Hanover and Holstein, but also from Oldenburg. Industry required horses to pull heavy loads, a role which was filled by the cold-bloods. Agriculture, too, made varied demands on the horse. Depending on the soil and the country, anything might be required from a team of Trakehners, Hanoverians, Holsteins or Oldenburgs to East Friesian horses, the heaviest of the German warmbloods. The fourth outlet, sport, was of little significance at that time, and little attention was paid to it when drawing up breeding policies.

Because of the differing requirements of the market, the breeding zones were obliged to specialise in order to fulfil the wishes of particular groups of buyers, and at that period individual breeds came to be referred to by their district of origin.

As a result of increasing mechanisation and technology, industry and the army were the first to drop out as buyers of horses from the provincial studs. There was then a surplus of horses, since remounts for the army were no longer required, and outlets were almost exclusively agricultural. As these, too, dwindled a dramatic fall in the horse population began. Not until people living in the world of high technology discovered in riding a sport with which to fill their increasing amounts of

245

leisure time did horse breeding begin to come into its own again.

In the middle of the 1950s a drastic change in breeding policy took place. Obviously those zones which had stock that was already close in type to the now highly sought after sporting horse were at an advantage. In the revised breeding tactics, stallions of three breeds were used as 'improvers': the Trakehner, the Thoroughbred and the Arabian. Moreover, in the period that followed there was much intermingling of breeding stock, something which has continued at almost the same level up to the present day. As a result of this, horses from the different breeding zones of Federal Germany are now much closer both in type and geneologically. It can be seen more and more from the displays put on by the different regional studs that the differences in type and quality are greater within one region than between different regions.

For these reasons, on 22 April 1975, the breed associations decided on a breeding policy for a *German Riding Horse*, which was to include the horses from all the regional warmblood breeding zones:

The aim shall be to breed a quality, correct horse with 'clearly defined lines' and ground-covering, elastic paces full of supple impulsion; a horse which because of its temperament and nature and its 'ridability' is suitable for any branch of riding.

This formula for a common breeding policy under the general heading of *German Riding Horse* does not in any way signify the breakdown of independent breeding zones with their old traditions, or the erosion of their functions and rights. On the contrary, it removes outdated barriers to shared responsibility and benefits, and creates an internationally recognised product.

Breeding Zones

The map on page 247 shows the areas covered by the nine regional breeding zones, represented by their brands. A

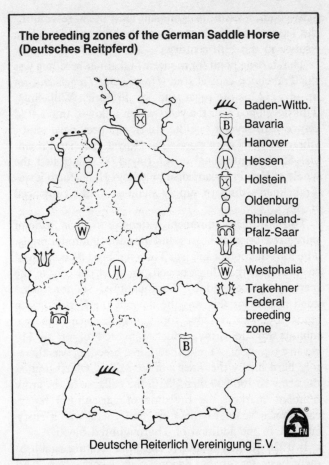

The breeding zones of the German Saddle Horse (Deutsches Reitpferd)

Baden-Wittb.
Bavaria
Hanover
Hessen
Holstein
Oldenburg
Rhineland-Pfalz-Saar
Rhineland
Westphalia
Trakehner Federal breeding zone

Deutsche Reiterlich Vereinigung E.V.

short section about each breed association is included below, but first of all those two groups which are active on a national level are discussed, namely Trakehners and Arabians.

9(4)i TRAKEHNER

The Trakehner's history is certainly the most varied of all the German horse breeds. It can be traced back to the

Schweiken, a small, insignificant local breed resembling the Tarpan and which was found by the crusaders in East Prussia in the 13th century.

The starting point for modern Trakehner breeding was the Trakehnen central stud (*Hauptgestüt Trakehnen*), set up in 1732, as the royal stud, by Friedrich Wilhelm I. This developed over the years which followed into a stud centre with several satellite studs, the provincial studs, where stallions were stood. The 'Royal Prussian Provincial Stud Regulations' of 17 July 1787 controlled the whole of East Prussian horse breeding. Henceforth it was Trakehnen's duty to supply stallions to the provincial studs.

To fulfil this requirement, extensive use was made of pure-bred oriental horses and English Thoroughbreds. The introduction of English Thoroughbred blood proved so successful that, for a period, up to 84 per cent of the mares were covered by Thoroughbred stallions. One good reason for this was the duty of the East Prussian studs to make available tough performance horse remounts for the army, which consisted of up to 110 cavalry regiments. Trakehnen horse breeding was therefore hard hit by the Treaty of Versailles, which limited the army to 100,000 men. With the collapse of the army remount market, the breeding of agricultural horses came once again to the fore, and there was a sharp cutback in the addition of Thoroughbred blood.

In 1926 the first stallion performance testing establishment was set up at Zwion, near Georgenburg. All potential provincial stud stallions were sent here for a year's rigorous testing. Only those stallions whose three basic gaits, and whose behaviour in harness, in heavy draught and under saddle, were satisfactory were accepted for stud.

Up until the end of the Second World War, East Prussia was the largest self-contained horse-breeding zone in the world. Even in 1939, 43,000 mares were covered, half of whom were registered in the stud book of the Prussian stud book society (*Stutbuchgesellschaft*). After the end of the war less than 1,000 breeding horses had reached the area which is now the German *Bundesrepublik*. Out of 18,000 registered brood mares, about 600 reached the *Bundesrepublik*, and of these only 18 were from the 350 strong herd of the central Trakehnen stud. The 1,300-km trek from East Prussia to West Germany had been the toughest performance test imaginable.

On 23 October 1947 the *Verband der Züchter und Freunde des Warmblutpferdes Trakehner Abstammung e.V.* or *Trakehner-Verband* (the Association for Breeders and Friends of Warmblood Horses of Trakehner Descent, or Trakehner Society) was set up as the successor to the East Prussian Stud Book Society (*Stutbuchgesellschaft*). After an initial drop in numbers for various reasons – in 1956 only 602 registered mares and 45 stallions were counted – the *Trakehner-Verband* grew to be the third largest breed association in West Germany, and now has more than 4,000 mares and nearly 300 stallions. Its main function – to preserve and promote the breeding of warmbloods of Trakehner descent – has succeeded beyond all possible predictions.

It is becoming apparent, particularly from Trakehner stallion licensing, which is centralised in Neumünster, that the Trakehner is capable of breeding true to type outside its original breeding area. It is worth noting that, no matter where they are bred, Trakehner stallions are only recognised if they are licensed at the central licensing session, where they can be compared with others of their age.

The Trakehner horse played a major part in upgrading the stock at the regional warmblood studs, particularly during the change-over in breeding policy. In a number of German studs Trakehner stallions founded their own stallion lines.

Perhaps the varied history of the Trakehner is best symbolised by the name *Tempelhüter*. Son of the

Thoroughbred Perfectionist and born in 1904, he first served at stud in Braunsberg, at the provincial state stud. In 1916 he became senior stallion at Trakehnen, where between 1916 and 1931 he covered 495 mares, who produced 333 foals, among them 65 stud stallions, 59 Trakehner brood mares and 195 auction horses (Köhler 1977). He was still alive in 1932 to see, on the occasion of the 200-year festival of the central Trakehner stud, the unveiling of his own memorial in front of the stud master's house. After the destruction of Trakehnen the statue was taken to Moscow, where it stands in front of the horse museum. After long negotiations the German Horse Museum in Verden succeeded in obtaining a cast of the original, which arrived in Verden in 1974 and now stands in front of the horse museum there.

9(4)ii ARABIAN

Allah spoke to the south wind, saying, 'I will cause a creature to come forth from you; take substance!' and so the Arabian horse was born. This story mirrors the legends which have grown up around the Arabian horse, who obviously has the same origins as other breeds. The golden age of the Arab began with Islam and was due to the many advantages gained by fast, agile troops during the Islamic wars of the faith. Soon afterwards, with the spread of Islam, the first Arab horses arrived in Europe, predominantly in Spain and southern France. Further influences can be traced to the crusades, continuing into the 13th century. Hence the Arab exercised an influence on the European breeds, not least the English Thoroughbreds, much earlier than it would have done by means of planned, peace-time imports.

The breeding of Arab horses can be said to have begun in Germany in 1810 with the founding of the Weil stud in Neckartal by King Wilhelm I of Württemberg, as he later became. This stud influenced the most eminent breeding areas in Europe until it closed down in 1932. However, the valuable stock was not lost but was found new homes. The stud's success, and more especially the Arab horse itself, inspired numerous smaller breeders, so that Arab breeding in Germany today is a small but not insignificant force. The *Verband der Züchter des Arabischen Pferdes*, the breeders' association, has in its stud books at present 295 stallions 'and 1,039 mares. The association's stud book comprises the following sections:

Pure-bred Arabian (German initials: AV)
The ideal pure-bred is the classical type of desert Arab bred by the Bedouin: small tapering head, with a dished face; small muzzle and broad forehead; prominent eyes; small ears, height between 145 and 158cm; very intelligent and of good disposition.

Horses who were imported from the East bore the abbreviation 'Or. Ar' (Original Arabian) after their names, and their descendants 'AV' (*Arabisch Vollblut* – Pure-bred Arabian).

Arabian (A)
The aim is to breed a horse in a 'bigger frame', which still has clearly identifiable Arab characteristics.

Anglo-Arab (AA)
The Anglo-Arab should combine the advantages of both breeds, those of the Arab (AV and A) and those of the English Thoroughbred. Neither the proportion of Arab blood nor that of Thoroughbred must be less than 25 per cent.

Anglo-Arab Half-bred (AAH)
The Half-bred Anglo-Arab may contain up to 25 per cent genes of another breed.

Part-bred (V)
Horses in this category also appear in a section of the stud book of another breed association. They must contain at least 50 per cent of the above-mentioned origins.

The Arab breeders' association carries out a central stallion licensing session every year. The stallions have to undergo the same performance tests as those carried out in warmblood breeding.

The Arab horse has had an enormous influence over a long period on warmblood breeding. After the up-grading process has finished Arab blood is only intro-duced, for various reasons, in strictly controlled doses. However, its influence will remain, as is testified by the example of the successful Hanoverian stallion Kurier von Kurde (AA). Another memorable example is Burnus (AA), sire of numerous performance horses.

The Arab is also particularly important in pony breed-ing because of its good temperament and disposition. The Arab influence is becoming more and more appa-rent, particularly in the German Riding Pony (*Deutsches Reitpony*).

9(4)iii HANOVERIAN

As far back as the 15th century there were the beginnings of organised breeding in the Hanoverian breeding area, in the Hoya district. How highly the lower Saxons esteemed the horse was apparent not only from the crossed horses' heads on the gables of their houses, but also from the fact that the horse featured on the coat of arms of the ruling dynasty, the guelphs.

It was the state stud at Celle which did most to influence the development of Hanoverian horse breed-ing. The stud was founded in 1735, by King George II of Great Britain and the Duke of Brunswick-Lüneburg, with 12 stallions, who stood for the first time in 1736.

Unlike Trakehnen, Celle has never been obliged to make money to fill the coffers of the ruling dynasty. Celle was founded 'for the good of the subjects'. This was reflected in the order that farmers' mares were to be given priority over those belonging to the nobility and officers. Up until 1770 most of the stallions who stood at Celle came from Holstein, though there were also

Danish, East Prussian, Neapolitan and Andalusian, as well as a few English stallions among them. In spite of heavy losses during the Napoleonic wars, the influence of the Celle stud on horse breeding in Lower Saxony continued to grow. Stallions kept privately in Lower Saxony frequently provided more horses for agricultural work than did the state stud, but they hardly figured at all in the development of actual Hanoverian breeding (Schlie 1967).

At the beginning of the 19th century the Celle stud drew its supply of stallions primarily from Mecklenburg. It also obtained numerous stallions from England, most of them Yorkshire Coach and Cleveland Bay horses. There were also a few Norfolks. The breeding policy in Hanover was both to produce a strong warmblood horse to meet the requirements of agriculture, and to provide remounts for the army. In contrast to the Trakehners, however, the emphasis was always on the former. There was a glut of horses just after each world war because the army ceased to buy up the horses bred by the regional studs. The change in breeding policy after the Second World War was triggered off by the Swiss buying remounts for the cavalry from about 1948 onwards. Although these purchases of remounts brought a little relief to the market, the Hanoverian breeders suffered just as much as other horse breeders from the advancing mechanisation of agriculture. By 1963 the Celle stud, which in 1948 still had 539 stallions, had a stock of just 149; in fifteen years it had disposed of 75 per cent of its stallions – although this was obviously also a unique opportunity for selection in the breeding of the Hanoverian.

The revised breeding programme involved the use of Thoroughbred, Trakehner and Arab blood, and in this the Hanoverians were lucky to have the benefit of some very good East Prussian stallions who had finished up at Celle and Hunnesrück after the flight from East Prussia. Today, with more than 16,000 registered brood mares and 256 stallions, 83 per cent of whom are at Celle, Hanover is numerically by far the largest breeding zone. With its stallions Hanover has influenced not only the other West German breeding zones but also numerous other countries whose horse breeding is based on the Hanoverian.

The Westercelle stallion testing station, which was founded in 1927 and in 1975 moved to Adelheidsdorf, has influenced much more than Hanoverian horse breeding. With a capacity for more than 100 horses, Adelheidsdorf is the largest testing station in the *Bundesrepublik*.

Mention must also be made of the stallion rearing centre at Hunnesrück, which since 1921 has been responsible for supplying Celle with stallions. As has been stated, many of the stallions at Hunnesrück came from Mecklenburg. However, at the beginning of the 1920s, owing to inflation the German studs were passed over by foreign buyers. This led to a significant reduction in the amount of young Mecklenburg stallions bought by Hunnesrück, which instead turned its attention to stabilising prices at a time when German-bred foals were very difficult to sell. Hunnesrück has now reverted to its original function of a stallion-rearing centre.

9(4)iv WESTPHALIAN
With almost 10,000 registered brood mares, the Westphalian breeding zone is the second most powerful warmblood breeding zone in the *Bundesrepublik*. Although the founding of the Warendorf state stud in 1826 and the stallion licensing decree a year later can be considered as the beginning of organised horse breeding in Westphalia, breeding there was experimental for some time after this date. Since Westphalia was never a 'remount province', more emphasis was placed on agricultural use than in any other breeding zone. Even after the beginning of organised breeding, there was still an enormous diversity of breeds of stallions there: Thor-

oughbreds, Trakehners, Hanoverians, Oldenburgs and East Friesians were used. Towards the end of the 19th century the use of East Friesian and Oldenburg blood was stepped up. However, the use of these stallions did not prove satisfactory, and Anglo-Norman stallions were brought in to try to restore characteristics which had been lost, for example boldness, clean legs and paces. In the event, the use of these stallions was almost as unsuccessful as that of trotter stallions.

In 1904 the *Westfälische Pferdestammbuch* (Westphalian Geneological Register) was founded. At the members' convention, in 1920, it was decided to organise warmblood breeding along the same lines as in Hanover, which was the turning point in the history of the Westphalians. Westphalia now influences other zones with its breeding stock in the same way that Hanover does. It should be mentioned that during the changeover in the breeding programme Westphalia did not introduce East Prussian blood.

The sale of Westphalian horses which, because of the high standard of riding in the province, traditionally took place mainly direct from the stud, is supported by regular auctions in the Halle Münsterland. A third alternative was provided in 1977 with the setting up of the *Zentrum für Ausbildung und Verkauf Handorf* (Handorf Training and Marketing Centre) near Münster.

Westphalian horses have recently achieved a high level of success in sport, examples being the World Champions Ahlerich and Fire.

Westphalian horse breeding was greatly influenced by the founding in 1826 by the Prussian stud authorities of the Warendorf state stud, with 140 stallions. Westphalian performance testing is linked to the stud, although since 1982 this has also taken place in the Pferdezentrum Münster-Handorf. Since 1968 the *Deutsche Reitschule* (German National Riding School) has been annexed to it. Here professional riders, qualified amateurs and competition specialists are trained and examined.

9(4)v HOLSTEIN

Largely surrounded by sea, Schleswig-Holstein was destined by nature to be a horse breeding area on account of its climate and its high proportion of grazing land. According to Thun (1976), the first flowering of the Holstein horse was back in the early middle ages, when it was supported by the four powers: the monasteries, the nobility, the Danish monarchy and the peasantry.

In more recent times the Holstein has influenced horse breeding in other areas of Germany, including, as has already been mentioned, Hanoverian breeding at the time of the founding of the Celle state stud. Holstein breeding policies, in common with those of other breeds, took into account the interests of both the army and agriculture, with their differing requirements.

Since the high demand for Holstein horses had resulted in their being in short supply, in 1867 the Prussian breeding authorities set up the Schleswig-Holstein state stud at Traventhal. Naturally the stud continued to pursue the aim of producing horses for use by the cavalry, which did not completely fulfil the needs of the farming fraternity. In 1891 they set up their own Holstein association, the *Holsteiner Verband*, and in 1894 added to this the Elmshorn riding and driving school, which was responsible for training and marketing and also for keeping the stallions. Thus the people of Holstein did not have the same positive contact with their state stud as, for example, those in Hanover and East Prussia had with theirs. This relationship did not improve very much when the stallions had to be sold to the state stud after the Second World War. It must be mentioned that in Holstein for a long time there were two warmblood associations, that of the highlands and that of the marshy lowlands, and that these did not merge until 1935. The recession in horse breeding in the 1950s and 1960s finally led to the state stud being dissolved, its stallions returning to the ownership of the association. Holstein is the only breeding zone in the *Bundesrepublik* where the association looks after its own stallions. It is still based at Elmshorn.

The foundations of the revised breeding programme aimed at producing the modern riding horse were fast coach horses, who had, however, already shown that they possessed riding horse qualities. Up-grading was achieved by liberal use of English Thoroughbred stallions, so much so that at times it was feared the Thoroughbred would take over completely. At present the Holstein association is at the end of a consolidating phase, during which, through methodical counter-selection, the valuable genes of the original Holstein population have been restored. Although this endeavour has not been directly helped by the introduction of Anglo-Norman blood, a small number of stallions of this breed have given good results and have influenced Holstein horse breeding for the better.

Considering the fact that the Holstein breeding zone, with approximately 2,900 mares, can in no way compare numerically with the Westphalian or indeed the Hanoverian zones, it is noteworthy that Holstein has at almost all periods produced large numbers of performance horses. This was evident not least at the 1982 World Championships, when Holstein horses won silver medals in all three disciplines.

9(4)vi OLDENBURG

Oldenburg horse breeding has been favoured not only by natural conditions, but also by a continuous line of sovereigns who looked more than kindly on this activity. The first who deserves a mention is Count Johann von Oldenburg, who in 1580 imported oriental, Spanish and Neapolitan horses. However, the first great flowering of the Oldenburg took place under his son, Count Anton Günter (1603–67) known as the 'Stable-master of the Holy Roman Empire'. The Count further promoted horse breeding by founding schools where farmers could be instructed in the keeping and use of horses.

In 1819 the first licensing law was passed, and in 1820 the first licensing session took place. In 1861 came the publication of the first volume of the Oldenburg stud book, and 1897 was an all-important year for it saw the passing of the Oldenburg horse breeding law, which in theory still holds good today. The Oldenburg brand, also introduced in 1897, is still in use today in the same form.

The Oldenburg horse was for a long time the most uniform in type and geneology. The aim was to breed a heavy coach horse, equally suited to hard work on the land and to making up an imposing team to draw the ruler's coaches. From, at the latest, the beginning of this century until the end of the 1960s an absolute minimum of outside blood was used. The use of the Derby winner Lupus (TB) did as little towards changing the direction of Oldenburg breeding as did the Anglo-Norman Condor, only serving to introduce foreign genes into the Oldenburg stock which had otherwise remained pure. After the Second World War it was the Oldenburg which was being bred the most extensively around Germany and abroad. It was held in the highest repute.

It is, therefore, in no way surprising that in the traditional breeding zone the change in the breeding programme was very late in starting and involved massive doses of Thoroughbred blood, a process which continues today. Oldenburg is at present going through a consolidation phase, assisted in particular by stallions from Hanover and France. At present there are 102 stallions standing at stud in Oldenburg, which has always had a flourishing private stallion industry. Of these, eight (i.e. 8 per cent) are Thoroughbreds, one is a Trakehner, eight are Anglo-Normans, two are Anglo-Arabs, 39 are Hanoverians (i.e. 38 per cent) and 40 are Oldenburgs (i.e. 39 per cent). The successes of the Oldenburg horse in competitions show that this experienced, handy breed has managed the transition into the modern riding horse in a very short time.

9(4)vii RHINELAND

For a long time Rhineland was the leading coldblood breeding area in Germany. Coldbloods were superior to warmbloods on the heavy, fertile land of the Rhine plain, so that in 1876 a policy of breeding Rhenish horses along the lines of the Belgian coldbloods was initiated. The Rhenish-German coldblood, bred from Belgian foundations, achieved world-wide renown. Naturally it was the coldbloods which were hardest hit by advancing mechanisation. Attempts to produce F-1 hybrids for use as riding horses by crossing Rhenish coldbloods with highly bred stallions failed on account of the immense weight of the Rhenish.

Although the Rhenish breeders could hardly fail to appreciate that it was impossible for the breeding of coldbloods on an agricultural basis to continue, they were not prepared to give up horse breeding entirely. So they turned to warmblood breeding instead. With a high level of technical knowledge, and an equally high outlay of capital, the Rhenish breeders bought from the top breeding zones the foundations for what is now the Rhineland warmblood. This horse compares very favourably with the top breeds, as has been shown by the performance of the breeding zone at the state stud displays. In the Rhineland breeding area there are some excellent Trakehner as well as numerous Hanoverian and Westphalian stallions. The Northern-Rhine/Westphalian state stud at Warendorf has also considerably influenced the positive development of Rhineland horse breeding.

9(4)viii HESSEN

Made up of small farms, Hessen was never a natural horse breeding area. Nevertheless, in 1982, with approximately 4,000 registered brood mares, Hessen lay in fifth place numerically in the *Bundesrepublik*. In quality, too, the German Riding Horse from Hessen can hold its own with the other breeding zones.

At the beginning of this century Hessen was still

largely a coldblood breeding zone. When it later began warmblood breeding it was on Oldenburg foundations. It experienced a great deal of difficulty in changing over to the modern breeding programme, which involved the use of Thoroughbred and Trakehner blood. The Dillenburg stud played an important part in this, as indeed it continues to do today. The central Prussian stud at Beberbeck must also be mentioned, because until it was dissolved between the two world wars it provided a large proportion of the stallions for Dillenburg.

9(4)ix BADEN-WÜRTTEMBERG

In 1978 the Baden-Württemberg breeding association was formed by merging three associations: Württemberg, South Baden and North Baden. Württemberg horse breeding has long suffered not only from the vicissitudes of the climate but also, and above all else, because of the political situation. In spite of this the central stud, which is the state stud at Marbach an der Lahn, is the oldest of the German state studs, having been founded in 1573. The first encouraging results were destroyed by the thirty year war.

Until the 1960s the Württemberg warmblood consisted of a cross between Norman stallions and indigenous mares, who contained oriental blood. Agricultural use featured in the forefront of the breeding policy. The people of Württemberg liked to describe this agricultural horse as a 'gentleman-farmer'.

Large quantities of the best type of Trakehner stallions were used in the revised breeding programme. For this reason Baden-Württemberg can also be said to count as a Trakehner breeding area, although Trakehner blood is no longer being used to the same extent. In the central stud, the Marbach state stud, performance testing of the young Baden-Württemberg stallions also takes place. It should be mentioned that the young breeding stallions are no longer licensed at two and a half years but a year later, after performance testing, which in this area, with its exceptionally difficult terrain, is the most demanding in the whole of the *Bundesrepublik*.

9(4)x RHINELAND-PFALZ-SAAR

The Rhineland-Pfalz-Saar breeding association was created in 1977 from the merger of the two breeding associations Pfalz-Saar and Rhineland-Nassau. This breeding zone on the French border has suffered a great deal from political circumstances, as has the Zweibrücken state stud, which is some 200 years old and which has changed hands repeatedly between France and Germany. This, definitely the smallest of German state studs, not only issues the characteristic regional brand but also has a marked influence on breeding in the region. Rhineland-Pfalz-Saar is a young, up-and-coming breeding zone of German Riding Horses.

9(4)xi BAVARIAN

In the past when warmblood breeding in Bavaria was mentioned, it was almost exclusively the Rottal, a tributary of the river Inn, which came to mind. Originally based on English half-breds, Normans, Zweibrücker stallions and Clevelands, the Rottaler drew very close to the Oldenburg following the use of Oldenburg stallions. Present-day breeding of the German Riding Horse is based largely on Hanoverians and Westphalians, and on Thoroughbreds and Trakehners introduced for upgrading purposes.

The traditional Bavarian state stud at Landshut was moved in 1980 to Schwaiganger, where the Bavarian authorities are constructing a horse breeding centre which should serve as an example to the rest of the horse breeding world, just as Bavaria has often pointed the way in other spheres of animal breeding. The Bavarian stallion performance testing takes place on the Olympic ground at Munich-Riem, also the site of the Bavarian Riding Horse auctions.

261

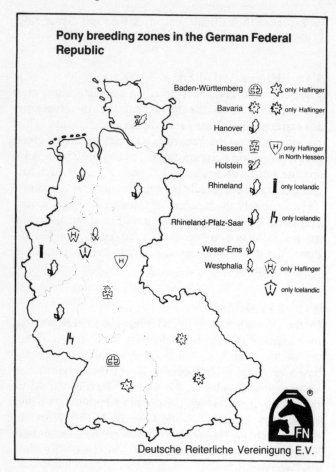

Pony breeding zones in the German Federal Republic

Baden-Württemberg — only Haflinger

Bavaria — only Haflinger

Hanover

Hessen — only Haflinger in North Hessen

Holstein

Rhineland — only Icelandic

Rhineland-Pfalz-Saar — only Icelandic

Weser-Ems

Westphalia — only Haflinger

— only Icelandic

Deutsche Reiterliche Vereinigung E.V.

9(5) Ponies

The ponies bred in Germany today are mainly of British and Scandinavian origin, though to a limited extent ponies from East and South European countries and native large pony breeds, such as the Haflinger, the Dülmen and Nordkirchen wild ponies, also feature.

9(5)i HAFLINGER

The Haflinger was first bred in the mountains and valleys of the South Tyrol. Hafling itself, on a plateau near Meran, still has its own stallion station and herd of mares. Today the Haflinger pony is found all over the world, and has gained friends in many countries thanks to its kind temperament, its attractive chestnut colour and flaxen mane, and its strong constitution. Originally the Haflinger was a sure-footed mountain pack-horse. Transporting loads in the mountains and the difficult terrain of the high-lying areas was among its tasks, as well as working the mountain fields.

Haflinger breeding areas in Germany are the Bavarian Alps, the Allgäu and, since the last war, Hessen and Westphalia, where Haflingers came to be used largely as small agricultural horses. Nowadays the Haflinger is mainly a leisure horse for riding and driving. For several years attempts have been underway, especially in Bavaria, to up-grade the Haflinger by the use of Arab blood, and some useful riding ponies ('Arabo-Haflinger') have resulted from these crosses.

9(5)ii NORWEGIAN FJORD

The Fjord pony comes from the Fjord region of West Norway. In its homeland it is known as the 'Westland horse' and is used primarily in agriculture. After the last war the Fjord spread throughout the whole of North and West Germany as a robust, frugal pony for light agricultural work. In addition to its attractive appearance, with its striking colour, its upright mane and an eel-stripe extending right down to its tail, it is a very economical, good-natured pony, soundly and solidly built, with a very straight top line. Above all, the loins should be well muscled. A strong neck, handsome head and lively eye are distinguishing characteristics.

The mechanisation of agriculture meant that this breed, too, was no longer required to work the land, so that attempts began to adapt it for riding purposes. Good results were achieved in the Hessen breeding zone by selective breeding from the light, elegant types. This resulted in the production of useful riding ponies, who are employed today mainly for leisure riding. The use on Fjord mares of stallions of other breeds such as the Arab or the English Thoroughbred was successful in only a few cases.

9(5)iii ICELANDIC

Horses have been kept and bred on the island of Iceland since 941 AD. They were taken there by the Vikings to be used as pack ponies and also for meat, and having survived their Spartan environment, have emerged as undemanding, tough animals with plenty of spirit. In its homeland the Icelandic has been bred without any admixture of outside blood for about 800 years.

The breed is characterised by its special gaits: apart from the ordinary basic walk, trot and canter, the Icelandic also has the ability to pace or tölt, the latter being a type of fast, four-beat walk. Long distances can be covered at the tölt without fatigue to either horse or rider. The Icelandic stands approximately 125 to 140cm high. There are two basic types, the rather more elegant, smaller type and the solid, heavier type. Although any colours are permitted, chestnuts are by far the commonest.

Over the last ten years the breed has become widespread in Germany and Western Europe. A riders' and breeders' group is responsible for organising competitions specially aimed at the Icelandic on a federal level, and also on a West European level. There are pacing and tölting races, as well as other competitions, such as obedience tests and so on. The shows are large, with a high level of entries and much enthusiasm on the part of the owners. Owing to its specialised gaits, the Icelandic is particularly suited to leisure riding. It should not be crossed with other breeds, otherwise its original characteristics will be lost.

9(5)iv WELSH

The commonest riding ponies in Europe today are the various types of Welsh pony, which originated in Wales. It developed over the centuries into a highly esteemed pack and draught pony which was much in demand, and was also used as a pit pony. The original Welsh Mountain Pony has been improved over the years, first of all with Arab blood, and it is to the Arab that it owes its prevalent grey colouring. Welsh ponies are lively and alert and, although wilful, they have a kind temperament. Today in their homeland they are divided into four sections, depending on size and also on the admixture of outside blood.

Section A, the Welsh Mountain Pony, has a small, finely modelled head with large eyes, and a strong, solid body with very hard, slender limbs, although some are more solidly built and have a small tuft of hair at the back of the fetlock. It stands up to 122cm* and is bred in all colours except piebald and skewbald. Welsh Mountain Ponies have been imported into Germany and have been bred there since 1965. The breed has established itself extraordinarily quickly.

Section B, the Welsh Pony, which is bred up to 137cm in England, is very much in demand. The question of type in this breed is constantly under discussion, and it is apparent from looking at this somewhat larger pony that it has been influenced much more by outside blood than the Section A, and that, as the size has increased so the Welsh Mountain Pony characteristics have been lost. In Germany Section B ponies established themselves quickly, since they are very suitable as sporting mounts for children.

Alongside the Section B Welsh Pony is bred the *Section C* Welsh Pony of Cob Type. These ponies derive mostly

* In Britain the height limits sometimes vary from the average sizes stated in this German book.

from Section A or B crosses or through crossing with Welsh Cobs. They are more sturdy generally and are solidly built. In type they are closer to the Welsh Cob than to the Section A and B ponies.

In England the Section D Welsh Cob is above 137cm (usually between about 142 and 158cm) but there is no upper limit. The Welsh Mountains have been the home of the Welsh Cob for many years. Cobs are strong and tough, with a flowing, ground covering action. Because of their jumping ability they are good ponies for cross-country riding and hunting.

9(5)v NEW FOREST

This most primitive of pony breeds has been preserved in the New Forest, a district west of Southampton, over the course of centuries. The ponies run completely free in the forest, winter and summer alike. To keep the breed going, stallions are put with the free-roaming herds. The stallions must be approved beforehand by the authorities. Studs, which have been set up on the edge of the New Forest area, breed from actual forest-produced stock, their aim being to try to improve the breed further and to produce a suitable mount for adults and youngsters alike.

The New Forest Pony stands between about 130 and 148cm high and is found in all colours except piebald and skewbald and blue-eyed cream. It is an ideal pony for young riders since its size enables it to cope with the demands of present-day competition riding. It has a very kind temperament and can be ridden by children as young as ten to twelve years. However, it can also be used as a riding animal by older children and even adults.

The New Forest has a typical pony face – sometimes with a rather long head – and is solidly built. It is exceptionally receptive and therefore is suitable for dressage and jumping. However, its origins and its natural ability also make it suitable for hunting.

9(5)vi DARTMOOR

This attractive pony, originating from the Dartmoor area of south-west England, stands between about 116 and 127cm. The preferred colours are black, brown and bay, with as few white markings as possible. Its original environment has enabled it to survive in very harsh conditions, and it is able to carry heavy loads over long distances. The breed has only achieved limited popularity in Germany, yet because of its friendly nature and kind temper it is an ideal first pony for children. It has also shown itself to be a good pony for crossing with larger stallions to produce Riding Ponies.

9(5)vii CONNEMARA

This pony takes its name from the region of Connemara on the west coast of Ireland. It varies considerably in appearance, since it may stand between about 132 and 147cm and comes in different types. It is conditioned by the harsh living conditions of its homeland, where until very recently it was left to run wild, often never seeing a stable. Today the Connemara enjoys enormous popularity. It established itself very quickly outside Ireland, especially in the USA, and also in England and on the Continent. It has gained a good foothold in German pony breeding circles, too.

Connemaras are compact ponies, very deep through the girth, strongly built and 'standing over a lot of ground'. They have well set on necks, muscular, sloping shoulders, correct limbs and excellent paces. All colours are permittçd except piebald and skewbald. Duns are commonly found, and in more recent times, greys have gained in numbers. Their particular talent for jumping can be attributed to their Irish origins.

Since hunting is very popular in Ireland, Connemara ponies are bred specially for the qualities this requires. Hence they are good, steady ponies for cross-country riding and are suitable for carrying youngsters as well as adults for long distances over uneven terrain. It is perhaps not generally realised that the Connemara is commonly used as a base for breeding hunters.

9(5)viii GERMAN MOORLAND PONIES

In Germany there are only two native pony breeds, the Dülmen and the Nordkirchen, both of which come from Westphalia. Moorland ponies have bred in Merfelder Bruch, near Dülmen, for over 600 years, the first recorded sighting being in 1316. Over the years there have been frequent admixtures of outside blood, namely English pony stallions and Eastern European Koniks. Nordkirchen ponies were once bred by the Duke of Arenberg. A small stock of them is still kept and bred today in private hands.

The Dülmen and Nordkirchen ponies used to be popular for light agricultural work. Nowadays there are some pleasing, elegant children's riding ponies among them, the result of successful crosses carried out in Westphalia with Arab stallions. The size of the moorland ponies is approximately between 125 and 140cm. Common colours are blue or yellow dun with an eel stripe, and zebra marks on the forelegs.

9(5)ix GERMAN RIDING PONY (DEUTSCHES REITPONY)

In Germany, as in the other European countries, a variety of different crosses has finally resulted in a pony breed in its own right, with its own specifications and ideals. The model for the German Riding Pony is the British Riding Pony, which has evolved from crosses between different breeds. In England these Riding Ponies are bred principally by crossing Arabs and Thoroughbreds with the so-called basic ponies, which are usually pure-breds belonging to one of the native pony breeds. In Germany these procedures are imitated, and very successfully. Westphalia in particular has made a name for itself in this field.

However, Riding Ponies are also bred in the other

regions of the *Bundesrepublik* and the best ones are as good as successful English ponies. The use of Arab stallions has proved particularly successful. The aims in breeding are clearly defined: to produce a pony suitable for competition, for use particularly by young riders and children, and which can cope with the many aspects of equestrian competitions. The most desirable height is 140cm and above. The pony must also have a kind temperament, good conformation and good paces, and be solidly built.

9(5)x SHETLAND

The Shetland, one of the smallest pony breeds in the world, is to be found today in all countries, both in and outside Europe. Shetland ponies are native to the Shetland islands, where they were used for general-purpose work in a very poor agricultural economy. However, they later quickly became established outside their homeland as popular companions for children. They also make particularly good driving ponies for adults.

The average height of a Shetland is about 101.50cm. Variations do occur, from a miniature pony of about 75cm to a large Shetland standing some 115cm. However, the British Shetland Pony Stud Book Society does not include these variations, specifying that Shetland ponies must not exceed 106.5cm. Although black is the foundation colour, Shetland ponies may be of any colour. Piebalds and skewbalds are very popular and recently there has been a good market for palominos, duns and chestnuts.

The Shetland Pony should have a small, quality head; small ears; small muzzle, with large nostrils, and large, kind eyes. The mane should fall on both sides of the neck and the tail should reach the ground. The summer coat is smooth and silky. The winter coat should be very thick with a good under-layer, thus enabling a pony to spend the whole winter out of doors. A Shetland should have a lively, merry temperament, but must also be quiet and well-behaved. Ideal conformation includes a short, strong back; good depth of girth; sturdy, powerful legs; a pronounced 'double rump' ('pony croup'), and small, hard, open feet which will carry the pony easily and safely in all gaits.

9(6) Coldbloods

The coldblood category comprises all horses belonging to a group of breeds which have a high bodyweight and are bred for heavy draught. In languages other than German the terms 'heavy horses' and 'draught horses' are also used. The golden age of the coldblood was the second half of the 19th and the first half of the 20th centuries, numbers being regulated by the requirements of industry and agriculture.

Owing to mechanisation, the coldblood horse has been almost completely superseded in Germany. At present there remains in federal Germany only a residual stock of 1,100 mares and 70 stallions. It is to be hoped that it will be possible to preserve this small stock. However, in some Western countries the coldblood breeding industry continues to thrive. In France, Belgium and Italy, for instance, coldblood horses are bred for meat, and the quality of the meat and the daily increases in production suggest that horse meat is becoming a serious challenge to the beef industry. German eating habits rule out this use. Attempts at crossing coldbloods with Thoroughbred stallions with a view to producing active riding horses were unsuccessful. This can be attributed partly to the particular characteristics of the coldbloods bred in Germany, but also to the fact that there was plenty of Riding Horse stock already available.

Nowadays the coldblood is used to a very limited extent on the land, but it is being channelled into forestry work and into special assignments such as tree nurseries, where it has a use even in a high technology situation. Another important use is for advertising purposes, for example in teams of dray horses. In England the cold-blood has become a popular show and display horse, its public appeal being on a level with that of top equestrian sports.

The Rhenish-German coldblood, with its stallions standing 160 to 170cm and weighing 1,000kg, is no longer bred in Rhineland. There are still 18 stallions and 126 mares in Westphalia, but the coldbloods bred there fall a long way short of the size and weight of the Rhenish Coldbloods.

Even the numbers of the once famous Schleswig Coldblood have fallen to only 4 stallions and approximately 50 mares.

Numerically the coldblood is best represented in Bavaria, where there are 27 stallions and about 650 mares. The demonstration by the Southern German coldbloods at the State Studs Display in Munich in 1976 showed that the small stock of coldbloods which remains is of very high quality indeed.

The Black Forest Chestnut breed in particular deserves a mention: this lightweight, clean-legged cold-blood was formerly suited to the hilly terrain and small farms, and is used today as a driving horse and pack horse in the Black Forest area, where it serves as a tourist attraction.

9(7) Performance Testing and the Breeding System

There is a long tradition of performance testing in horse breeding. Although the racing of horses certainly grew out of a love for competition, and not as a means of evaluating the breeding potential of the animals concerned, the latter was a welcome by-product, as it were. The importance of the horse in war led finally to the rapid introduction of performance testing into the warm-blood breeding industry. The requirements of agriculture, which differed considerably from those of the army, then served to modify the make-up of the tests. When the policy changed completely in favour of breeding riding horses, there was a complete revision of performance criteria. In the modern riding horse breeding system there are now many different performance tests, the significance of which is described in the following section.

Riding Horses
Riding horse performance testing presents the breeder with a problem. There are now many facets, not just one, to be considered, since the aim is to produce a horse who can take part in many fields of activity. In addition, conformation and appearance are of tremendous economic importance. Another problem is that hardly any of the performance characteristics, and in particular none of the essential ones, can be measured objectively.

The following plan shows the inter-relation between the assessment of conformation and performance at the various stages of the selection procedure. The procedure shown on the plan relates to stallion selection:

First step
   Assessment of foals before weaning from the point of view of pedigree and conformation.
Second step
   The same criteria are used for the assessment which takes place at two and a half years.
Third step
   Performance testing, at testing station, in individual disciplines.
Fourth step
   Evaluation from competition results of progeny.

At present undoubtedly the most important aspect of performance testing in riding horse breeding is the testing in different disciplines undergone by the young stallions at the testing station. Firstly, it allows sufficiently reliable data to be obtained; secondly, it enables the subsequent selection to take place relatively early on, so that there is no big 'generation gap'. In order to obtain reliable statistics, however, the individual tests must take place in conditions which are as far as possible standardised, that is at a station where sufficient numbers of horses are being tested, and within a specified period. The length of time allowed for testing must be kept as short as possible so as not to make it too expensive, but it must be as long as is necessary to produce meaningful results. As things stand at the moment, a period of 100 days is considered the minimum and has been prescribed as such for stallion licensing purposes. Through repeated assessments of the stallions by several judges in separate assessment processes, and the use of experienced test riders – for example to judge how easy the horse is to ride – the testing establishments are endeavouring to increase the repeatability of subjective criteria to the extent where genetic differences can be found between the stallions. All procedures which lead to the objective judging of performance receive backing and financial support from the Deutsche Reiterliche Vereinigung.

All potential warmblood and Arab stallions are required by law to undergo the 100-day testing. The minimum threshold for selection is laid down at 1.0 standard units, and this mark is achieved by about 28 per cent of the group. Also provided for is *performance testing within the framework of public competitions*. However, for many reasons this method of testing stallions is to remain restricted to exceptional cases.

Of ever-increasing importance is the *evaluation of stallions from the competition results of their progeny*. Every time a horse is placed in a competition it adds to the stud value of its sire. In 1977 35,000 horses took part in 15,940 competitions and obtained 117,862 places. These figures, as well as the latest results of enquiries in France and Germany, allow us in Germany to look ahead with confidence. A precursor to stud value ratings for stallions is the *Yearbook II – Breeding (Jahrbuch II – Zucht)* in

273

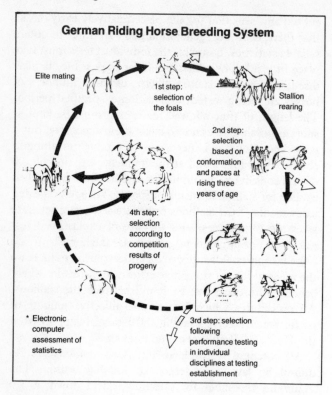

German Riding Horse Breeding System

Elite mating

1st step: selection of the foals

Stallion rearing

2nd step: selection based on conformation and paces at rising three years of age

4th step: selection according to competition results of progeny

* Electronic computer assessment of statistics

3rd step: selection following performance testing in individual disciplines at testing establishment

which the stallions are given a placing in each discipline according to the winnings of their progeny.

It is obvious from the breeding system which has been described that one of the most essential conditions for its success is the use of performance-tested parent stock. However, the *performance testing of mares* poses special problems, because for both biological and financial reasons it is not feasible to submit mares to lengthy testing at a testing establishment. Experiments carried out by some of the breed associations in this field gave very good results but were of no direct significance owing to the small size of the group tested. For this reason the field test for mares is of particular significance. However, this simple test, involving a minimum standard in the three basic paces and a willingness to go in harness, does not provide much to go on. As a result a performance test has been devised which corresponds in its structure and requirements to the riding horse test, but is based on meeting a certain minimum standard.' This test is not a legal requirement, but some breed societies use it for certain registrations.

Coldbloods

In the golden age of coldblood breeding, performance testing of this breed group was more vehemently discussed than that of any other. Particularly spectacular are the heavy draught tests, with the horse harnessed to a vehicle specially designed to measure pulling power. Nowadays coldblood stallions are legally required to reach a minimum standard pulling the draught-testing device: they must cover, in walk, with three halts followed by immediate move-offs, a distance of 1,500m in 19 minutes, with a pulling resistance of 20 per cent of their bodyweight, or 1,000m in 12½ minutes, with a pulling resistance of 25 per cent.

Pony Breeding

Pony performance testing takes the form of field tests. Testing at a testing establishment seems unacceptable, firstly because of the costs involved, and secondly because of the difficulty in bringing together an evenly matched group of riders for the purpose. Tests are based on meeting a required minimum standard. Depending on his height, a pony stallion must cover under saddle 300m in walk, 750m in trot and 1,500m in canter in the following times:

Height at withers in cm	*Time per section in minutes*
up to 127	4
from 127 to 137	3½
over 137	3

The difference in use is taken into account as well as the size. Hence, Haflinger and Fjord stallions may as an alternative be tested harnessed to sledges in the same way that coldbloods are tested. For Icelandic ponies the trot is replaced by a tölt section.

Over and above the minimum legal requirements, the pony breed associations are endeavouring to gauge the inner qualities through an additional test in dressage and jumping.

9(8) Keeping Breeding Stock

9(8)i REQUIREMENTS FOR BREEDING

As an agricultural enterprise horse breeding is based on viability, which can only be achieved if good breeding stock is used. In Germany brood mares must be registered in the stud book of a state recognised breed association. It is the breed associations which are responsible for issuing foal pedigree certificates. Moreover, it is the breeders' society, through its appointed agents, which has the sole right to brand the foals. A pedigree certificate is only issued to a foal whose dam is registered in the stud book and whose sire is licensed and recognised by the breed association. A foal without a pedigree certificate is worth considerably less. Hence it is extremely inadvisable to use at stud mares who are not registered in the stud book. Mares can be sent to stud for the first time at the age of three. Sending them earlier is not recommended since it impairs growth. Usually they cease to be fertile at about twenty years of age, though in certain cases they can be used for longer. This is particularly the case with pony mares.

9(8)ii OESTRUS, MATING AND PREGNANCY

During oestrus ('heat'), a ripe egg is released from the ovary (ovulation). For successful fertilisation it is essential that the mating takes place as short a time as possible before ovulation. This point can be determined with reasonable certainty by the veterinarian through follicle examination (ovarian palpation), which is particularly advisable in the case of mares who are difficult to get in foal. An outward sign that the mare is in oestrus is 'winking' the vulva. The mare also becomes restless and excitable. However, these signs are not always very obvious. It is therefore strongly advisable to try the mare repeatedly with the stallion.

On average oestrus lasts from three to nine days, but it may last for fourteeen days or even more. Usually the mare peaks on about the fourth day after the beginning of oestrus. Long oestrus periods often occur early in the year. The mare is more easily got in foal in a short oestrus. The sperm of a healthy stallion remains fertile for twenty-four to twenty-eight hours. The mare should therefore be covered several times during oestrus: on the third day after the beginning of oestrus and thereafter every two days until she 'rejects' the stallion (end of oestrus). More than three matings within one oestrus period reduces the mare's chances of becoming pregnant owing to the increased risk of infection.

Since economic viability has a lot to do with the mare's fertility, breed associations and studs, both state and private, require for all except maiden mares and mares with foals a veterinary certificate to say the mare is free of infection and fit for breeding. The veterinarian establishes this by means of a smear test. The ovaries should be examined at the same time, because the mare cannot conceive if they are inactive.

If the mare has not come into oestrus again by about three weeks after covering it is the first sign that she may be in foal, though unfortunately this cannot always be relied on. It is therefore a good idea to establish at the first possible opportunity whether or not the mare is definitely in foal. There are four ways of doing this:

1 Veterinary examination of the rectum (rectal

examination) from approximately the third week of pregnancy onwards;

2 Testing for pregnancy hormones in the blood (45th to 120th day of pregnancy);

3 Testing for pregnancy hormones in the urine (from the 120th day of pregnancy onwards).

4 Use of ultra-sound scanning.

The average gestation period of the mare is 333 days, that is a good eleven months, though it may vary by a month or more. Since mares slip their foals very easily, strenuous exercise, such as competitions and hunting, should be avoided with in-foal mares. However, light exercise is beneficial right up until foaling.

Normally the mare comes into oestrus nine days after foaling. Opinions differ as to whether the mare conceives more easily in the second oestrus period after foaling. When the mare should be covered is decided by the point in the breeding year at which it is hoped she will foal.

9(8)iii FOALING

Obvious signs that foaling is imminent are the dropping of the pelvic ligaments and the formation of the so-called 'resin drops' on the udder ('waxing up'). However, these signs cannot always be relied upon. Some mares do not produce the wax-like substance on the udder, others do so weeks before foaling.

A few days before foaling the mare should be brought into a spacious, disinfected foaling box. In a normal birth, assistance usually gets in the way. When, in individual cases, it is necessary, the strictest standards of hygiene must be observed. If it has not broken spontaneously during delivery, the placenta should be ruptured at once, otherwise the foal will suffocate. It is wrong to sever the umbilical cord immediately: it usually ruptures of its own accord at the correct point. If it does not do so, it should be twisted off with clean hands at the point where a small indentation is visible. After it has severed, the stump should be dipped in tincture of iodine or disinfectant. The foal should be rubbed dry with straw, which stimulates the breathing. If the afterbirth does not come away within two to three hours, the veterinarian must be informed. He should come in any case the next morning to give the foal a precautionary antibiotic injection.

The foal must drink the colostrum as soon as possible. The intestinal wall is only permeable to the antibodies for thirty-six hours after birth, and these antibodies are important for building resistance against certain diseases. Within twenty-eight days of the foal's birth the breeding association must be informed so that the foal can be registered and branded.

The contact between foal and man should be established at an early stage. With knowledgeable instruction, the foal gets used to man's touch in no time and quickly learns to wear a foal slip, have its feet picked up and even to be led beside its dam.

9(8)iv TURNING THE MARE AND FOAL OUT TO GRASS

Keeping a horse at grass is the healthiest and most natural form of management. When rearing a foal it would be better to be without a stable than without grazing. It is wrong to turn out the mare and foal intermittently so that they can 'let off steam': they may then stand sweating in the cold or in a draught and catch cold.

The foal can be turned out with his dam as soon as he is steady on his feet. If several foals are reared together, they play together, which promotes the growth of tendons, joints and muscles. Foals are educated through their association with others of their own age and with 'grown-ups'.

9(8)v WEANING

At five to six months of age the foal should be weaned

and kept in a group made up of other weanlings. Keeping a foal on his own is only recommended where the foal is rejected by the group and cannot develop properly. Growing horses must be allowed sufficient exercise, including in winter. A spacious, airy covered yard or a stable with an exercise area (small paddock) in front of it will serve the purpose. Foals are better able to tolerate cold than they are damp and draughts.

9(8)vi GELDING

Colt foals who are not potential stallions are gelded at about one year old. With a horse who has developed normally it is not a good idea to wait any later, otherwise stallion characteristics will begin to develop. The horse will also start to behave like a stallion, which is undesirable in a riding horse. Moreover, rearing ungelded colt foals requires more care and expertise than rearing geldings. Gelding also means that foals of both sexes can be kept together. In Germany the castration procedure is governed by Paragraph 6 of the Animal Protection Act.

9(8)vii FOOT CARE

The feet should be trimmed regularly, beginning when the horse is a foal. Minor faults in the position of the feet and the stance can be corrected by the blacksmith much more easily in growing horses than in adults. It is a good idea from an educational point of view to pick up the feet of even young foals and to accustom them to the halter and to associating with man. This makes things much easier not only when the foal has his feet trimmed for the first time, but also at a later stage when he is shod, ridden, transported, etc.

9(8)viii THE MANAGEMENT OF YEARLINGS AND TWO-YEAR-OLDS

For the management of young horses up to the age of three, the same principles apply as described in the section 'Turning the mare and foal out to grass'. When to turn them out and when to bring them up is very much dependent on the location, and rigid guidelines cannot be given. Turning the horses out should be preceded by about fourteen days' preparation: more forage, less concentrates and exercise in an enclosure in front of the stable. If the grazing is 'good, concentrates are not necessary for horses destined to be riding horses; however, minerals should always be available and mineral licks have given good results in this respect.

If an open-fronted field shelter is available to provide protection, mainly from rain and strong winds, this inexpensive, healthy system of management can be made available for longer periods of the year. The ideal is for youngsters to be turned out regularly even in winter. This is particularly beneficial to the development of tendons, muscles and joints. Over-rich feeding, in particular the feeding of high-protein concentrates accompanied by insufficient exercise, can lead to metabolic disturbances such as laminitis and azoturia.

9(8)ix PARASITE INFESTATION

The more horses there are in a field or stable, the greater the risk of parasite infestation. Infestation with worms (strongyloides, large and small strongyls, ascarids, stomach bots) lowers the horse's general resistance more than is often acknowledged. The presence of worms causes a marked loss of performance, high food intake and anaemia. Because of his lowered resistance, the horse becomes very susceptible to other diseases. Symptoms of heavy worm infestation include loss of condition, dull coat and tail rubbing. However, no horse should be allowed to reach this stage. Following an examination of the droppings, regular dosing with wormers (anthelmintics) is essential.

Brood mares

In cases of heavy worm infestation the development of the foetus is impaired, and abortion may occur. When

281

and how often to worm the mare should be discussed with the veterinarian. Usually, three doses are necessary: at the earliest six to eight weeks after the beginning of pregnancy; during pregnancy, and four to six weeks before the end of pregnancy. However, not every type of wormer is suitable for unrestricted use on in-foal mares.

Suckling foals and weanlings

The first worm dose should be given at five to seven days and the second at approximately four weeks. Thereafter dosing every eight weeks up to the age of one year is recommended. It is not unusual for a foal to die from a heavy worm infestation, or for serious permanent damage to be caused, especially in the blood vessels, liver, lungs and parts of the kidneys.

Yearlings and upwards

Three to four worm doses per year are necessary following examinations of the droppings. If the horse is stabled all year, at least four doses are necessary, while if the horse is partly in and partly turned out, three doses per year are required.

Adult horses should be wormed at least twice yearly, at the latest two weeks before being turned out or brought in from grass, so that they do not infect their new environment with worm eggs or worms in later stages of development. Boxes should be thoroughly cleaned out and disinfected after each worm treatment. Regular collection of droppings from the field is also recommended in so far as this is feasible from the point of view of the labour involved.

Index

Index